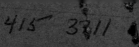

BY L. E. SISSMAN

Dying: An Introduction (*poems*) *1968*

Scattered Returns (*poems*) *1969*

Pursuit of Honor (*poems*) *1971*

Innocent Bystander: The Scene from the 70's (*essays*) *1975*

Hello, Darkness: Collected Poems 1978

Hello, Darkness

Hello, Darkness

The Collected Poems of
L. E. SISSMAN

Edited and with a Preface by

PETER DAVISON

An Atlantic Monthly Press Book
LITTLE, BROWN AND COMPANY · BOSTON · TORONTO

FIRST EDITION

Library of Congress Catalog No. 78-54091

T 05/78

Dying: An Introduction
The author wishes to thank the following publications, in which many of the poems appeared, for their kind permission to reprint them here: *The Atlantic, Boston, The Harvard Alumni Bulletin, The New Yorker,* and *The Review* of Oxford University, England.

Scattered Returns
The author wishes to thank *The Atlantic, Boston, Harper's, Harvard* and *The New Yorker,* in whose pages many of these poems appeared originally.

Pursuit of Honor
Of the poems in this collection, twelve appeared originally in *The New Yorker;* one in *Harper's;* four in the *Atlantic,* including the title poem.

The following posthumous poems appeared in *The New Yorker:* "Spring Song," "August: A Jingle Man," "Under the Rose: A Granfalloon for Kurt Vonnegut, Jr.," "Amazing Grace," "Love Day, 1945," "New York: A Summer Funeral," "Temporary Measures: A Book of Hours," "Cockaigne: A Dream," "Negatives," "December 27, 1966," "Homage to Clotho: A Hospital Suite," and "Cancer, A Dream"; in *The Atlantic:* "On Picking and Smelling a Wild Violet While Wearing Driving Gloves" and "Tras Os Montes"; in *The Times Literary Supplement:* "The Clearing in the Woods"; in the *Boston University Journal:* "American Light: A Hopper Retrospective."

ATLANTIC–LITTLE, BROWN BOOKS
ARE PUBLISHED BY
LITTLE, BROWN AND COMPANY
IN ASSOCIATION WITH
THE ATLANTIC MONTHLY PRESS

*Published simultaneously in Canada
by Little, Brown & Company (Canada) Limited*

PRINTED IN THE UNITED STATES OF AMERICA

"Did Shriner Die or Make It to New York?"
A Preface

SISSMAN and I were nearly exact contemporaries: he was born six months ahead of me, on New Year's Day, 1928. We both came, as people say in New York, from Out of Town (I from Colorado, he from Detroit), and were schooled there. We were both half-Jewish, both attended Harvard, attempted New York, settled ultimately in Boston. From what he tells us of his life, he had a hothouse childhood and a precocious youth. Profiles seldom fail to mention his having been a Quiz Kid on national radio, and that, at thirteen, he won through to the National Spelling Bee in Washington, where, as he recalled later, he "bested some poor little girl from Kentucky on an easy word ('chrysanthemum,' as I remember) and became the National Champion, the emolument of which office included a $500 Defense Bond, a wooden plaque with two bronze owls on it, and an all-expense-paid trip to New York." The preciseness of observation is characteristic, but not what follows. "My main reaction to all this was to lose my lunch more frequently than usual, a long-standing symptom of my revulsion to performing in public, and to conceive a lifelong hatred for the exploitation of the young."

Such remarks ought to lead us even farther back in time. Louis Edward Sissman was an only child, of parents who seem to have been peripatetic, homiletic, and remote. His mother urged him to accomplish much. Like other gifted only children, he developed Interests — cars, planes, technologies, and varieties of expertise — that enabled a boy to go it alone, under warily benign parental eyes. I am told that the elder Sissmans were specially alert, even perhaps cranky, about diet. When young Louis (as they called him) finally left home, bright boy, to go to Harvard, his filial letters would report faithfully on the wholesomeness of his food intake. The letters also requested, with preternatural insistence, money.

"My parents, who were constitutionally opposed to the idea of property, fearing its potential stranglehold on their freedom, never owned a house while we lived [in Detroit]. Instead, they rented run-down but commodious buildings which could house both my father's business and our living quarters. This neatly avoided the problem of living in the suburbs and at the same time put me in more than nodding touch with the heart of a city. . . . Still, I lacked more than the merest trace of a sense of belonging until, in 1944, I made the trip east to Boston.''

Though Sissman and I attended Harvard at the same time, and although our backgrounds, our interests, our tastes, and even our friends overlapped, we never met there, nor for nearly twenty years afterward; and then our friendship, though more than professional, could not be described as intimate. I suspect that most of Sissman's friendships — with men at least — contained an element of wariness. Though much admired and beloved, though given to deep and explicit courtesy and capable of conferring a sense of warm camaraderie, he was not easy to get close to. His friends, therefore, seem to know very little about his life as a whole, but rather, each of them, about his or her part in it. His sense of personal privacy was acutely developed, yet it may have been linked to his artistic gift by a reverse gear, for his poetry, or at least that part of it written after 1963, had a very high autobiographical content.

Our knowledge of his earlier years, if we can clear a view unadorned by the foliage of his verse, might reveal a root-and-branch structure something like this: Young, left-handed Lou Sissman arrives at Harvard in November of 1944, full-grown (six-four, two hundred pounds) but not yet seventeen. His assigned roommate is "a tall, courtly, withdrawn youth who was so steeped in the Brahmin tradition that he sometimes seemed barely able to function in the real world." He also welcomed the cheerfulness of the Irish maid assigned to clean his college rooms: "To me she was helpful, sensible, motherly, always forgiving: a kind of foster mother in my strange home, and one who never demanded the things my real mother did. . . . I never saw any reason to reconsider my vision of Boston as bound up in those two people." Boston had set its seal upon his heart, and both his life and his work would be played out mostly against its background. Except for "a short, unhappy stint in New York," he would live in or near Boston till his death.

This sixteen-year-old freshman became a seventeen-year-old sophomore. Poems written in the 1960s testify to college escapades, observations and debauches, romantic pursuits of knowledge and honor. In 1946 the overstimulated eighteen-year-old was booted from Harvard, doubtless with good reason and probably with excellent effect. He got himself a job as a stack boy in the Boston Public Library, found a series of furnished rooms around

Boston, and wrote home regular reports on his diet and health and regular requests for money — each request gravely particularized as to the benefits that would accrue. By the time Louis Edward Sissman was readmitted to Harvard in 1947, he was ready for more serious work. The furnished rooms had stirred up poetry. His teachers, John Ciardi, Andrews Wanning, and Theodore Morrison especially, commented encouragingly in the margins of "my dense, clotted, intentionally obscure verse of that period." His poetic technique set and was varnished: he received Harvard's Garrison Poetry Prize. On his graduation *cum laude* in 1949, a year late, he was elected Class Poet. He had also married for the first time, in 1948.

The chronological record now blurs a little. A fortune is sought, but not found, in New York. The National Spelling Bee Champion becomes for a while a copy editor at a now-defunct book publishing house, but beats a somewhat ignominious and unemployed retreat to Boston in 1952. He works to elect John F. Kennedy to the U.S. Senate. He takes odd jobs — for instance, selling vacuum cleaners. Eventually he lands in an advertising firm and likes it. He mingles with the motley population of the "wrong" side of Beacon Hill. But although this swathe of experience would emerge piecemeal in poetry written in later years, almost no poetry seems to have been written now, for perhaps a decade. Seen in hindsight his poetic silence is so curious as to be nearly as deafening as the seven-year silence that befell Wallace Stevens after *Harmonium*. Yet four significant changes occurred, more or less concurrently.

Sissman mastered the craft of advertising and proved himself capable of making a good living at a business he succeeded and delighted in. He married for the second time in 1958, this time very happily. (There were no children of either marriage.) And at some stage (students and scholars may one day divine when, but I do not know) Louis Edward Sissman ceased being Lou Sissman (the home and college nickname) and became Ed Sissman, the business and literary nickname. Ed and Anne Sissman moved after their marriage to the country an hour west of Boston, significantly near the village of Harvard, Massachusetts.

Before the end of 1965 Sissman had compiled, in spite of a busy career, at least one typed volume of poetry. Some of it, true, had been revived from college notebooks. His recent work, however, dealt with the bone and marrow of his own past, Ed Sissman writing about the life of Lou Sissman and more than once in the poetry referring to himself as "Mr. Edwards." And then in the autumn of 1965 he discovered he had Hodgkin's disease, a disease which had once been "routinely fatal," but whose cure had by this time progressed far enough to give him an extra decade. Illness did not, except for periods of hospitalization, radiation, and chemotherapy, stop or slow his output of poetry and, later, prose. For the rest of his life he wrote like one possessed of a knowledge remote from most of us, the knowledge of real time. His new poems only apparently resembled the thickly textured formalities of his undergraduate writing, for they had been summoned for a purpose as mortal as Proust's.

The 1950s, as some of us know first hand, imposed certain terrible disciplines on people and on poetry. The early sixties, when Sissman began to write again, saw publication of the breast-baring, bottle-draining confessional poetry of Robert Lowell, Anne Sexton, John Berryman. The year 1963 saw the deaths of Robert Frost, William Carlos Williams, Theodore Roethke, and Sylvia Plath. Poets were now expected to throw over the "constraints of closed forms," to question the past, to face down the Self. But approaches varied. Perhaps the reason Sissman and I were drawn together as author and publisher was that our work had certain resemblances. My own first book of poems, published in 1964, matched the work he was doing in private, insofar as it was written in rhyme, in blank verse, in stanzaic regularities. I have a clear memory of reading my first Sissman poem, and of my reaction, probably in 1965, when "The Marschallin, Joy Street, July 3, 1949" was published in *Boston Magazine*. What a title! And what a strange, elongated, heavily epigraphed ruminative monologue this was, of a woman named Mona Mountjoy, no longer young, watching the Cambridge Independence Day fireworks across the Charles River from her Beacon Hill bedroom window! Whad did lines like these have to do with the poetry deemed appropriate to the time?

A small white integer appears,
Bears a huge school of yellow pollywogs,
And, with a white wink, vanishes.

This portrait of a fading beauty dreaming of her past, her lovers, her town house, her city, her declining years, framed itself in a gold filigree of formal verse. It would take me a while, and it has taken the world longer, to get used to the sound of it. The poem was unsettling. Its deft way of speaking, both in the woman's voice and in the poet's, evoked a past that was neither sentimental nor tragic, neither frozen in ridicule, nor gasping in self-punishment, nor drenched in emotion. It was, as John Updike would later remark, "a middle tone."

By the time Sissman and I met at last, I had already read a number of his poems in the *New Yorker* and elsewhere. He turned out to be a long, slightly lopsided man, grave, formally dressed, extremely courteous, even owlish, so polite as to lend me confidence in my own opinions. Sissman's accumulated manuscripts proved that this pawky gentleman had already the makings of a book. Esther S. Yntema at the Atlantic Monthly Press helped me advise the author during 1966 and 1967 to winnow out his better (usually later) poems from his less good (and usually earlier). From his first volume, typed up before his 1965 illness and entitled *Homage to Cambridge,* we ultimately selected only ten poems out of thirty-eight manuscripts for book publication.

The first published book was entitled *Dying: An Introduction.* Such a title would prove a hard act to follow. While it was being prepared for publication (not long after Ed's fortieth birthday in January, 1968), he continued writing, not only poems but now reviews for the *New Yorker,* in addition to his highly pressured advertising work. By now he was creative director for the Boston office of Kenyon and Eckhart and would later hold a similar position with Quinn and Johnson. His first bout with Hodgkin's disease was over, but there would, as he could well imagine, be others, and he had much he wanted to write. After reaching that first grim awareness of the limitations of time, he began to write like what he was, an innocent man possessed. Possessed of a certain knowledge that things could not last, but possessed too of a wide-ranging engagement with the world around him — marriage, the advertising business, politics, hobbies, photography, old cars, new cars, food and drink, travel, but, above all, the life of words and their ability to make arrests. His work brought him prompt recognition of one sort: a Guggenheim Fellowship in 1968, an award from the National Institute of Arts and Letters in 1969, a cherished invitation to be Phi Beta Kappa Poet at Harvard in 1971. Some fellow-poets praised his accomplishment, but the moral terrorists who dominated the poetry business of the time withheld their accolades.

Prior to his death in 1976, Sissman published three more books: *Scattered Returns* (1969), *Pursuit of Honor* (1971), and a book of essays selected from his five years of monthly *Atlantic* columns of the same name, *Innocent Bystander* (1975). After the end of 1974, to his chagrin, he was unable to write more poetry, though he continued to write successful prose until the last months of his life. Nearly all the poems published in the posthumous section of *Hello, Darkness* were written between 1970 and the cessation of poetic capability. The collected poems as a whole were written, with the few exceptions I have mentioned, in the dozen years between 1963 and 1974.

I have examined all the manuscripts I could find in his own files, or others, and decided, perhaps arbitrarily, that he would have wanted to collect mostly the poems from this period. Since he trusted me to edit his books when he was alive, I must believe that he would not have appointed me literary executor if he hadn't wanted me to exercise discretion in the selection as well as the arrangement. Most of the poems remaining from Ed's first, collegiate, "literary" career are in my opinion best left uncollected. If posterity thinks me wrong, posterity can look them up at the Houghton Library, Harvard University, where they repose. I have also decided to exclude, with a couple of exceptions, the occasional pieces he dashed off on the typewriter or inscribed on the flyleaf of a book: such pieces were often private, though endearing, and Ed valued privacy.

In his life as in his work, Sissman was grave and formal, with a wry, ingratiating sense of humor. He never played the literary Brahmin in spite of his precocious learning. He dedicated his poem "Scattered Returns" to one "who knows how it is to be young and old." He was a divided, complex man: businessman and poet, infant prodigy and late-bloomer, a slowly dying man trying to press the flowers of his youth, a man as humorous as he was persistent, with the courage not only to be himself but to take himself with a certain wry modesty.

John Updike, to whom with Anne B. Sissman I am indebted for counsel and support in editing this book, has justly written of Sissman's poetry: "The metrical form becomes a shimmering skin of word play, compression, antic exactitude, sudden sweet directness, swoops and starts of rhythm. Though possessing the declarative virtues of prose — hospitable, even, to dialogue and narrative suspense — his poetry is always poetic." *Antic exactitude* says a great deal, an exactitude born of the obsession to recapture a past that might suddenly escape. It could, on the whole, be done to the life, only one day at a time, with poems specifically labeled as to place and date, and dedicated to those who might share the memory. But at least once, in "A War Requiem," Sissman, achieving his highest level of ambition and accomplishment at once, managed to evoke the historical forces that had dislocated an entire generation, his and mine. Born in the twenties, bred in the thirties, bewildered and polarized by the war, stunned by the evasions of the fifties, and coming of age, if ever, in the sixties, he concluded:

> I warm myself in isolation . . .
> >   I hide
> Out in my hideout from the memory
> Of our unlovely recent history . . .
> >   I see,
> By luck, a leisurely and murderous
> Shadow detach itself with a marine
> Grace from an apple tree. A snowy owl,
> Cinereous, nearly invisible,
> Planes down its glide path to surprise a vole.

The poem is dated 1969, when New England saw, not only a southward wave of snowy owls, but signs that the Vietnam war would not quickly cease to be murderous. Standing by, as this sharp-eyed, worldly Innocent did with all senses open, he was not likely to be surprised by death, or murder, when it approached. In his last poems, some of them dreams or even nightmares, which he foresightedly entitled "Hello, Darkness," he watched the snowy owl as it, nearly invisibly, nearly inaudibly, planed down. And he might have grinned a little at the memory that the National Spelling Champion had been awarded a plaque with two bronze owls on it, and an all-expense-paid trip to the Big City.

Peter Davison
Gloucester, Massachusetts
October 30, 1977

Contents

Editor's Preface   vii

DYING: AN INTRODUCTION

PART ONE

Going Home, 1945   3
Parents in Winter   11
East Congress and McDougall Streets, Detroit, May 25   13
Henley, July 4: 1914–1964   15
A College Room: Lowell R-34, 1945   16
The Birdman of Cambridge, Mass.   18
The Savage, Gore Hall G-31   18
Up All Night, Adams House C-55   20
The Museum of Comparative Zoology   20
Stillman Infirmary   22
New England: Dead of Winter   23
In and Out: Severance of Connections, 1946   24
In and Out: A Home Away from Home, 1947   26
Midsummer Night, Charles Street   28
Two Encounters   29
Death City, 1949   31
Peg Finnan's Wake in Inman Square   32
A Day in the City   33
Sweeney to Mrs. Porter in the Spring   35
On the Island   37

PART TWO

The Tree Warden   42
String Song   44

Our Literary Heritage 46

Just a Whack at Empson 51

Dear George Orwell, 1950–1965 52

Peace Comes to Still River, Mass. 53

Chamber Music, Bar Harbor, Off-Season 54

The Marschallin, Joy Street, July 3, 1949 55

A Common Prophecy 61

Bethlehem State 61

Sondra Dead or Alive 65

Man and Wife 67

Two Happenings in Boston 67

Provincetown, 1953 70

The West Forties: Morning, Noon, and Night 73

The Nanny Boat, 1957 77

Love-Making; April; Middle Age 82

Dying: An Introduction 83

Canzone: Aubade 87

SCATTERED RETURNS

I. SCATTERED RETURNS

A Deathplace 93

The Harvest, State Street 94

Scattered Returns: Three Derivative Poems 95

Sonatina: Hospital 98

Patrick Kavanagh: An Annotated Exequy 99

An Unknown Western-Union Boy 101

Lüchow's and After 101

Small Space 103

The Veterans: A Dream 104

Bathing Song 106

Elegy: Evelyn Waugh 107

Visiting Chaos 108

Upon Finding *Dying: An Introduction,* by
L. E. Sissman, Remaindered at 1s. 109

The 20th Armored: A Recurrent Dream 110

The Cinematographers, West Cedar Street 111

Clever Women 112

Edward Teshmaker Busk   113

Safety at Forty: or, An Abecedarian Takes a Walk   114

Solo, Head Tide   115

Pepy's Bar, West Forty-eighth Street, 8 A.M.   116

With Dr. Donothing at Farney End   116

Lettermen   118

Nocturne, Central Park South   120

The Village: The Seasons   120

II. A WAR REQUIEM

Fall Planting   126

Wintertime and Spring   131

High Summer   136

Harvest Home   141

In the New Year   147

PURSUIT OF HONOR

Notes on *Pursuit of Honor*   150

The Big Rock-Candy Mountain   151

An E-Type on the Interstate   156

Among Schoolchildren   156

Cock Robbins Opens in New York   159

An American in Evans Country   160

First N.Y. Showing   161

Manchester: Night   161

The New York Woman   163

Mouth-Organ Tunes: The American Lost and Found   165

The Dump: A Dream Come True   167

Tears at Korvette's   169

The Time in Venezuela   170

Letter from Coast to Coast   170

New Year's, 1948   174

Dying: A Resurrection, 1969   179

Pursuit of Honor, 1946   180

In Bardbury   196

Convenient to Victoria   197

An Arundel Footnote   198

A Life in Alabaster Street 199

A Loss of Largess; Its Recapture (And Point After) 200

Excuse for an Italian Sonnet 201

J.J.'s Levée, 1946 202

In Baltimore — Why Baltimore? — Did Kahn 203

Inflation 204

Empson Lieder 206

A POSTHUMOUS COLLECTION

I. DESCRIPTIVE AND SATIRICAL

Getting On: Grave Expectations 213

Spring Song 214

August: A Jingle Man 215

On Picking and Smelling a Wild Violet
  While Wearing Driving Gloves 216

Under the Rose: A Granfalloon for Kurt Vonnegut, Jr. 217

The Clearing in the Woods 219

American Light: A Hopper Retrospective 220

Model Rooms 223

Amazing Grace, 1974 224

Man in the Street 225

Work: A Sermon 226

An Anniversary: A Lucubration 227

The Better Half 230

The Persistence of Innocence 231

II. NOSTALGIC AND NARRATIVE

A Comedy in Ruins 232

Love Day, 1945 234

At the Bar, 1948 241

The Escapists, August, 1949 242

New York: A Summer Funeral 244

A Late Good Night 251

Going Back: A Word with Leslie Vandam in New York 253

The Mid-Forties: On Meeting No One in New York 255

Notes Toward a 25th Reunion   256
Temporary Measures: A Book of Hours   257

III. LIGHT AND DREAMY

Concerto for the Left Hand Alone   264
Boston–Chicago, May 11   265
Praeludium, North River   265
Matter of Britain: Some Fragmentary Souvenirs   266
A Private Line   267
To Your Uterus; an Uncompleted Call   268
Packing Material: Excelsior   268
Dear John   269
Cockaigne: A Dream   270
Three American Dreams: A Suite in Phillips House   272

IV. HELLO, DARKNESS

Negatives   275
December 27, 1966   276
Homage to Clotho: A Hospital Suite   277
Cancer: A Dream   281
Tras Os Montes   284

Dying:
An Introduction

For Anne

PART ONE

Going Home, 1945

Home is so sad. It stays as it was left . . .
— *Philip Larkin*

I. GETTING THERE

1. Night

"En route aboard the Twentieth Century
Limited," says the club-car notepaper.
With a glad cry, I take a seat and write
Six crested notes to six deserving friends
Who need a lesson in my eminence,
Or on whose female persons I have vain
Designs. Speaking of female persons, who
Is that old-fashioned girl three seats away,
With maraschino-cherry lips and teeth
As white as lemon pith, with ice-blue eyes
And amber Bourbon hair? Must be Bryn Mawr.
Above my station, which is G.C.T.,
And, at the other end, Fort Street. I cock
An innocent index at the bar waiter,
And call, in a bass tenor, for a Scotch
And branch water. (I hope that branch water
Is carried on crack trains. I think of it
In pear-shaped bottles, like Perrier.) The black
White-coated waiter makes ironically
Over my disarray. "Mix, sir?" "Uh-huh,"
I grunt. Branch water gets no rise,
Not even one eyelid bat, from Bryn Mawr.

I give up and tack back to my roomette,
Where Webster waits to take me by the throat
And threaten me to sleep. "Or with his nails
He'll dig them up again." Amen. I doze,
Until, in the marshalling yards of Buffalo,
The nails of couplings dig me up again.
Up the trick curtain; under it, the moon
Face of the station clock beams a huge One
Into my dilatory pupil. Sleep
Returns for his lost westbound passenger
And hustles him aboard. They couple up
Another Hudson 4-6-4 and I awake
Again. The clock says two. We're off. Good night.

2. *Dawn*

Morning is not a matter of whiskbroom
Paradiddles on sack-suit shoulders; not
A throb of chocolate voices in the men's
Washroom; not an aubade of good cigars
Smoking on sink rims while their masters shave
In undershirts, pending suspenders; not
Steam rising from the ranks of sinks where jokes
Go off so limply at this hour — "Mister,
Your sign fell down!" (Laughter) — and one man drinks
Rye by himself in a toilet stall; morning is not
That any more at all, but a shave alone
In my roomette and a walk to the dining car,
And breakfast in silence on the Century.

3. *Noon*

Nous sommes arrivés. The old Lafayette
Coach which my dad affects awaits without,
While my dim mother pins me in a grip
Of flesh and blood. Just two semesters stand
Between me and these twin authorities,
The moon and sun, ruling me night and day
In opposition and conjunction. Now

I stoop to inspect their tiny orrery,
Worked by a crank from higher up, a god
From the Machine-Design Department. We
Climb in the fatal car and head for home
Through widened streets lined with diminished shops,
Patrolled by shrivelled people, shrunken kids,
And miniature dogs. Waste paper blows
For miles along the thoroughfares toward
The straightedge of the horizon, where the world,
Seeing me entering my father's house,
Awaits my resurrection in the fall.

II. AT HOME

  1. The Room

The next of kin is marched into a dark,
North-oriented room where trumpet vines
And overhanging eaves restrain the light,
There to confront the body of his past:
A matter of identity. Look, those
Are spectacles that were his eyes. That book
Was his vocabulary. That wall map
(Out of the *Geographic*) was his world.
That copy of "Jane's Fighting Ships" was all
His insular defense. Those model planes —
Stormovik, Stuka, ME-109 —
Were his air arm, which tirelessly traversed
The compass rose around its dusty strings.
Who was this recent tenant of my room?
Intelligence demands an answer. "Why,
I never saw the boy before in my life."

  2. The Folks

My father casts a stone whose ripples ride
Almost to my unhearing aid, the ear.
My answering fire likewise falls short. Between
Us lies no-generation's land, a waste

Of time. Barbed wire and trenches separate
The conscript class of 1895
From that of 1928. I see
My father, in a tall examination room
Gaslit by fishtail burners, demonstrate
The differential calculus; he sees
Me boozing with low types in Central Square
And touching tasty women on the quick.
(Not such a bad idea, Dad, after all.)
Had he his way, his little mathemat
Would be devouring sums and public praise
Like any Univac; and had I mine,
My dad and I would be out on the town,
Like as a brother act in our black ties,
Clubbable, bibulous, sly, debonair.
Fat chance of that. Across the timing gap
No blue spark fires. We talk in circles which
Are not contiguous. It is too bad
Our purposes for others founder on
Their purposes for us. Now, take my dad.

3. *The Date*

Hat holds me at an angle to survey
My metamorphosis from local boy
To Eastern College Man. Light years away,
Her once and future beaux from Tech and State
Back, blinded, into corners of the room,
Bedazzled by my meteoric rise.
All night, respectfully, their voices flat
As the land's lie, they ask me what it's like
Back there, incredulously fingering
My J. Press jacket, softly crying "Cool!"
Like pigeons. And the girls! Such nattering —
Which even bird conventions cannot touch —
Alarms my keeper, Hat, to vigilance
Over her showpiece, lest I taste too much
Of all I'm offered. But it doesn't matter;
The *pièce de résistance* is Harriet later.

4. The Chum

It's Harvard vs. Williams at the D.-
A.C. Out of my corner armchair, I
Dance nimbly to clasp hands with Richie B.
Mackenzie, my old challenger. Now he,
The shorter fighter, boards his bicycle,
And pedals up to me. Right cross; we shake,
Break clean. On to the greater battle, where
The muffled musketry of cutlery
Rattles a rapid fire above the dull
Trench-mortar thuds of crockery. "A dry
One with a twist." "Bourbon and branch water."
"Blue points." "Cracked crab." "The grayling amandine."
"Filet mignon. Pommes allumettes." "Roquefort."
"Blue cheese." "Rosé?" "Rosé." "There's no place like —"
"Cambridge. Boy, what a wild —" "Woman I met
At Bennington." "I'll tell the world they put
Out. Why —" "They don't pass out, I'll never know."
"Two great big townies —" "Landed on their ear
Outside the bar. From Rensselaer." "No kid?"
"I swear." "Rum cake." "Profiteroles."
"Cointreau." "Martell." "Gentlemen's grades. Three C's,
A D." "Still worse — two D's. On pro." "No kid?"
"I'll pay." "Let me." "I'll pay." "Let me." "O.K."
The winner and still champion is me.

5. The Town

In this al fresco gallery of Sheelers —
Replete with stacks and tipples, ramps and hoppers,
Vents, derricks, ducts, louvers, and intercoolers —
I wander lonely as a cloud. Here is the beauty
Of this ridiculous, gas-smelling city.
Not those gilt towers stuck up so proudly
To spell a skyline, not those too loudly
Dulcet and unobtrusively huge houses
Dotting the northern suburbs. No, the heart
Of it is where its masters' love is:
In the cold-rolling mills, annealing rooms,

Pickling and plating vats, blast furnaces,
Drop-forging shops, final-assembly lines:
Wherever angular, ideal machines,
Formed seamlessly of unalloyed desire,
Strike worthless stereotypes out of the fire.

6. The Room, 8/31

Lieutenant Kije, for the twentieth time
On record, tramps the dogged August night
In glacé top boots, jangling all his high
Orders of Irony and Satire. My
Suffering mother passes through the wall
A muffled *cri de coeur:* "Turn that thing down,"
To which I courteously defer. The summer stands
Suspended in its bowl, and also runs
At a great rate down the drain somehow, dragging
Me into fall. There still remain these nights
Of close restraint in heat, a camisole
Of dampness wired for the amazingly
Loud sound of streetcars roller-skating; for
The shocking sight of their electric-blue
Stars overhead; for their galvanic smell
Of ozone; and the unforgettable scent
Of air-conditioned drugstores, where the pure
Acid of citrus cuts across the fat
Riches of chocolate, subjugates perfume
(Evening in Paris), soap, iodoform.
Back in my heated room with the night game
And Nine Elizabethan Dramatists,
I chill myself with Webster. In the twelfth,
August strikes out and thunders to the showers.

III.   AWAY

1. Packing

Admit the sophomore's impediments
In the Caesarean sense: the stuff I lug
Wisely and foolishly out of the breach

In Mother's privet hedge, in Father's picket fence.
Item: one pair of officer's pink pants
Left over from R.O.T.C.; one tam
Worn by the Pictou Highlanders and me;
One six-foot Princeton scarf; one pair sweatpants;
Two white bucks aged to grey; one copy each
Of "Dubliners," "Wind in the Willows," "Kim,"
"Tropic of Cancer," "House at Pooh Corner," "Teen-
Age Etiquette," "Ulysses," "Leaves of Grass,"
"A Child's Garden of Verses," "Four Quartets,"
"Tarr," "Peter Rabbit," "Lady Chatterley";
One Remington Electric Shaver; six
Giant Almond Hershey Bars; one roll of Tums;
One jar of Mum; one tube of Pepsodent;
One guest bar of Camay; two Trojans; three
Packs of Balkan Sobranie cigarettes;
A secret diary (three entries), and
A tangled mass too numerous to list.
I genuflect on the stuffed leatherette
Until the straining snap locks creak and catch;
Then I pick up my bags, one in each hand,
And take the first step to Jerusalem,
New England's green and pleasant land.

2. *Parting*

"Caoutchouc," I comment, flexing my big feet
In their new gum-boots. "Are you catching cold?"
Mother demands. "Uh, no. Just practicing
A new word." "Good. Do you have everything?"
"Uh, yes. Umbrella, earmuffs, undershirts —"
"The marmalade!" "Oh, hell!" "Your grandmother
Will just be sick. She got it from Dundee."
"Ship it." "It's glass. I can't." "Here comes the train.
Son, have a good year," my poor father says.
His eyes belie his smile. But he's a good,
Though steady, loser. Now, fraternally,
He takes my hand in the firm, funny grip
Of the Order of Fathers and Sons. My mother plants
A moist and plosive kiss across my ear,
Mumbles, and sheds a shiny patent tear.

3. Starting

Gathering way, we step out of the station
Gingerly, silver showing at the forefoot
Of the long engine, and a curl of cream
Whipped at her whistle. How superior
It is to pass clean through the roots of each
Bystanders real life and leave the city
In the lurch like a wife. My guilt is packed
In with my sweatshirts in the baggage car;
I travel light. Brick tenements sprint by,
All up to here with melodrama, kids,
Mice, misery. I blink and miss a block,
Yawn and omit a mile. Now the Toltec
Pyramids of plants appear and pivot by.
Soon rolling mills give way to fields of rye.
It's reading period: "Wish me good speed;
For I am going into a wilderness."
The sun goes west; the sky goes black; it is
Full tide 'tween night and day. Just in the nick,
Bosola, in a mist, I know not how,
Receives his mortal wound at cocktail time.
I home in on the club car, straightening
The rucked-up jacket I've been reading in,
And take a seat with *Fortune* on my knee.
The waiter fetches Scotch and branch water.
Say, who's that Highland tycoon's fetching daughter
In a dress-Stewart skirt, with Shetland hair,
Eyes like a loch, breasts like a ben? She's mine,
Assuming I can take a dare. With luck,
From now until tomorrow is today,
From here over the hills and far away,
We'll kiss and play and possibly make free,
En route aboard the Twentieth Century.

Parents in Winter

I. MOTHER AT THE PALACE, 1914

In ragtime, when my mother ran away
From flat Ontario with Art to play
A fair Ophelia on the two-a-day
Time of that time, she was just seventeen
And far behind her figure and her face
In bearing, aim, and point: one more good kid
To swell a progress or to farce a scene
With slim impersonations of a race
Of royal losers, which is what she did.

Until, until. Until, in Buffalo,
The Rep played out its string and let her go,
And she tried out before the morning show
By gaslight in the cold Academy
For right end in the chorus, which required
An elemental sense of rhythm, and
A dauntless liking for variety,
And a good pair of legs, which she had. Hired,
She danced split weeks across the level land.

In Dayton, at the little Lyceum,
She was first billed with Andy as a team —
Shannon & Anderson — a waking dream
Worth thirty dollars weekly. Soon, in Troy,
Her act was spotted by Gus McAdoo,
Who made her both a single and a star
At twenty; and, in the blood-tasting joy
Of early triumph, barely twenty-two,
She played the Palace just before the war.

The times forbid me to imagine all
The grandnesses of that high music hall
Upon her opening, when, at her call,
Packards and Pierces inlaid new-laid snow
With their non-skid tread, largely loitering
While their Van Bibber owners drank her in

Through two-power pearl Zeiss glasses, in a glow
Of carbon-arc limelight wherein she sang,
En Dutch girl, to those white fronts that were men,

"When I wore a tulip." Many a rose
Made its red way toward her ravished nose
With its eleven peers and one of those
White cards of invitation and entrée
To a man's world of idleness and grace,
Leather and liquor and less fluent night
Exchanges than one would expect, and day
After day embowered alone to face
Oneself returning singly from the night.

"You great big beautiful doll," she sang, but "No,"
She said to her appraisers, who would go
To any lengths for her after the show.
I wonder why she did. Perhaps she saw
No commonness in their inheritance
And her upstart career; perhaps she felt
The condescension in their bids, their law
Of put and call. Instead, she chose to dance
And sing on in the hand that chance had dealt.

I wonder, too: was it her Irish pride
That made her tell the man she would not ride,
And so turn down a rôle with Bonafide
Films, Limited, and so turn down a road
That was to lead to giving up the stage
And taking up the piano, to her glory,
And winning the Bach prize, and having sowed
Such seeds and oats, at last to marriage,
And so to me? But that's another story.

II. FATHER AT PACKARD'S, 1915

The brick plant like a school. The winter set
Of East Grand Boulevard. The violets
Of dawn relent to let us see the first
Shift of its students hurrying to class
Distinction in the undistinguished mass

Concealing offices and cubicles,
Great drawing rooms with draftsmen on their stools,
Foremen's rude cabins bringing outdoors in,
Craftsmen's workbenches littered with their trim
Brushes and colors, and, in Main, the lines
Of workers in their hundreds vanishing,
With our perspective, at the end of all
The crucial stations in their longsome hall.
Here comes my father. Look how thin he is.
See snowflakes flower on the blank plat of his
Forehead. Note his black hair. In hand,
He has already all the instruments
(Pre-war and German in their provenance)
To tap and die a life. Intolerant
To the last thousandth, they encompass all
Protracted elevations of his soul,
And in their narrow ink lines circumscribe
The isometric renderings of pride
Which will propel him through the glacial years
While he designs the sun and planet gears.

East Congress and McDougall Streets, Detroit, May 25

Now winter leaves off worrying our old slum,
And summer comes.
Already docks,
Daisies and dandelions, thistles and hollyhocks
Begin to camouflage the tin in vacant lots.
(Some vegetable god ordains these plots
Of plants to rule the earth.
Their green clothes mask the birth-
Marks of a blight.)
Look down the street: there is nobody in sight
As far as Mount Elliott Avenue (where
We kids in knickers took a double dare
To hop a Grand Trunk freight;

Where, every night,
Those marvellous whistles came from).
This dead kingdom,
Composed of empty shanties under the sun,
The arc lamp swinging overhead (the one
That hung there in 1930), the same sidewalks
Of dog-eared squares of slate marked with the chalks
Of the persisting children, the sad board
Fences which shored
Up private property falling into the alley,
This was Jerusalem, our vivid valley.

In our dead neighborhood
Now nothing more can come to any good.
Least of all the Victorian orphanage that still stands
Behind an ironic fence on its own grounds
Diagonally opposite.
The convict children have forsaken it:
In one mad prison break, foiling their guards,
They burst out from its wards —
Long as the Hall of Mirrors, high as a kite,
Carved like a cuckoo clock, capped with grey slate —
Leaving an archive of curses on its walls,
A dado of dirt at hand height in its halls,
And a declivity in each doorsill.
Now the street-Arabian artillery
Has lobbed a brick into each gallery
And opened every window from afar.
Each outer door, ajar,
Is a safe conduct to the rat,
The mouse, the alley cat.
Under its exaggerated eaves,
The orphanage endures. Here nothing leaves,
Nothing arrives except ailanthus trees.

My thirst for the past is easy to appease.

Henley, July 4: 1914–1964

Fifty years after Capt. Leverett Saltonstall's Harvard junior varsity became the first American eight to win the Grand Challenge Cup at Henley in England, Saltonstall . . . will lead his crew back to the scene of its triumph. Every man who pulled an oar in the victorious 1914 Harvard crew, as well as the coxswain, is not only alive but is preparing to return to Henley on July 1. They will take to a shell again on the picturesque Thames course during the forthcoming regatta.
— *The New York Times*

Fair stands the wind again
For nine brave Harvard men
Sung by both tongue and pen,
    Sailing for Henley
Fifty years after they
Won the great rowing fray
On Independence Day,
    Boyish and manly.

On Independence Day
Fifty light years away
They took the victor's bay
    From mighty Britain.
They were a City joke
Till they put up the stroke
And their strong foemen broke,
    As it is written.

Leverett Saltonstall
Is the first name of all
That noble roll we call,
    That band of brothers.
Curtis, Talcott, and Meyer,
Morgan and Lund set fire
To England's funeral pyre,
    They and three others.

That young and puissant crew
Quickened their beat and flew
Past all opponents, who

Watched them in wonder.
Fifty years later, we
See them across the sea
Echo that memory
Like summer thunder.

Fair stands the wind again;
Thames, bear them softly, then.
Far came these rowing men
In every weather.
What though their stroke has slowed?
(How long they all have rowed!)
Oarsmen, accept our ode,
Blades of a feather.

A College Room: Lowell R-34, 1945

A single bed. A single room. I sing
Of man alone on the skew surface of life.
No kith, no kin, no cat, no kid, no wife,
No Frigidaire, no furniture, no ring.

Yes, but the perfect state of weightlessness
Is a vacuum the natural mind abhors:
The strait bed straightway magnetizes whores;
The bare room, aching, itches to possess.

Thus I no sooner shut the tan tin door
Behind me than I am at once at home.
Will I, nill I, a budget pleasure dome
Will rear itself in Suite R-34.

A pleasure dome of Klees and Watteaus made,
Of chairs and couches from the Fair Exchange,
Of leavings from the previous rich and strange
Tenant, of fabrics guaranteed to fade.

Here I will entertain the young idea
Of Cambridge, wounded, winsome, and sardonic;
Here I will walk the uttermost euphonic
Marches of English, where no lines are clear.

Here I will take the interchangeable
Parts of ephemerid girls to fit my bed;
Here death will first enter my freshman head
On a visitor's passport, putting one tangible

Word in my mouth, a capsule for the day
When I will be evicted from my home
Suite home so full of life and damned to roam
Bodiless and without a thing to say.

FOOTNOTE: MRS. CIRCASSIAN

An orphan home. But into this eclectic
Mass of disasters sails Mrs. Circassian,
Maid without parallel, queen beyond question
Of household gods, gas and electric.

She puts the room right with a basilisk
Look, pats it into shape like a pillow;
Under her hard hand, the Chinese willow
Learns how to live with an abstraction. Risk

All and win all is her maiden motto,
Which makes mere matter fall into its place,
Dress right and form platoons to save its face,
And suffers Pollock to lie down with Watteau.

The Birdman of Cambridge, Mass.

How odd, in his odd trousers and odd coat,
Herron appears to strangers in his field.
Standing stock-straight in brown, he may not yield
Even his presence to intruders. Note,

However, the harsh characteristic cry
He often utters to his kind; his old
And drafty house, forever damp and cold;
His grey legs, Shetland jacket, and tight tie.

All fine field marks, but nothing to his grin,
Bent and concealing a long rusty laugh,
His long-nosed long head stuffed with birdman's chaff —
A perfect specimen of the odd man in.

The Savage, Gore Hall G-31

(For H.B.)

The poor Near North Side Bigfoot In-di-an,
Deadeye, draws back the arc of aching steel
Another eighth of an inch. Cochineal
Glimmers and trembles just across the span,

A foot from its blank target. Now his thumb
Cranks the Nth degree of pitch onto the blade
Of the minute ballista which has laid
Siege to the Tabula Rasa since the drum

Of Bigfoot first flammed into old Newtown.
Splat. Now the missile which he has let fly

Colorfully crosses the gap, hits the bull's eye,
Dum, dum, with its soft nose, spreads and runs down.

Stand back to see what Deadeye is up to:
Attacking, in his irregular uniform
Of jeans and moccasins, the still white form
Of his opponent, shot and bleeding through

The canvas ever more copiously.
Fighting for altitude, a lumpen moon
Clears the horizon like a free balloon
With squarish corners and tacks up the sky

Which is jet black. The Indian, one, steps back,
A sight in his war paint, ultramarine
Streaks on his forehead, madder and chrome green
Spots on his cheekbones, gouts of crimson lake

In his ink hair. Perfumed by turpentine,
But white and tame again, he puts on clean
Field's clothes and claims his old seat on the machine.
Together, Deadeye and I step out to dine.

Behind us in the dark, the painted moon
Keeps rising in the artificial sky
Until at last it cannot tell a lie
And lights that landscape up as bright as noon.

Up All Night, Adams House C-55

Dead on the dot of dawn, the Orient
Express steams in the window where we sit.
Its headlight hits Henry Kerr right in the eye.
Lightened by loosing the sandbags of sleep,
We bob about C Entry's ceilings like
So many free balloons, still full of gas
From yesterday, while out in Plympton Street
The air, recharged with light, proclaims today
To its great public, and one rusty ray
Of sun, noon-bound, takes hold on Randolph Hall,
And caroms down, diluted, into all
Shades of Aurora on the brick sidewalk
Beside the charcoal street, all business —
Coal carts, milk wagons, and newspaper trucks —
At this ungodly and almighty hour.
"Kant," Henry tries to say, producing just
A peanut-whistle husk, but we all know
Which *philosophe* he means. "I don't buy Kant,"
Says Parsons. "Now, you take Descartes and see —"
"*You* take Descartes," I interrupt, and down
The lees of my rum Coke. "Let's all get down
And eat before it gets too jammed, and take
A walk." "All right, let's go!" Each with his green
And inky copy of the *Crimson* in
His inky hand, a badge of editors,
We march like marshals down the dusty flights
Of stony steps to the subalterns' mess,
In clouds of power and manly sleeplessness.

The Museum of Comparative Zoology

Struck dumb by love among the walruses
And whales, the off-white polar bear with stuffing
Missing, the mastodons like muddy busses,
I sniff the mothproof air and lack for nothing.

A general grant enabled the erection,
Brick upon brick, of this amazing building.
Today, in spite of natural selection,
It still survives an orphan age of gilding.

Unvarnished floors tickle the nose with dust
Sweeter than any girls' gymnasium's;
Stove polish dulls the cast-iron catwalk's rust;
The soot outside would make rival museums

Blanch to the lintels. So would the collection.
A taxidermist has gone ape. The cases
Bulging with birds whose differences defy detection
Under the dirt are legion. Master races

Of beetles lie extinguished in glass tables:
Stag, deathwatch, ox, dung, diving, darkling, May.
Over the Kelmscott lettering of their labels,
Skeleton crews of sharks mark time all day.

Mark time: these groaning boards that staged a feast
Of love for art and science, since divorced,
Still scantily support the perishing least
Bittern and all his kin. Days, do your worst:

No more of you can come between me and
This place from which I issue and which I
Grow old along with, an unpromised land
Of all unpromising things that live and die.

This brick ark packed with variant animals —
All dead — by some progressive-party member
Steams on to nowhere, all the manuals
Of its calliope untouched, toward December.

Struck dumb by love among the walruses
And whales, the off-white polar bear with stuffing
Missing, the mastodons like muddy busses,
I sniff the mothproof air and lack for nothing.

Stillman Infirmary

Clowning with you, I fell into Lake Waban
In late November and ended up in Stillman.
Was a loose kiss in the dark Agora
Worth such an earache and so much penicillin?

Why, yes. Where else was my grandmother's house
Open for business? Where else was the "in"
Sheet signed by three white shifts of nursing mothers?
Where else was food so innocent and filling?
Where else could wards make only children brothers?
Where else, if you were young and weak and willing
And suitably infected, would they ease you
Of all impediments except your childhood,
One almost insupportable snatch of river
Twisting to westward, and the smell of woodwork?

Today some civil servant must deliver
Us from all this strong languor and abolish
Our ultimate retreat, which he has done.

Passing the site, driving along the river,
I see apartments sprung up from the ashes
Of my late childhood. Farther east, the skyline
Is made and broken by a topless tower
Of wet white concrete painted by Dong Kingman.
Its name is Hygiene. Its mauve curtains shelter
New men who need not ever go to Stillman.

Clowning with you, I fell into Lake Waban.
I wonder where you currently are matron.
I wonder if you ever think of clowning.
I wonder if I could have stayed in Stillman.

New England: Dead of Winter

Whether this impulse was a "renaissance" or only an "Indian summer,"
as Mr. Santayana has called it . . . the impulse existed and the movement was real.
— *Van Wyck Brooks*

Augustin Dunster Saylor Sayward now
Undoes his side door to the likes of me,
And hands me up into his rarefied
And rubber-smelling entry, where a pride
Of marble literary lions cows
Me in the antlers of an oak coat tree,
Vetting the unlicked cub for keeping size.

Homer, whose head is twice the span of mine,
Looks down on me in spades with twice-blind eyes;
The Bard looks dirks. Professor Sayward comes
Hotfoot to claim me. His whole household hums
The high harmonics of a mighty line
He is the end of. Only empty skies
Exist past the slim volume of his smile,

Still cased in its worn pink dust cover.
We walk upstairs in the eclectic style
Of Colonel Captain Doctor Saylor, who
Came back from Lexington and Canton blue,
Wore blue again before the war was over,
And left two blueblood legs on Malvern Hill.
The study: in a cunning China trade,

The rude West was exchanged for Eastern guile,
Which, when transported and translated, made
This faded, dazzling room of overripe
Blue, gold, and amber fruit the prototype
Of all Chinesery, set off with tiles,
Italicized with a bronzed Tuscan maid,
Completed with a period Morris chair.

Above the Gothic desk, the dull-gold wall
Displays the leonine and dogged stare

Of Augustin the First, the ur, the great
Augustin Dunster Saylor, where too late
The sweet birds sang of Arthur in his hall,
God in his Heaven, Saylor in his chair
Of English Literature in Harvard Yard.

"My grandfather was great," his scion mutters.
I answer that he was indeed a bard.
(Unlike Professor S., industrious
And able critic of illustrious
American authors, save his forefathers.)
He jots an introduction on his card —
"Do show your work to dear Professor Dix" —
And bows me out to nineteen forty-six.

In and Out: Severance of Connections, 1946

1. Civis

Walking the town as if I owned it all —
Each lilac leafing out in Brattle Street,
Each green vane in the hollow square guarding
The gargoyles on Memorial Hall, each inch
Of rubber tubing in the Mallinckrodt
Chemical Laboratory, each
Particle who would learn and gladly teach,
Each English bicycle chained to its rack,
Each green bag humping on its scholar's back,
Each tally for a Cambridge traffic death,
Each boyish girl who makes you catch your breath,
Each Argyle sock, each Bursar's bill, each ounce
Of shag, each brick, each doctorate — as if
I owned the entire spring-wound town, I walk
Up the north path to University Hall.

2. *Magister*

The Master's teeth squeak as he sprinkles me
(Too hot to handle) with a mist of spit
That dries quite coolly. "Edwards, I've got some
Rough news for you." In his glazed, padded, blue
Old double-breasted serge suit and his bat-
Wing bow tie (navy, with pink polka dots),
He lets me have it right between the eyes,
His aces on the table, man to boy.
"Look, if there's one thing I can't tolerate
It's smart guys that won't work. The deans are soft
On geniuses. Not me. What we need more
Of is Midwestern athletes who get C's."
He stands up to reveal that his brown vest
Is perfectly misbuttoned. "Now, don't think
That I'm the least bit sorry about you.
I'm sorry for your mother and your dad.
You let them down. Now, you get out of here
And do something worthwhile. Work with your hands.
Stick with it two years. Maybe they'll take you back.
Okay, fella? That's it. Now let's shake."
We shake. I shake in secret with the shame of it.

3. *Exilium*

The ghost goes south, avoiding well-worn ways
Frequented by his friends. Instead, he slips
Into loose shadows on the sunless side
Of the least-travelled street. But even there,
One with a bony finger points him out
And pierces him with questions. Zigzagging,
He hedges hastily back to his route,
Which leads on past his windows, tendrilly
Embraced already by the outriders
Of summer's ivy, past his pipes and books
And dirty shirts and mother's picture, past
The dining hall where his name is still good
For a square meal, no questions asked, and past
The common room which is too good for him.
Across the Drive his beast heaves into view:

A monster boathouse lolling on the bank
Of the high river, backside in the water.
Inside, he greets the landlord's black-haired daughter,
Miss Jacobs, with a nod, and goes upstairs
To put his chamois-seated crew pants on.
Then, past the ranks of Compromises, he
Walks out to the land's end of the long float,
Selects his Single, and stands out to sea.

In and Out: A Home Away from Home, 1947

1. One O'Clock

With gin, *prosciutto,* and Drake's Devil Dogs
In a brown-paper bag, I climb the Hill
On Saturday, the thirty-first of May,
Struck by the sun approaching apogee,
Green comments issued by the Common trees,
Mauve decadence among magnolias,
The moving charcoal shadows on the brown
Stone of the moving brownstone where I live,
And a spring breath of Lux across the Charles.
My key mutters the password; I step in
To the dense essence of an entire past:
Rugs, chicken, toilets, Lysol, dust, cigars.
Through that invisible nerve gas (which leads
In time to total incapacity),
I climb the two flights to my little flat.

2. Two-Thirty

Done with the Devil Dogs, I take the brush
Out of the tooth glass and decant my first
Gin of the afternoon. In half an hour
She will be here. All is in readiness:
The bedspread taut, the ashtrays wiped, a glass

Swiped from the bathroom down the hall, a small
Plate of *prosciutto* canapés. Now Fu
Manchu reclines at ease in his hideaway,
While his nets, broadcast, sweep their victim in
To an innocuous address on Pinckney Street.
Now Lou the Loser uses all his ten
Thumbs to count up the minutes till she comes,
Or till (more likely, with his luck) she never shows.
The gin sets up a tickle in my toes.
I blow my nose. The room is hot. A fly
Does dead-stick landings on my neck. She's late.

3. *Three-Ten,* et seq.

The doorbell rings. I barrel down the stairs
To meet the coolest copy I have seen
Of Sally on the steps. Up in my room,
I fix her gin and secretly survey
This manifestation by which I have so
Astoundingly been visited: a girl.
She walks on her long legs, she talks out loud,
She moves her hand, she shakes her head and laughs.
Is this mechanical marvel to be mine?
Quite paralyzed, I nod and nod and nod
And smile and smile. The gin is getting low
In my tooth glass. The hour is getting on.
Gin and adrenalin finally rescue me
(With an assist from Sally) and I find
My lips saluting hers as if she were
My stern commanding officer. No fool,
She puts us on an equal footing. Soon
My strategies and tactics are as toys
Before the gallop of her cavalry
That tramples through my blood and captures me.

4. *Five-Fifty*

Later, as racy novels used to say,
Later, I turn to see the westering sun
Through the ailanthus stipple her tan side

With yellow coin dots shaped to fit her skin.
This Sally now does like a garment wear
The beauty of the evening; silent, bare,
Hips, shoulders, arms, tresses, and temples lie.
I watch her as she sleeps, the tapering back
Rising and falling on the tide of breath;
The long eyelashes lying on her cheek;
The black brows and the light mouth both at rest;
A living woman not a foot away.

The west wind noses in at the window,
Sending a scent of soap, a hint of her
Perfume, and the first onions of the night
Up the airshaft to where I lie, not quite alone.

Midsummer Night, Charles Street

The one untuned clock bell, ten minutes slow,
Tolls curfew for all tenants. The black bars
Exhale us into the dark street. Below,
The gutters swallow water; above, the stars

Roll in their ball race, bearing the dead weight
Of stricken hours below. Cancer, the Crab,
Surveys his citizens, who, huddled, wait
For the last word, the last light from a cab

To form our faces, the last touch of hands
Laid on our sleeves, the *dernier cri* of night.
We must ascend alone into the lands
Upstairs we live in. The initial flight

Is granite, which our crampons lace with sparks
Like kitchen matches'. The next flight is brick,
Glacé like ornamental walks in parks,
Offering no purchase to our pitons. Kick

A foothold in the sheer face, belay up
Over the lip of the third stage, rigid wood.

Last up a scant lath chimney to the top,
Where, sweated, scared, made up with dust and blood,

We face at length again the nightly sky,
Where our sign reigns alone, picking us out
Of our crowd on the Hill, who singly lie
About us in a similar case, no doubt.

Two Encounters

I. AT THE INN, 1947

Your mink scarf smells as if it smoked cigars,
And soot clings in the corners of your eyes,
And cold has cancelled your pale cheeks in red,
And you stand faintly in a veil of Joy,
And your kid gauntlet grips a round red bag,
And your lips taste of roses and Nestlé's
Milk-chocolate bars, and your long arms entail
My foreign body in the turning world.
One washroom later, in the oaken Inn
Where things transcend the bogus and return
To old simplicities aimed at and missed,
At least today, at least with you beside
Myself with love on the ridiculous
Oak settle picked as earnest of the past,
I see your color come back in the murk,
Drawn by a dark and blood-suborning drink.
I can't describe your long-shanked leverage
To move the world at that tart, flowering age:
The brief and just trial balance of your power.
However, I recall that at that hour —
After one drink, before the Dartmouth game —
You looked at me forever with an eye
Of tourmaline without a fleck or flaw,
Set in a mount of bone as plain as steel
And flesh as scanty and as beautiful

As a March pasture following rock ledge
Into a scythe of shadow, where the snow
Melts late, if ever. In that fixing glance
Framed by your hair as brown as beaver, I
Saw one faint faltering, one evidence
That even empires nod, that sceptres sway.

II.   AT THE FAIR, 1967

Dark lady of a dozen sonnets I
Endited in a winter and a spring,
We meet now in an altered circumstance
Across the floor far later in the dance —
Midnight approaches with its pumpkin car
To carry us away — and gravely tread
One tune together before partners change.
How you are changed and you are still the same:
Girl thirty-nine and woman twenty-one
Inseparably telescoped in one
Tall matron whose each mannerism rings
A dim bell in the back room of my mind.
With my wife and your daughter we attend
A spring fair: gangs of randy neon light
Seize your town common for one gaudy night
And set the Tilt-a-Whirl and Ferris wheel
Rotating to calliopes and screams
Above fluorescent grass. In the bookstall,
We find your former husband's fifteenth class
Report with Veritas stamped on its spine,
Price .25. His name does not appear.
Time shifts, but '47 was his year,
I think. Back in the pitch-black air
You ask me if I'll take a ride with you.
The Tilt-a-Whirl. Of course I will. The red
Sea of kid faces parts to let us through
And we sit in a narrow gondola,
Confined by a crossbar. The whirl begins:
First horizontally, then up and down.
Rim-tilted, lit in green and gold, the wheel
Drops out from under us. Kids yell.
I wince and grip the bar. I'm falling off.
What idiots! You laugh. I laugh and swear.

I'm really losing it. You grab my arm.
We laugh together, turning in the air,
Really alarmed, far too old to be here,
Glad when it ends and we can leave the park
After one night, like the fair, to the dark
We are accustomed to. Shaken, I'm glad
We did it, though. To hold your airborne arm
Twenty years later is to ride the calm
World's rim against the gravity of time.

Death City, 1949

(For C.A.S.)

Victorian urban redevelopers
Plotted a garden city for their hearse,
Drawn by four dapple greys, and its fast freight
Delivered from his home almost too late
But in the nick of time. Inveterate
Death dealers keep a large supply in stock,
All shapes and causes: falling, drowning, shock,
Birth and old age. Locust and Ash
Is the busiest corner in town, with the Cash
Memorial Block (of polished travertine)
Diagonally opposite the Lean
Spire, a split chocolate-covered brownstone fang.
On the next corner clockwise, the whole Lang
Family makes its white sepulchral home.
Finally, a pergola from Rome
(Grosser than Greece's) raises a Flaxman frieze
Over its rivals. On their marble knees,
Fat Vestals weep one who, the only son
Of a Senator, father of another one,
Was tantalized by the Pierian spring
Lifelong and died dehydrated. The thing
About this city is its arrogance,

Its cold assumption we would want to dance
To its dead march, sing to its dirge. Look out!
A Stygian barge appears and comes about
Two feet from us, its belly full of men, its black
Fluke raking us, its transom lettered Cadillac.
Charles, in a city where the only weeds
Are worn by widows, where the only deeds
Are done and done, they have no need of us.

Quitting a city which is dangerous,
Let us get on the Huron Avenue bus
And ride to our reprieve in love and pity
For the free burgesses of our death city.

Peg Finnan's Wake in Inman Square

At last his old nag's dead. In Finnerty's
Front parlor she looks up at the three-light
Pot-metal ceiling fixture, painted white,
While marble cake and whiskey are consumed
By Looney, Moriarty, Sweeney, Burke,
Costello, Mrs. Riordan, O'Rourke,
Ann Casey, Leary, Finnerty, McCue,
Finnan himself. He cries a tear or two
In freedom's honor and looks after her
As, rippleless, she slips away from shore
And puts a gulf between them, even while
Her brazen, toothless turtle's beak still smiles
With undertaker's rigor and her guile.
Finnan, unchained, still hears the passing bell
Of her bronze voice commanding him to tell
Why he was late, why he drank up his pay,
Why he forgot to bring her back *Screenplay,*
Why he missed Mass, why he made up to Dot
McCann on Inman Street, the dirty slut,
Why he got fired from Harty's. The last Pope,
A Sacred Heart, a cover from the *Globe*
Depicting John F. Kennedy look down
Upon their confrontation. Finnan's eyes,

Opaque and pale as first-communion skies,
Blink as he chases cake with whiskey. Out
He goes, unhampered, into a fall night
Of oak leaves on the move, and walks the street
Unsteadily toward the third-floor flat
Where he will drink his gin tonight alone,
In silence, free, poor fish, and far from home.

A Day in the City

(Boston – New York)

I. A TASTE OF QUEENS

The dead in Queens lean westward from their stones,
Bidding granitic and marmoreal
Adieux to their descendants, who go west
A better way across the bridge to lodge
Like unspent bullets in high offices
And spiring living rooms up in the air.
Low grow the tenant cabins, stucco, brick,
Half-timbered, double-numbered, where the quick
Who were not fast enough groom their feat sons
To leap the river, and, for love or money,
Fall stunningly upon the stony city.
Here Maple Towers (Now Renting 3-Rm. Apts.)
Now towers without a tree, its swimming pool
A blue oasis in the asphalt plain
Where caravans of Carey busses ply
From Flushing to their caravanserai
In that grey fret of city over there,
Bearing us strangers straight to our desire.

II. THE AMAIR TOWER

Amair, whose lightfoot jets transship today
Across the Pole to where tomorrow starts,
I do not like your *pied-à-terre* which squats,

Arrived and immemorial, upon
Diminished traces of that lovely grey
Novembrist town bespoke by the old school
Who specialized in rainy afternoons
Enclosing incandescent *thés-dansants,*
From which the singles and the couples went
On by tall lemon cab to their affairs
Down at the Café Brevoort or upstairs
Above the Plaza's tiles and palms. Now I
Am escalated to a mezzanine
From which I will be launched into an air —
Which fifty stories circulate — as rare
As the rich breath of couchant unicorns
Or levant chairmen at the dormant board,
Whose low end I will sit at and, like Molly,
Bloom into smiles and, yes, say yes to folly.

III. HIGH PLACES

Sitting in conference with the president,
I am at first a trifle hesitant
To pierce his thin-skinned sphere with my harsh voice
And possibly dissipate his corporate choice
Of fruitwood furniture and cosmic view —
Look! Look! Canarsie! Inwood! Greenpoint! Kew
Gardens! United Nations Plaza! — true
Embodiment of everything that's ex-
Travagant in American life but sex,
Which is supplied in minims by Miss Hatch
Outside his office door to each fresh batch
Of clients, underlings, and impressees,
Who, on his bounty, sail the seven seas
Of his blue, black, calm, manic, angry moods,
This king of men and emperor of goods.
We talk across two tankards of his pale
Impeccable imported English ale,
Which break out in a fine cold sweat, like me,
In his stern presence. Can my dim words be
Reaching their destination? Yes, sir. He
Nods in his waking sleep and sanctifies
My views in every echelon of eyes.

IV. EAST FORTY-SECOND STREET

Acutely, the late sun interrogates
The street held in its custody, casting
New light on western faces, shadowing
Each subject with the long arm of the law
Of relativity, gilding the back,
Benighting the east front of everyone.
In front of Longchamps, on a burning brass
Standpipe stained orange by sundown, a tall green
Girl worth her weight in meadows, orchards, trees
Sits waiting for her date to claim her long
Cool fall champaign, capped by black scuds of curls,
And stage a pastoral with her as Phyllis
And him as Colin, awkward, forward, witty,
Against the pre-cast forest of the city.

Sweeney to Mrs. Porter in the Spring

In Prospect Street, outside the Splendid Bar
And Grill, the Pepsi generation —
The beardless, hard-eyed future of our nation —
Rolls casually south out of the slum
From which it will go far,
Leaving an old country where spring has come.

It is not obvious about the spring.
You have to know the signs: a hoist of wash
On every back-piazza line, a sash
Propped open with an empty pint of cream,
A comic softening
Of the wind's blade to rubber, an old dream

Of something better coming soon for each
Survivor who achieves the shores of May —
Perhaps a legacy, a lucky play

At dogs or numbers, or a contest prize.
Lady Luck, on the beach
Between assignments, does not hear their cries,

"Me! Me!" like gulls'. She never will. The old
Diminish steadily in all but years
And hope, which, uncontrollable as tears,
Racks them with life. Just look at Mrs. Porter,
Preparing to unfold,
In the dark bar, a letter from her daughter,

A beauty operator in Ladue,
And to remasticate the lovely tale
Of ranch and Pontiac, washed down with ale
Cold from the Spendid bowels, while waiting for
Her unrefined but true
Love's shape to shade the frosted-glass front door.

Meanwhile, Sweeney, Medallion 83
(A low old-timer's number), wheels his hack,
In Independent livery, past a back-
Projected process shot of Central Square,
To where his love will be,
Impatient to resume their grand affair.

She, like a pile of black rugs, stirs to hear
His two-tone horn just outside, heralding
The coming of both Sweeney and the spring.
Inside, he greets her as before, "Hi, Keed,"
While Wilma lays his beer
And whiskey down between them and gets paid.

His knotty fingers, tipped with moons of dirt,
Lock on the shot of Seagram's, which he belts
And chases with a swig of Knick. Nobody else
Could comfort them except their old selves, who
Preserve, worn but unhurt,
The common knowledge of a thing or two

They did together under other moons.
Now the Splendid night begins again,
Unkinking cares, alleviating pain,

Permitting living memories to flood
This country for old men
With spring, their green tongues speaking from the mud.

On the Island

To an isle in the water
With her would I fly.
— *W. B. Yeats*

1. Friday Night

We issue from the meat of Pineapple Street,
Skipping in unison in the jet rain to
The cadence of our footsteps left behind
Just momentarily as we bound on
To water, laughing, soaked, four-legged and
Three-armed, two-hearted, Siamese, unique,
And fifty put together. On the Heights,
We embrace like trenchcoats on a rack at Brooks.
You taste like lipstick, wine, and cigarettes,
And, now quite irrecoverably, you:
A tear in the material of memory
No reweaver can match. Nevertheless,
I feel your rainy face against mine still,
Hear your low laugh join boat hoots in the night
(One Song, one Bridge of Fire! Is it Cathay?),
And see, just past the corner of your eye,
Our city momentarily at bay.

2. Saturday Morning

Starting for Paumanok from Remsen Street,
Taking my Buick, leaving your La Salle,
Putting the top down in the false-spring light
Of February second, following

The "27" signs — Atlantic Ave.,
Rockaway Parkway, Linden Boulevard,
And Sunrise Highway finally at noon —
We leave the city we did sometime seek
In favor of the fish-shaped fastnesses
Due east, beyond the sounding wave
Of outer suburbs rushing up the shore
To flood the flat potato country with
The family of man. Past Babylon,
We run at last aground on the pre-war
Simplicities and complications: farms
Looked down on by great houses in the style
Of Insull, piles of those who made a pile
In Motors, Telephone, and Radio,
And dropped it all down the defile
Between decades, where all our fortunes go.

3. Saturday Afternoon

Patchogue, my dear, offers a white-faced bar
With a black heart. In its interior
You are more beautiful than you really are,
More *dégagée,* more *jeux sont faits,* world-wearier.
That artificial night, with evident aim,
Plinks out my daylit thoughts and goes to black,
Where, in the tarry sky, the Bull, the Swan
Couple illegally till dawn
With lavish princesses and Spartan queens,
As I autistically do
With you, while you invent a terrible drink —
A pilot biscuit drowned in gin and It,
Dubbed a Wet Blanket, in a whiskey glass —
Before my wondering eyes. With a bright crack,
A back door opens and the atmosphere
Of night blows out as sharply as a tire,
Revealing a slack rank of garbage cans
Out back, and a red carpet underfoot.
You look yourself again; I start to feel
Like death in the afternoon. Let us be gone.

4. *Saturday Evening*

Night, like a funeral, comes marching in
On muffled heels, its west-bent coffin met
By gathering naked bulbs and neon tubes
Along Sag Harbor's streets. Beyond the pale
Pearl light of day's regrettable demise
The whalers' churches and town halls rise up like white
Whales surfacing, their sugarloaves of white
Mammalian clapboards sailing on a grey,
Calm main of mud. These Puritanic arks,
Fane and profane, holy and secular,
Divide their flocks into white Sunday sheep,
Ripe to be fleeced of grace, and weekday goats,
Alert to steal their wool. A vesper bell,
Like a late bird, sings curfew to the town,
Turning our steps to where, in tongues of fire,
A stammering sign defines the Grande Hotel.

5. *Saturday Night*

Now, wearing my discounted wedding ring,
Still foggy with disuse, you face the desk,
Where the Korean War loudly bombards
The *Daily News* with black. The manageress,
A human hatchet in a florid dress,
Takes five from me for her best double. We
Go up and up to that sidereal
Address, where all the bentwood furniture,
The stunted metal bed, the chiffonier
Graced with our pint of Partners' Choice, but scarred
By all the post-coital cigarettes
Of sadder, wiser transients, the ashtray
("Momento of Peconic Bay"), the tin
Wastebasket lithographed with pennants, yours
Included, all call time and freeze till we
Move on. The four-light window, featuring
A huge streetlamp dead center, resonates
To the first wave of onshore rain as we

Resume our elevating, ludicrous
Posture of love. Dear Jane, the prize is far
Too near for me to melt with laughter now,
But there's a whoop down in my throat. Later,
And cooler, rubbing Lucky Strike ash in-
To my bare chest, I'll tell you what I mean:
The fact that I, unhandsome, awkward, pale,
And you, Vassar or no, too ample for
An age of skin and bone, should tumble for
Love seven stories high, with eyes as blue
As tropospheres, with dazzling teeth the size
Of cornerstones, and noses straight as dies:
The cliché of the first-class citizens.

6. *Monday Morning*

The party's over now. In a tense white
Ruffled blouse, you look as different from last night
As day. I swallow the last scratchy crumbs
Of my last baking-powder biscuit, and
Leave your place, touching for the first time now,
Noting my fingermarks on the front door.
Once more unto the breach: at the St. George
We sound the hellmouth of the I.R.T.
And ride the hissing, green, Draconic train
Under the river. *Wicker, wicker* goes
The air compressor at a stop. You sit
On shiny wicker, looking at my feet;
I hang from a chipped white-enamel strap
Marked Rico No. 12. Quite soon, at Wall
Street, we get off. Now leaving Trinity
Out of the corner of my eye, I spin
Behind you into the loud lobby of your tower
Where banks of Gothic elevators rise,
Absurd, on high. You turn and face me now,
All Bala-Cynwyd in your Peter Pan
Collar and single string of pearls, dear Jane.
"It's no go, Lou." "But wait — " "But why?" "But I — "
"I know, but it won't ever work. You know
That I have certain standards." "Pouring tea."
"Yes, pouring tea. And you just don't, that's all.

You just don't care." "But I can try." "Unh-uh.
Look, Lou, let's stop this." "Can't I see you once?
Just one more time? Tonight?" "No. I'll be late
For work upstairs. Goodbye." Now that I know
I won't see you again, an awful pain
Of deprivation twists my abdomen.
The lancet doors squeeze shut between us, and
Lights track your progress overhead as you
Devise me to myself. Jane, for the gift
Of you at first, then us, and lastly me,
My thanks, since even such off-islanders
As I can profit by a visit to
The fish-shaped island, population two.

PART TWO

The Tree Warden

I. A FAREWELL TO ELMS

In late July, now, leaves begin to fall:
A wintry skittering on the summer road,
Beside which grass, still needing to be mowed,
Gives rise to Turk's-caps, whose green tapering ball-
Point pens all suddenly write red. Last year,
The oriole swung his nest from the high fan
Vault of our tallest elm. Now a tree man
Tacks quarantine upon its trunk. I hear

An orange note a long way off, and thin
On our hill rain the ochre leaves. The white
Age of a weathered shingle stripes the bark.
Now surgeons sweat in many a paling park
And bone saws stammer blue smoke as they bite
Into the height of summer. Fall, begin.

II. THE SECOND EQUINOX

Perambulating his green wards, the tree
Warden sees summer's ashes turn to fall:
The topmost reaches first, then more, then all
The twigs take umbrage, publishing a sea

Of yellow leaflets as they go to ground.
Upon their pyres, the maples set red stars,

The seal of sickness unto death that bars
The door of summer. Bare above its mound

Of leaves, each tree makes a memorial
To its quick season and its sudden dead;
With a whole gale of sighs and heaving head,
Each ash attends its annual burial.

The warden, under a boreal blue sky,
Reminds himself that ashes never die.

III.   DECEMBER THIRTY-FIRST

The days drew in this fall with infinite art,
Making minutely earlier the stroke
Of night each evening, muting what awoke
Us later every morning: the red heart

Of sun. December's miniature day
Is borne out on its stretcher to be hung,
Dim, minor, and derivative, among
Great august canvases now locked away.

Opposed to dated day, the modern moon
Comes up to demonstrate its graphic skill:
Laying its white-on-white on with a will,
Its backward prism makes a monotone.

In the New Year, night after night will wane;
Color will conquer; art will be long again.

IV.   MAY DAY

Help me. I cannot apprehend the green
Haze that lights really upon the young
Aspens in our small swamp, but not for long.
Soon round leaves, as a matter of routine,
Will make their spheric music; and too soon
The stunning green will be a common place.

Sensational today runs in our race
To flee the might of May for willing June.

To reach a bunch of rusty maple keys,
Undoing a world of constants, more or less,
I tread on innocence. The warden sees
In May Day the historical success
Of labor; a safe date for planting trees;
A universal signal of distress.

String Song

> And, if he then should dare to think
> Of the fewness, muchness, rareness,
> Greatness of this endless only
> Precious world in which he says
> He lives — he then unties the string.
> — *Robert Graves*

I.

First, it is fundamental to realize
No two of anything may be alike.
That dawn out there that paints those loitering skies
Around St. Ceil's pale lemon, and tints white
Pilasters on its spire the tastiest lime,
Cannot come up the same another time
On morning's fruit machine, no matter how
Close the clock comes to telling the same hour.
The day shift moves the lingerers on now,
Into the shadow of the whited tower,
Whence they will not return another day
To interpret the same plot with the same play.

II.

A thousand bells belabor noon
And send it, beaten, to my room

On Canting Hill. I knock off work
And look out over Broome, Newkirk,
And Canterbridge, my mother's slum
From which my bleeding blessings come:
My ignorant and able art,
My aptitude to play the part
Of artist, my self-seeing eye.
Under the chimney-sweeping sky
Ten thousand houses smoke soft coal
And tap ash on my father's goal:
A terrace house exactly like
Ten thousand others, and a bike
Made by the gross in Brummagem.
In Milliard Street, our Hill's main stem,
I spy a hundred lines and queues
Of Catholics, Protestants, and Jews.
To work: now drying on the rack,
My sable brushes call me back
To carry out my grand designs
With infinite curlicues and lines.

III.

Looking straight down into Singleton Street,
I see one policeman tacking north in blue,
One Witness offering Watchtowers opposite,
One ray of sun striking my house askew,
One clock hitching itself, hand over hand, to six,
One couple walking south.
Allow me, as a colorist, to describe:
She wears an ivory mackintosh, an alizarin hat,
Viridian pumps too good to eat. Her face is flesh.
His, on the other hand, is a tint of scarlet lake.
He wears an umber overcoat, jet shoes, a raw-sienna hat.
In shadow, all the tones are muddier;
In sunlight, all are biassed toward orange.
At this routine, immemorable moment,
The ragman's nag sways by with slow, arhythmic beats,
Pursued by cries of iron tires and ''Rags!''
As usual on our street at six o'clock.

IV.

Just a black whisker in the top-right corner, and
My signature — "K. Zauber" — at the bottom, and
"The Way of the World" is done. The icy coffee in
The paper cup I hold in my cold, painted hand
Turns out to float a long-dead cigarette, which I
Almost ingest. The thing is done. I turn my back
On the dead square of canvas, which looks far too red
In incandescent light, and look out at the sky,
Now clamping down its curfew on all light resorts.
Night turns too solid places, squares, and terraces —
Thick cubic miles of intricate, Baroque decay —
Into an inverse star map which exhaustively reports
New constellations on a scale of one to one.
There is The Cloverleaf, where superhighways run;
There is Dad's Sunday Suit, three stars to form the fly;
There is The Steering Wheel, made of a rotary;
There is The Burning Cross in runway-marker lights;
There is The Model in the bosom of the Heights;
There is Self-Portrait, witty, pointed, populous
Abstraction of myself in the metropolis.

Our Literary Heritage

I. RIVERSIDE DRIVE, 1929

" 'Good-by, Ralph. It should end some other way.
Not this,' Corinna said. 'Now go away.'
No. Rhymes. It's ludicrous. Try 'Dear, good-by.'
No. Repetitious. Maybe 'Dear, farewell.'
No. Stagy. Out of character. Oh, hell.
Time for a drink.'' The Smith-Corona heaves
As he retracts his knickerbockered knees
To rise. Outside, a southbound tug receives

The sun broadside, and the bold Linit sign
Pales on the Jersey shore. Fresh gin, tk-tk-
Tk-tk-tk-tk, quite clearly fills his glass
Half full from the unlabelled bottle. Now
His boyish fingers grip the siphon's worn
Wire basketweave and press the trigger down
To utter soda water. One long sip
Subtracts a third of it for carrying.
On the way back, he pauses at the door
Beside his football picture, where a snore
Attests that all is well and promises
Him time to work. To work: before the tall,
Black, idle typewriter, before the small
Black type elitely inching on the blank
White sea of bond, he quails and takes a drink.
First, demolitions: the slant shilling mark
Defaces half a hundred characters
With killing strike-overs. Now, a new start:
" 'Good-by, Ralph. I don't know why it should end
Like tihs,' Corinna said. 'But be my freind.' "

II. HOTEL SHAWMUT, BOSTON, 1946

(From a commercial travellers' hotel,
Professor S. jumped straight down into hell,
While — jug-o'-rum-rum — engines made their way
Beneath him, one so cold December day.)

While he prepares his body, cold gears mate
And chuckle in the long draught of the street.
He shaves; his silver spectacles peruse
An issue of *The North American Muse*.
He uses Mum; outside him in the hall,
Maids talk their language; snow begins to fall.
He puts on his old clothes. The narrow room
Has nothing, nothing to discuss with him
Except what time you should send out your suit
And shoes for cleaning. Now he stamps his foot:
Outside the window, not saying anything,
Appears a seagull, standing on one wing;

A long-awaited colleague. With glad cry,
Professor S. embraces the white sky.

While S. demolishes a taxicab,
His spectacles review the life of Crabbe.

(From a commercial travellers' hotel,
Professor S. descended into hell.
But once in April in New Haven he
Kissed a friend's sister in the gloom of trees.)

III.   DEUS EX MACHINA, FLUSHING, 1966

La Guardia. Knee-deep in storyboards,
I line up for the shuttle, which arrives
Outside the gate and off-loads shuffling streams
Of transferees — each in his uniform
Of sober stuff and nonsense, with a case
Of talents at his side — who pass our line
Of sombre-suited shuttlers carrying
Our cases on. Then one appears, a rare
Bird in migration to New York, a bare-
Crowned singer of the stony coast of Maine,
And of Third Avenue in rain; a bard.
The way of the almost-extinct is hard.
He peers through tortoise-shelly glasses at
The crowd, the place, the year. He is not here
And is. In his check jacket, he describes
An arc of back and arms as he proceeds
Between two city starlings, carrying
His store of songs in a beat leather grip
And a dried drop of his brown lamb's blood on
His wilted collar. A *Time*-reader in
Glenurquhart plaid identifies his bird —
"Godwit, the poet" — to a flannel friend.
The bard stalks on on his two legs, aware
He has been spotted; in, I'd say, some pain
At an existence which anticipates
Its end and in the meantime tolerates
Intolerance of the wing, the whim, the one
Unanswerable voice which sings alone.

IV. LAMENT FOR THE MAKERS, INCLUDING
ME: 1967

New-minted coin, my poet's mask
(A small denomination in
Demotic nickel, brass, or tin)
Passes from hand to hand to hand
Beyond my six acres of land.
Did I desire such currency
Among the meritocracy
Of tri-named ladies who preserve
The flame of art in mackled hands,
Of universitarians
And decimal librarians
Who shore and store up textual
Addenda, of asexual
Old arbiters and referees
Who startle letters with a sneeze,
Of critics whose incautious cough
Halts a new wave or sends it off
To break on uninhabited shores,
Of publishers, insensual bores
Procuring art — "A maidenhead!" —
To Jack the Reader, of well-read
Young underfaced admirers who
Impinge on undefended you
At readings in all colleges?
No, I did not; but knowledge is
All-powerless to seek redress
For injuries to innocence.
I think continually of
Abjurers, who, fed on self-love,
Housed in an incommodious cave,
Clothed in three-button sackcloth, crave
Indulgence of no audience
But their own laudatory ears.
Alack, this anchoritic few
Dwindles; these ticking times are too
Struck with celebrity's arrears,
And heap past-due advances on
The embryonic artisan;
All hours from dawn to night are lauds,

All auditors are all applause
(However electronic), all
Tempters conspire in Adam's fall.

The world turned upside-down, without
A beast in view, without a doubt,
Recalls its exiles and bestows
On them the palm, the bays, the rose
(Art sick?), the Laurel Wormser Prize,
Whose debased dollar only buys
More nods, more goods, more fame, more praise:
Not art, as in the rude old days.

Now worldward poets turn and say,
Timor vitae conturbat me.

Just a Whack at Empson

We rot and rot and rot and rot and rot.
Why not cut badinages to the bone?
Alas, cockchafers cuddle. We cannot.

We recognise the hand upon our twat;
Unfortunately X is always known.
We rot and rot and rot and rot and rot.

Unfortunately X is always not
Quite what we had in mind to end our moan.
Alas, cockchafers cuddle. We cannot.

Why must we be contained within our pot
Of message which we have so long outgrown?
We rot and rot and rot and rot and rot.

Your physic beauty made my inwards hot
Whilst talking to you on the telephone.
Alas, cockchafers cuddle. We cannot.

Each greening apple has its browning spot:
"The rank of every poet is well-known."
We rot and rot and rot and rot and rot.
Alas, cockchafers cuddle. We cannot.

Dear George Orwell, 1950–1965

Dear George Orwell,
I never said farewell.
There was too much going on:
Crabgrass in the lawn
And guests to entertain,
Light bantering with pain
(But wait till later on),
Love nightly come and gone.
But always in the chinks
Of my time (or the bank's),
I read your books again.
In Schrafft's or on the run
To my demanding clients,
I read you in the silence
Of the spell you spun.
My dearest Englishman,
My stubborn unmet friend,
Who waited for the end
In perfect pain and love
And walked to his own grave
With a warm wink and wave
To all; who would not pull
The trigger on the bull
Elephant, and who,
Seeing his foe undo
His pants across the lines,
Did not blow out his brains;
Who served the Hôtel X
As low man, slept in spikes
With tramps, in Rowton Houses
With pavement artists, boozers,
Boys, insomniacs;
Who spat on shams and hacks,
Lived in a raddled flat
Passing trains hooted at,
And died for what we are.
Farewell, Eric Blair.

Peace Comes to Still River, Mass.

Down at Fort Devens guns begin again:
I hear the thirties rattle, and the thin
Patter of rifles, each manned by a man
Invisible, disposable, and in
Our first line of defense, the paper says.
Now howitzers inflame our darkling days,
Exclaiming downrange in an O of fire
Upon their targets, and a virid flare
Gives the high sign to go on making war
In earnest of our inner truce. Once more
My quondam dean in University Hall
Stands in the breach of peace, whence he will call
Down fire on the bald, woolly heads of all
Professors of the other point of view,
Who, flanked and enfiladed and too few,
Will soon throw down their dated arms, of course,
And yield themselves to a superior force
Of well-drilled intellectual police,
Sworn on our honor to enforce the peace.

Chamber Music, Bar Harbor, Off-Season

Vivaldi's pizzicato winter falls
On my bared head, as on the tangerine
Tiles overhead, with a soft pluck that calls
Off summer, plain and Indian, to bring
On All-American autumn, full of tears
For all America's bright college years.
An instance: take this mouldering hotel,
Built as a monstrous cottage by a swell
Manhattan traction millionaire in 1910,
And now far past its hour; or take this room,
This second chamber: nobs bathed in its long,
Crazed tub with nickel fittings, and were clothed
In white tie, studs, and pumps by a slight man
(The Unknown Servant), and went down to dine.
Was not their bravery of living fine?
The closet holds a lockbox for their jewels;
The ceiling is as high as their desires;
The fireplace, dead, is ample for their fires;
The bed and desk conform to their taut rules.
Outside, the maples shed stars in the pools
On the decedent lawn. The chamber group
Strikes up its water music on the roof
Encore, fretting fleeting, immutable
Silver-toned strings tuned at the cedar eaves,
Bowed by the balustrade, frayed on the ground.
Likewise impermanent and perpetual,
What will we leave half as ebullient,
Triumphal, potent, personal as this
Old place, old pergola, old hearth, old house?
Roll on, then, fall, sole death we can remember,
Routing the summer in our rented chamber.

The Marschallin, Joy Street, July 3, 1949

Manchmal hör' ich sie fliessen —
unaufhaltsam.
Manchmal steh' ich auf mitten in der Nacht
und lass die Uhren alle, alle stehn.
    — *Hofmannsthal,* Rosenkavalier

The penal gaol of Mountjoy, gaol 'em and joy.
    — *James Joyce*

1 .

At 2200 hours, a silver flare
Profusely illustrates the western air,
Sending poor Mona Mountjoy to the heights
Of her tall town house overlooking Joy
And Pinckney Streets. Her long and shapely brown
Hands, dusted with the first faint liver spots
As if by accident, pick up her husband's Zeiss
Night glasses and range in on Harvard Square,
Bearing 290 at ten thousand yards.
Fire one! A small white integer appears,
Bears a huge school of yellow pollywogs,
And, with a white wink, vanishes. The boom
Takes twenty-seven seconds to arrive
Across East Cambridge as the crow flies. Now
A star shell bursts northeast. Dim in the south,
Dorchester Heights replies, and at her feet
The Common coughs up its first rocket of the night,
A red stem blooming in an amber star,
Which splits (by fission) into asterisks
As numerous and green as grass. At last
Her Major General has gone west tonight
(Though only literally), riding in a Jeep
Like any of his boys, and soon will sleep
Or lie, not unaccompanied, in the red
Light of a motel sign in Plattsburgh, where
He bivouacs for the morning march to Drum.

The Major General is gone; alas,
Without replacement. Ian Quinn tonight
Is racing for Bermuda in the moon
Which rises earlier for seafarers
Bound east. Northwest, an imitation moon
Sails over Cambridge and divides itself
Impartially in seven satellites
White as the Pleiades. A Common sun
Rim-lights her long face with its Sayward nose
And dark-blue Dunster eyes. A river wind
Stirs her half-silver hair, switches her dress
Around her knees, whistles a winter air
Among the guy wires. Dimly, deep downstairs,
A doorbell rings beneath the rocketry,
And Anna goes to answer. At this hour
Who would walk up the steep side of Joy Street
To call on her? Bad news? A telegram?
A yellow pang? No, now they use the 'phone.
She steps into the black trap to the top
Story, her long legs in up to the knee;
Then she is a tall torso, and then she
Takes her blond disembodied head below.
The dark fifth-story boxroom is still hot.
A fan croons in the maid's room on the fourth.
Her own third-floor bedroom is dark and still.
The upstairs parlor is lit by one lamp.
The downstairs one contains her husband's Uncle Will.

Returning, he says (over a long Scotch
Which he has made himself, apparently),
Returning from a meeting at the Union Club
Of the Parnassian Sodality
(Where, with his classmates of the Class of '94,
He sang, "Drink to Me Only with Thine Eyes,"
"We'll Go No More A-Roving," and, to close,
"Fair Harvard," in his obbligato voice);

Returning across Beacon and up Joy
Toward his little flat in Myrtle Street,
He thought to stop and call upon his niece,
And tell her his good news. (Out of one eye
She spies his dog-eared yellow calling card
On Anna's silver tray.) Good news indeed:
Will has determined to become betrothed,
At last, at last, to a lady of family.
One Mona knows; a famous beauty; young.
(He punctuates his points with a gold cane.)
In fact, Will says, his trustee's voice a thread
Of cunning whispering out of his starred face:
In fact, he is effecting nothing less
Than one more union of the Mountjoy line
With, — yes, the Saywards. Here is her picture,
Which a few hours ago at a rendezvous
She pressed into his hand; her miniature.
Mona takes the smudged half-column cut
Clipped from this morning's *Herald* society page.
"Post-deb," it says, "assists at fashion tea."
The girl is Sally Sayward, her own niece.
His eyes as blue as starry chicory flowers
In vacant lots, his purple smile as warm
As summertime, his manners beautiful
As any plate in *Godey's Lady's Book,*
He rises now to take his leave. "Enough,
My dear, of my good news. I must be off.
Good night, good night." Above Will's trilby hat,
The roof of Pinckney Street is shot with fire.

    4.

The fireworks are not done. She goes upstairs
To her housetop again. A grunt of rain
Clouds in the west announces the intent
Of the deluge to fall on schedule,
As promised on the radio. The Park
Commissioners of Cambridge show at last
The color of their money in a green,
Red, azure, nude, cerise, and chartreuse blast,

Whose elegant ballistics shame the moon.
Its third stage, firing, adumbrates the flank
Of the first nimbus cloud, whose sheer freeboard
Goes straight up twenty-seven thousand feet,
Past cumulus to cirrus. She remarks
The coolness of its first forerunning winds,
Their spearheads bypassing strong points of heat.
On such a night she met the General,
Disguised as Minot Mountjoy, bond broker,
Concealing the identity of the head
Of Hall & Mountjoy; equally disguised
As Captain Mountjoy of the 26th,
Whose olive shoulderboards sustained the pips
Which would grow into the commanding stars
Of 26th Division, National Guard,
Through the good offices of thirty years.
On such a night in 1922,
She met Mountjoy in summer's high estate,
An awkward Sayward daughter now a swan,
A beauty, twenty, and imprisoned him
With her short blond bob and her long dark laugh,
As he imprisoned her in the high place
She occupies alone on Joy Street now.

5.

Someplace, apparently Arlington, begins
Its own fire fight in the northwest. On such
A night, too, she met Ian Quinn. In June,
The Eastern Yacht Club is lit up at night
With amber lanterns where the members dance
Indoors and out; there, just two years ago,
She first danced with him. In the low light, she
Carried her forty-five years well; and he,
Worn with ten years at sea and four at war,
Looked older than his thirty-three. Two years,
Two years now they have occupied plotting
To intersect their courses on a chart
Awash with obstacles: stubborn routines
Running abysmally deep; mutual friends

Marking their channel everywhere like rocks;
Exhausting care and caution forming bars
To their resolve. (Against this set the shock
Of his hands on her bare arms in the dark
Hotel room after a month's absence, or
The quick kiss — "Watch my lipstick!" — at her door,
Containing a month's worth of intimacy.)
Nevertheless, the end is perfectly clear.

6.

Its magazines hit by a lucky shot,
The first cloud bursts into internal fire,
Suddenly started, suddenly put out.
When will his skillful, luckless shot hit her?
Soon. Only this morning, in her hand mirror,
She read between the lines state's evidence
Amassed by forty-seven years. No doubt
She dreamt again last night of waking in the small
Of the night's back and stopping all the clocks,
Upstairs and down, because she could not bear
To hear time running through its tidemarks. All
The signs are negative; the hour glass drops
To storm point; still the thunderheads come on.

7.

The Common finishes its business
For one more year with an immense barrage
Of small white rockets with a terrier's sharp
And penetrating bark. In the bright lights
Of their impermanent sky sign can be seen
One tear in her eye, to memorialize
The fact that one day, now, tomorrow, or
Next year, he will leave her for someone else
Younger and prettier, as her glass predicts.
Stupid to speculate: but if she had
Her wrenching wish, it would be Sally Sayward,
Her gawky niece irradiating love,
Her silly self at twenty over again.

8.

Before its time, chain lightning makes next day
Out of tonight, then fuses all its lights
With a white snick and a black avalanche,
Burying here and now and far away.
So time utters an annual report,
Heard loud and clear, on its last fiscal year
In the man market, on its day-to-day
Quotations, on its gains in brick and clay,
Its wins on the Exchange and in the Court
Of No Resort. The last man-made stars burn
Out in the west, the last spectacular
Dwindles to darkness in the captured fort.
The dandelions of light now go to seed.
In Joy Street, Mona Mountjoy, like the year,
Ends her summation and begins to turn
Toward the dockets of more pressing need:
A house to keep, a failure to hold dear,
A fiction to maintain, another year
To fill with guest appearances, each day
Farced full, penned black and blue, marked with a mort
Of dates, engagements, living tongues to learn
At Berlitz, trips to take, and friends to mourn.
Being herself, she takes it well indeed;
She has had all the fireworks she will need.
She goes belowstairs, an unbroken reed,
To put her windows down against the rain.

A Common Prophecy

Crossing the Common, instep-deep in leaves,
To see my man for governor, I hear
A stentor's voice across the amber sheaves
Of summer underfoot: a drone of fear

That could be newsboys heralding a war
Whose front might coincide with Tremont Street,
Knocking each English elm and Colonel Shaw
Into a cocked hat at my marching feet,

Which now tread out the vintage where the grapes
Of drought are stored for our posterity.
I isolate the voice. In marble drapes
Of muslin, on a platform of asperity —

A green bench — a white-headed sibyl stands
And damns us all. "Boston will be destroyed,"
She screams in a deep tenor, and her hands
Ring down our likely curtains from the void.

Bethlehem State

> In durance soundly cagèd
> On the lordly lofts of Bedlam,
>   With stubble soft and dainty,
> Brave bracelets strong, sweet whips ding-dong,
>   With wholesome hunger plenty.
> *— Old Song*

> *Et les moins sots, hardis amants de la Démence,*
> *Fuyant le grand troupeau parqué par le Destin. . . .*
> *— Baudelaire*

I. GERSON

You smile with all the irony of life,
Showing your teeth, on the stupidity

Of your unsubtle keepers. How can they
Use locks and laws to be your masters, these
Trusties and toadies, lackeys, state-lovers?
How can you bear such ciphers, noughts and crosses?
How can the bossed become their betters' bosses,
Saying, Now brush your teeth, it's time to dress,
Go to the toilet, meet your visitors?
No, no. These beefy clowns with broken veins
Across their faces, waxy, bony doctors
Who squat on some dark secret, flat-faced nurses
Abandoned to some shady appetite
Are nasty, brutish, short compared to you.
Your towering rages raise you high above
This sane and dwarfish rabble of your peers,
Or, anyway, contemporaries, who,
Seeing your danger, put you in your place
In the brown air of Bethlehem, compost
Of ethyl alcohol, warmed-up pot roast,
Sweat, rubber tile, and unclean urinals,
Gravy, mothballs, stale flowers, and funerals,
Where corridors connect with corridors,
And yellow halls run on to intersect
In interborough fissures of the mind;
Where, through a guarded door of steel, I find
You in the violent ward, as meek and mild
As any christom child, as my roommate
Of seven years ago. That was before
You packed more wings and spurs than I and flew
Onward and upward into the wild blue
Beyond where I could breathe in the thin air,
And melted in the sun and landed here.
Ah, Noah Gerson, grounded from your gross
Fugue into fancy, meet the plain people,
The drones who drag their bourdon out for life
And drown your voluntary. But you're safe:
They're all behind locked doors, and you sail on,
Still captain of your heart, aboard this ark
Whose passengers are your fellow-animals:
Rough beasts who slouched to Bethlehem to die,
Mild innocents immaculately conceived,
Old men, all veins, who babble of green fields,

Young fathers, short-haired mad executives.
Bon voyage, Noah, over a lost world.

II. BETHLEHEM

O little town of Bethlehem, N.Y.,
One Christmas past, another present, I
Stand once again on Cedar Mountain, and
Look down upon the old town which looks down
On the old Hudson from its barefaced bluff,
Whose summit brandishes Bethlehem State,
All cloud-capped mouse towers which encapsulate
Another of my fortune's hostages
Without a ransom note. Small, bitter snow
Ticks on my hatbrim, and the lights come on
At the end of another year in the toy town —
The red-and-green strings on the Bluevelt Street
Dime stores, a Santa Claus beneath my feet
In Rikerstown, a twinkling of lit trees
Up north in Haversack, and one magic
Pure-red festoon over the gilded name
Board of the old Columbiana Hose
Company No. 1 in Clinton Street.
Above its palisade, the hospital
Contributes "Merry Xmas" in white lights
Across its cruel and fanciful façade,
Whose dark, suggestive, and aberrant powers
Now toll me to its halls for visiting hours.

III. DR. CRANKHITE

Fourteen-foot-high ceilings. Mission oak.
Dooms of dark woodwork. Under one green lamp,
The rosy Doctor glows and stirs for me.
"Chief, Psychiatric Service," his nameplate
States, shaming me and my A.B. His hands
Manipulate a concertina made
Out of thin air as he explains, squeezing
Roomfuls of theory into pleasing

Musique concrète (which practicing perfects)
And drawing out, conversely, such sustained
Notes on the patient as would make a text,
And will, and will. But in mid-chord he stops,
Rapt on the podium before my eyes,
And ducks his knowing head and nods and sighs
"Electric shock," as cool as Boreas.
The chill freezes my face as he explains
Why, when our interest and patience flag,
Black magic is plugged in to stun the brain
And punish the offender. "Much improved.
Increasing manual skills. Depression, less.
Social adjustment, better. Danced last week.
On Tuesday, drew. All for the best. What else
Was there to do?" What else, what else? Thank you.

IV. MRS. EDWARDS

"O.K., Mr. Edwards, sit in here.
They'll have her down real soon." Ten minutes with
A coverless *Collier's* on the chill sun porch
Beside a spineless two-foot paper tree
With cardboard ornaments, and then I see
Her standing in the doorway, suddenly
Distant, diminished, vanished from herself,
Translucent, fragile, thin, invisible
The way she was short days ago. She sits,
A bird beside me on the wicker couch,
Shy, starving, who has put herself in danger
To take bread at my hand. And now I range
Over the pitiful subject matter I
Will be allowed to cover, hearing my
Words falling hollow down a well. She smiles,
As weathered as the winter sun which stands
Unmoved upon its solstice, as I hand
Her my square present in gold foil, which she
Cannot undo for her gross tremor. So
I open it to show the silver beads.
"They're beautiful. I'll put them on." Above
The issue bathrobe two sizes too big,
Below her thin and institutional

Cheek, on her young girl's neck, the necklace is
Stunningly wrong. What business has
Christmas coming around here, anyway?
Committed to forever and a day,
These inmates need no presents to destroy
The aimlessness of their routine, no holiday
To grant them crushing hope, no visitors
To exercise their wounds. It's time. She turns away
With a faint phrase I can't quite catch, and pads,
Beside her matron, down the vasty hall
Toward her quarters, till she is a small
White figure one in the far distance, where
We cannot touch each other any more.

Sondra Dead or Alive

I. CAMBRIDGE, 1955

The trouble was nobody laughed at her
Too witty poems when she read in 5
Harvard Hall. Professor Dix was there.
He smiled. Hardly a man is now alive.

Nevertheless, she is the talk of the town.
Or gown, at least. Divinity Avenue
Is bathed in her florescence. Down around
Memorial Drive she is a *succès fou.*

In her garden last night I laughed. Alas, too late.
I am afraid it came in the wrong place.
A poetess defends her puny kit
Fiercer than tigresses. Witness my face.

How can we classify this astonishing piece
Of resistance? Her underground effrontery

Is now quite superficial; underneath
The loud whalebone she is a quiet country.

Perhaps. Sumner, her husband, does not say
Word one. Burdened, he sometimes sighs.
Transfixed by his prize catch, day after day
He eats her with his macroscopic eyes.

II.   LE TOMBEAU DE SONDRA MANN

Outside the Ritz, half-past our fifth Martini
With a twist I hand you into your Healey,
Returning your spirituous kiss, not really
Caught in your gin as you turn up Newbury.

The blat of your exhaust scatters the leaves
Of a December *Herald* underfoot;
For halt pedestrians you give a hoot
And pop the clutch in potently, O brave

And disappearing racer, all too soon
Vanished beyond the end of Berkeley Street.
Now, queen and huntress in a bucket seat,
How come I pace your grave in the new moon?

ENVOY

As I sat in the Ritz-Carlton, drinking the crystal wine,
And outside in the world the old moon died, a silver rind,
They told me you were dead, chauffeur, and I, for auld lang syne,
Took one more cup of kindness for the coldness that was mine.

Man and Wife

You were a unit when I saw you last:
The handsome husband and the happy wife,
Which was an act; but tissue of the past
Between you, unseen, made you one for life,

Or so I thought. It seems that I was wrong.
Seeing you ten years later, the kids grown
And gone, the still light of the long
Living room coming between you, I should have known

The lines were down. Your life went on with such
Attention to unchange: each "darling" fell
With metered carelessness; each "please" with much
Conviction; each "thanks" rang true as a bell.

But when you walked me to the door to go,
I saw the fault between your faces. Oh.

Two Happenings in Boston

I. A DISAPPEARANCE IN WEST CEDAR STREET

Did Shriner die or make it to New York?
In his side room, across the hall from mine,
Wide windows air bare ticking. On a line
Outside, clean sheets flap. Samples of his work

Litter the closet: a barbed, wiry nude
In his hirsute pen line; a sketch of me
In ink and wash; a torn gouache of three
Pears on a windowsill. A cache of food —

Saltines, Velveeta Cheese, dried apricots —

Hid in a cairn of bags is now laid bare.
Also a bathrobe belt, one sock, a pair
Of sneakers with frayed laces tied in knots,

A paperback "Candide." Did Shriner die
While I was on the Cape? Did his cough stop
Dead in the welfare ward? Did a blue cop
Wheel Shriner out under the summer sky?

Did absolutely nobody appear
When they interred his box in Potter's Field?
(*I* would have been there.) Did nobody yield
A summer hat, a winter thought, a tear?

Or did he make it to New York? Did his
Ship dock at last at Fifty-seventh Street?
Did angels, agents, and collectors meet
His price for life? Is that where Shriner is?

Does he sit down now in Minetta's late
With mistresses and models on each hand?
And is he now an icon in the land
Of mind and matter southward of Hell Gate?

Grey curtains flutter. A tall smell of pork
Ascends the stairs. The landlady below
Tells me in broken English she don't know.
Did Shriner die or make it to New York?

II.   A READING IN HUNTINGTON AVENUE

Hernando Milton, scion of the grey
Daylight that realizes all the stale
Unprofitable flats of the Fenway,
Halftone from head to foot, beyond the pale

Of ordinary people, reads his play
Aloud in the Alliance of the Arts,
Heard out by the dried flower of the Back Bay,
In moulting foxes, as he takes all parts.

That phalanx of once-marbled womanhood
Whose forties closed their minds and shut their hearts
Adores to hear the son of the late good
Nan Makepeace, sadly laid low by the darts

Of two degenerative diseases; lewd
Behavior by her disappearing husband, missed
Alone by whisperers; extremely rude
News of her son; and one obituarist.

Hernando Makepeace Milton, known as Nan
(Just like his mother) to a little list
Of boys on Beacon Hill, reads with élan
To the foxed ladies who will miss the gist,

With luck, of his verse play, entitled "Pan
And Hemp," and wholly dedicated to
The keen sensations of a happy man
(Himself) while smoking hashish. No one who

Savors the sound of words like a devotee
Of the Alliance of the Arts dares do
More than lie back and let a lurid sea
Of tone colors ravish her hair-do.

The baby-blue spot points to the last dance
Spun out by Milton, whose whole face is blue
With that light and the onset of a trance
Of *cannabis indica*. The play comes true.

Provincetown, 1953

The terns and seagulls tremble at your death
In these home waters.
                                            — *Robert Lowell*

I. BACKS OF THE CAPE

Two people couple on the beach. Above,
A fish crow flies his pattern in a stack
Of seagulls, seeing flesh as carrion
On the flat sand below, between the blue
Brim of the ocean and its undertow,
And the drab green of scrub among the dunes.
The wind is west and hot. A charter boat
Winks on the outline of the world, and sand
Blows over rusty rails inshore. The white
Brick lighthouse on the point must wait for night
To say its message, though bare bodies flash
Their heliograph across broad day. Sea salt,
Sweat salt cement them, each to each, upon
The bright beach towel, and breath comes thicker till
Her legs lock, loosen, lock upon his legs,
And their love falls apart upon the sand,
Crossed by the shadow of one circling crow.

II. COMMERCIAL STREET

No weathered clapboard or white-painted stone
Is left unturned to profit in this old
Arcade of follies where fat trippers dodge
Long summerers in sneaks and amputee
Tan chinos severed far above the knee,
Who in their turn duck party-faced recruits
Straight from West Eighth Street in their chukka boots,
Who also *dos-à-dos,* this time with spare
Maids of the Cape who, single, mind the store
Less, on the whole, than liberties from their
Fresh boy friends lettered "P.H.S." The Pier
Offers escape through Off-Street Parking to
Some fishy old romance of tarry smacks

Champing at anchor in a lavender
Sea of dead squid trapped by the tide; but here,
Trammelled on every hand by souvenirs
And overseen by the grim Monument
(Upended splinter of a Romanesque
High school in Heidelberg, P.A.) and by
The Manor, borne up by its class of guest —
A summer swallow in a Madras vest —
And riding high on its paint Plimsoll line
Of freshness, we must face the peeling town:
Skeletal, florid, crass, alluring, dull,
Spontaneous, premeditated, whole.

III.   MANN'S PLACE

"Have you met Sondra?" "The entablature
Is filled with generals in relief." "I said, 'Look —
You can just shove your fellowship.' " "I love
That yellow maillot. Saks?" "The Pleistocene
Or earlier." "No. Double bitters." "Ham
Has played the Cherry Lane." "A Ford V-8."
"He had this great dead fish, my dear." *"Solfège."*
"No. She was Peter's cousin." "You have such
Astonishing green eyes." " 'Stuprate, they rend
Each other when they kiss.' " "No, please, no more
For me." "You just try teaching 101."
"Pure crimson lake." "Fourth down and two to go
And getting dark." "Say, who's your friend?" "Casals
Just swallows you in tone." " 'I do not hope
To turn again.' " "Oh, Harry's not so bad."
"Shut up." "There's something calm about you." "Where?"
" 'At the first turning of the second stair.' "
"Please, Michael, don't." "The Louvre." "Let's go outside."
"Her diction stinks." "My analyst just died."

IV.   THE KING ON A BIKE

Kings, queens, and aces shuffle on the scarred
Deck of the dance floor, drawing to each pair
The poker faces at the tables, where

Each name or number waits the call to dance
The permutations of the draw, the chance
To join another in a game of bluff
Against the world, which sees or calls enough
Sooner or later so we win or lose.
But now the operative term is choose:
One's dress, one's step, one's love, one's mind, one's mask
(Unfrightening, unlike one's face), one's task
To be evaded or embraced for life,
Erect, immutable, the stainless knife
That shapes us to a point or pares us down.

V.   RACE POINT: $5 PLANE RIDE

Down-ocean from our climbing Piper Cub
And its flat shadow skipping over dunes,
Skimming the yellow shallows of lagoons,
Skirting the ocean, green, blue-green, and blue,
The girl in our plane's belly sights a grey
Great tadpole shape and shouts, "A whale! A whale!"
A whale, indeed, proceeds across our tail
In keel-deep water, one infrequent fluke
Just punting him along. A whale: a fluke
Of ocean to remind the Cape people
Of the eroded point of the harpoons
Which rust above their mantels. The sole whale
Patrolling his home waters, the white light
Which signals the sand's end, the ultimate
Stone shack with two-throat foghorns on its rock,
All serve historic functions: statues all,
Alive or not, commemorate this point's
Last turn from the saline concerns of sea —
Fish, ships, storms, fresh names in the cemetery —
To the demands of land and their supply.

VI.   EPILOGUE: ROUTE 6

Only the contact patches of our tires —
Sixty square inches — bind us to the world
Which we pass over lightly late at night.
Route 6 unreels its story line in white
Morse dashes on a static brook of black.

Faint bluffs corroborate the presence of
A planet under us. In the dash light —
If I should dare to turn my head — I'd see
Who you are with me, whether blond or brown,
Blue-eyed or otherwise, plain, handsome, thin,
Short, tall, or in-between. Between us fall —
Across the strait tan seat of my MG —
Sands of the dunes of anonymity
Where we are set to track a barren mate,
A desert passenger whose drifted face,
An undeciphered stone, may be the one:
A matter of indifference to the sun.

The West Forties:
Morning, Noon, and Night

But nothing whatever is by love debarred.
— *Patrick Kavanagh*

I. WELCOME TO HOTEL MAJESTY
(SINGLES $4 UP)

On this hotel, their rumpled royalties
Descend from their cross-country busses, loyalties
Suspended, losses cut, loves left behind,
To strike it lucky in the state of mind
That manufactures marvels out of mud.
Ensanguined by a bar sign selling Bud,
The early-streamline lobby — in its shell
Of late-Edwardian ornament, with a bell-
Mouthed cupidon extolling every swag
On its tall, fruitful front (a stale sight gag
First uttered by the comic landsmen who
Compounded a Great White Way out of blue
Sky, gneiss, and schist a whole stone age ago,
Before time steeled the arteries we know) —

The lobby washes redly over guests
With rope-bound bags containing their one best
Suit, shirt, tie, Jockey shorts, and pair of socks,
Half-empty pint, electric-razor box,
Ex-wife's still-smiling picture, high-school ring,
Harmonica, discharge, and everything.
Amid the alien corn and ruthless tares,
I hear a royal cry of horseplayers
Winding their tin horns in a chant of brass,
Their voices claiming in the wilderness.

II. SAL'S ATOMIC SUBMARINES

The Puerto Rican busboy, Jesus, coughs
Above the cutting board where Sal compiles
An outbound order for the Abinger
Associates next door; then, carrying
A pantheon of Heroes in a brown
Kraft-paper bag, he sidles by the chrome-
Formica-plastic dinette furniture
And gains the world, where anti-personnel
Gasses from crosstown busses, vegetable
Soup simmering at Bickford's, and My Sin
Seeping from Walgreen's silently combine
To addle all outsiders. Only lithe,
Quick indigenes like Jesus (whose tan neck
Is thinner than my wrist) can long survive
And later even prosper in the air
Of these times' squares, these hexahedral hives
Where every worker bustles for his Queen.

III. PENNY ARCADIA

Like lava, rock erupts to fill the room
From each coäx-, coäx-, coäxial
Concentric speaker's throat, and rolls like doom
Over the unmoved pinball-playing boys,
Whose jaws lightly reciprocate like long-
Stroke pistons coupled to the Tinguely loom
Of augmented electric music, strong

74

As sexuality and loud as noise,
Which keens across the dingy room at full
Gain, and, its coin gone, as abruptly dies.

IV.   STAGE DOOR JOHNNY'S

Silvana Casamassima, Vic Blad
(The talent agent), Lance Bartholomey,
Piretta Paul, Max Dove, A. Lincoln Brown,
Samarra Brown, Lil Yeovil, Beryl Cohn
(Theatrical attorney), Johnny Groen
(The owner), Merritt Praed, Morty Monroe,
Dame Phyllis Woolwich, Sir Jack Handel, Bart.,
Del Specter (the producer), Coquetel,
Fab Newcomb, Temple Bell, Vanessa Vane,
Burt Wartman, C. R. Freedley, F.R.S.,
Alf Wandsworth (author of "Queer Street"), Mel Hess,
His Honor Judge Perutz, Merced McCall,
Tam Pierce, Bill Brewer, Tom Cobley, and all
The darlings, mirrored in their flourishing
Autographed caricatures on every wall,
Sail on, sealed in, important, bright, serene,
In league in Captain Nemo's submarine.

V.   M. WAX LOANS

Clear and obscure, elbows of saxophones
Shine out like sink traps in an underworld
Of pledges unredeemed: a spectral band
Of brass and nickel marching in the dark
Toward the morning and redemption, where
Known lips will kiss their reeds, familiar hands
Resume their old and loving fingering.
Unlikely: in a hundred rented rooms
From here to Ybor City, pledgors plan
What next to pawn: the Rolleicord, the ring,
The eight-transistor Victor radio,
The travelling alarm. Alarm creeps in-
To all their calculations, now the bloom
Is off their promise, now the honeymoon

Is over with a cry, and time begins
To whittle expectations to a size
Convenient for their carrying to pawn.

VI.   LOVEMOVIE

Before the glazed chrome case where Lovelies Swim
Au Natural, and under the sly lights
Which wink and bump and wink and grind, except
For those that have burnt out, the singing strings
Of Madame Violin essay "Caprice,"
Not missing many notes, considering
How cold it is outside the Lovemovie.
Stray pennies in her tin cup punctuate
The music like applause. Play, gypsies! Dance!
The thin strains of a Romany romance
Undaunt the ears of each peajacketed
Seaman on liberty, and of each old
Wanderer slowly losing to the cold,
And of each schoolboy who has come to see
Life in the flesh inside the Lovemovie.
Beneath her stiff green hair, an artist's grin
Knits up the ravelled cheek of Madame Violin.

VII.   THE ARGO BUILDING:
NEW DELMAN'S GOOD NIGHT

The last bone button in the old tin tea
Box of the Argo Building lastly sees
GNIVAEWER ELBISIVNI peeling off
His street-side window as he locks the door
Of 720 one more night, and struts
His septuagenarian stuff down
The corridor, past Aabco Dental Labs,
Worldwide Investigations, Inc., Madame
Lillé, Corsetiere, Star School of Tap,
Dr. O'Keefe, Franck Woodwind Institute,
Wink Publications, and Watch Hospital.
Up the wrought shaft, preceded by its wires
Ticking and twittering, the intrepid car

Rises like an old aeronaut to take
Its ballast-passenger aboard beneath
The pointed clear bulbs of its four flambeaux,
Sweetly attenuated art nouveau
Which was *vieux jeu* and is the rage, unknown
To old New Delman, whom it ferries down
In its black cage, funebrially slow,
To Stygian Forty-seventh Street below.

The Nanny Boat, 1957

Towards the end he sailed into an extraordinary mildness,
And anchored in his home and reached his wife
And rode within the harbour of her hand . . .
                              — *W. H. Auden*

                    Relish the love of a gentle woman.
                              — *John Cheever*

I. DOWN

        I .

A surf of people, backlit by the sun,
Washes across Atlantic Avenue
To Rowe's Wharf, where the Nanny Boat awaits
Its gilt-edged Friday-night commuters, borne
Out of the city on a roasting wave
Of Victor Coffee. Soon that city scent
Gives in to those of shore and sea. You step
Infinitely daintily, treading my heart
With your white size-five foot, aboard the boat
Bound for Nantasket and for night, where you
Will understudy seas in undulant
Compliance and reception, swamping all
My longboat adjectives. Cast off the bow
And stern lines linking us to the upright,
August, and sobersided city, and
Back half-speed out into the glassy reach —

Cased yellow by the molten sun — which leads
South to anonymous liberties, where town
Clothes come ungirt and naked bankers lie
Late on the sand beside associates.

2.

My Nikon neatly juxtaposes you,
Tall, dominant, with the recessive, squat
Skyline of Boston, in its unabridged
Wide-angle condensation. Click, and it
Is history, distorted, black-and-white,
And two-dimensional at that. (Think now,
Eight good years later, of those passages
To sea and not to sea, those passages
Between us which we shared with Spectacle
Island and Gallup's Island, those long green
Fluent quotations of cold fact and salt
Occurrences about the boat, which, aureous,
For the short span of sunset, blanched and went blue
When day was done.) Later, the running lights,
The dusty bulbs above the bar, the cream
Fluorescent strips refract on the night air
And make a great white, green, red, cream
Mirage on the horizon, even beyond
Hull Gut and Bumpkin Island. The Sturgeon Moon
Levers itself, yellow as piano keys,
Out of the eastern sea and stains the waves
Its summer color. Lovers, limited,
Perhaps, to this boat ride to demonstrate
Their aims, melt into one under the moon
Along the promenade deck; we, sedate,
Smoke, knowing we can well afford to wait
For spring tides in the middle of the night.

II.   THERE

1.

The far mirage is an oasis now:
Beyond World's End, the spitting negative

Image of the city we left at five
Takes shape in the solutions of the sea.
Black towers go white, and, shivering to the shore,
Lead our wide eyes up white towers in the air
Above the sky signs advertising love
In a lost language: O's of ferris wheels,
The cursive of the roller coaster, scrawls
Of neon on the rooflines of dance halls,
All ciphers for a scholar to decode.
Your face, a spectrogram, reflects their shades
Of meaning, green, red, white, as we slip in
To dock at this free port of noise, whose din —
Calliopes, pop records, human cries —
Projects the same sensational offer of
Love for mere money, though the easy terms
Are unintelligible through
The language barrier, *comprenez-vous?*
But on the dock, spelled out in silver light
Dispensed by Paragon Park, we read two old
Familiar names, Frannie and Ed, who wait
In the old yellow Willys wagon. Friends,
Greet two new voyagers to the World's End.

     2.

Out those wide windows Hingham paints itself,
Impeccably, if academically,
In the low-key, representational
Shades of a summer night. Well to the west,
A knot of lights, the Center, sends a line
In Morse across the water to Crow Point,
Calling my maritime interests to
Three granite islets, possibly archly named
Ragged, Sarah, Langlee, harboring
Just underneath my window. The moon's sway
As night-light laureate is threatened by
Arc lightning in the western front of cloud.
My host's voice calls me back. I wake and drown
In the dry world of letters. "Lefty, you
Don't really mean it about Gilbert, do
You, seriously, I mean?" "Why, sure I do,"
I say. "Come on, just tell me who

Else wrote a decent line of satire in
The bloody century. Why, Porter and
The Major-General are radical
Caricatures, Ed, archetypes.'' ''Go *on!*''
''No really.'' ''Hell, let's have a nightcap.'' ''Yeah!''
We toast our differences in B.P.R.
And Pierce's No. 6 commingled. Wug!
That's bracing going down. The evening ends
In inconclusion, as it should with friends.

3.

To quote my later self, ''I punctuate
Your long body with exclamations.'' Not
Terribly temperate; nor was I then,
Between a skinful of cheap rye and a
Head full of Great Ideas. Then there was you
To blame, with that invisible smirk
I could see as plain as anything in the dark,
And your slow pulse just slipping up the shore
And barely sliding back, and worst of all,
Your cool electrifying skin humming
With wattage waiting for the switch to close.
Fused and short-circuited at last, we doze
Until a jovial thunderclap hits home
And takes our pictures with a massive flash
That just goes on and on, while we sit up
Like couples caught by eyes in hotel rooms,
And face the music. Rain comes down like doom.

III.   BACK

1.

A bodkin through my head, I watch the view,
Which, as a dayscape, paints itself anew
(With cunning strokes around the shoreline), while
I wait for bacon frying. Mesmerized
By smoke from your bent Viceroy, you still sit
Cross-legged on the sofa, eyes at ease.

Soon we will fly from this well-ordered here,
Complete with friends, to an amorphous there,
Hull down on the horizon, where we will
Take steps to walk together or apart.
Whichever, in this moment I concede
Your beauty and necessity aside
From any need of mine, which makes my need
Decided and imperative. Be mine.

2.

Pink stucco steams behind us as we steam
Away from hot Nantasket, where the brass
Poles of the carrousels, the steering wheels
Of Dodg'ems, and the rusty grab rails on
The front of roller-coaster cars are all
Too hot to touch, and where the towering
Totems of Popeye, Jiggs, and Mickey Mouse
(Done by some village Lichtenstein, some mute
Inglorious Warhol using old house paint)
Peel in the August sun, while we creep in
To the tiny shade of the top deck, drinking
Warm, sticky Coke in paper cups. They pass,
The harbor islands, one by one, astern,
Rapt in a heat haze. The sleek, moneyed sea,
All gold and green, turns in its figured sheets
As it sleeps off a stormy night. We draw
The city slowly closer to our bow.

3.

All this our north stinks peace. The cabbage leaves
Downtrodden on the Market cobbles, and
The fish heads festering in garbage cans
Outside the shuttered fish stores lend their loud
Saturday odors to disturb the peace
Of Sunday in the city. Carrying
Your Winship overnight bag, I walk up
The shady side of every street beside
You, to the desert waste of Cambridge Street.

We brave the sun to cross. Around the bend
Under the El, and up West Cedar Street,
And up four flights to your apartment, where
You turn the fan on, and I'm home
At last with you the first time in my life,
My anchor, my harbor, my second wife.

Love-Making; April; Middle Age

A fresh west wind from water-colored clouds
Stirs squills and iris shoots across the grass
Now turning fiery green. This storm will pass
In dits and stipples on the windowpane
Where we lie high and dry, and the low sun
Will throw rose rays at our grey heads upon
The back-room bed's white pillows. Venus will
Descend, blue-white, in horizontal airs
Of red, orange, ochre, lemon, apple green,
Cerulean, azure, ultramarine,
Ink, navy, indigo, at last midnight.
Now, though, this clouded pewter afternoon
Blurs in our window and intensifies
The light that dusts your eyes and mine with age.

We turn our thirties over like a page.

Dying: An Introduction

Always too eager for future, we
Pick up bad habits of expectancy.
— *Philip Larkin*

I. RING AND WALK IN

Summer still plays across the street,
An ad-hoc band
In red, white, blue, and green
Old uniforms
And borrowed instruments;
Fall fills the street
From shore to shore with leaves,
A jaundiced mass
Movement against the cold;
I slip on ice
Slicks under powder snow and stamp my feet
Upon the doctor's rubber mat,
Ring and Walk In
To Dr. Sharon's waiting room,
For once with an appointment,
To nonplus
Ugly Miss Erberus.
Across from other candidates —
A blue-rinsed dam
In Davidows, a husk
Of an old man,
A one-eyed boy — I sit
And share their pervigilium.
One *Punch* and two
Times later comes the call.

II. PROBABLY NOTHING

Head cocked like Art, the *Crimson* linotype
Operator, Dr. Sharon plays
Taps on my game leg, spelling out the name,
With his palpating fingers, of my pain.
The letters he types are not visible
To him or me; back up the melting pot

83

Of the machine, the matrix dents the hot
Lead with a letter and another: soon a word,
Tinkling and cooling, silver, will descend
To be imposed upon my record in
Black-looking ink. "My boy, I think," he says,
In the most masterly of schoolish ways,
In the most quiet of all trumps in A
Flat, "this lump is probably nothing, but" —
A but, a buzz of omen resonates —
"I'd check it anyway. Let's see when I
Can take a specimen." Quiet business
With the black phone's bright buttons. St, ssst, sst.
An inside call. In coded whispers. Over. Out.
"Can you come Friday noon? We'll do it then."
I nod I can and pass the world of men
In waiting, one *Life* farther on.

III.   O.P.O.R.

Undressing in the locker room
Like any high school's, full of shades
In jockstraps and the smell of steam,
Which comes, I guess, from autoclaves,
And not from showers, I am struck
By the immutability,
The long, unchanging, childish look
Of my pale legs propped under me,
Which, nonetheless, now harbor my
Nemesis, or, conceivably,
Do not. My narcissistic eye
Is intercepted deftly by
A square nurse in a gas-green gown
And aqua mask — a dodo's beak —
Who hands me a suit to put on
In matching green, and for my feet
Two paper slippers, mantis green:
My invitation to the dance.
I shuffle to the table, where
A shining bank of instruments —
Service for twelve — awaits my flesh
To dine. Two nurses pull my pants

Down and start shaving. With a splash,
The Doctor stops his scrubbing-up
And walks in with a quiet "Hi."
Like hummingbirds, syringes tap
The novocaine and sting my thigh
To sleep, and the swordplay begins.
The stainless-modern knife digs in —
Meticulous trencherman — and twangs
A tendon faintly. Coward, I groan.
Soon he says "Sutures," and explains
To me he has his specimen
And will stitch up, with boundless pains,
Each severed layer, till again
He surfaces and sews with steel
Wire. "Stainless." Look how thin it is,
Held in his forceps. "It should heal
Without a mark." These verities
Escort me to the tiring room,
Where, as I dress, the Doctor says,
"We'll have an answer Monday noon."
I leave to live out my three days,
Reprieved from findings and their pain.

IV. PATH. REPORT

Bruisingly cradled in a Harvard chair
Whose orange arms cramp my pink ones, and whose black
Back stamps my back with splat marks, I receive
The brunt of the pathology report,
Bitingly couched in critical terms of my
Tissue of fabrications, which is bad.
That Tyrian specimen on the limelit stage
Surveyed by Dr. Cyclops, magnified
Countless diameters on its thick slide,
Turns out to end in -oma. "But be glad
These things are treatable today," I'm told.
"Why, fifteen years ago — " a dark and grave-
Shaped pause. "But now, a course of radiation, and — "
Sun rays break through. "And if you want X-ray,
You've come to the right place." A history,
A half-life of the hospital. Marie

Curie must have endowed it. Cyclotrons,
Like missile silos, lurk within its walls.
It's reassuring, anyway. But bland
And middle-classic as these environs are,
And sanguine as his measured words may be,
And soft his handshake, the webbed, inky hand
Locked on the sill, and the unshaven face
Biding outside the window still appall
Me as I leave the assignation place.

V. OUTBOUND

Outside, although November by the clock,
Has a thick smell of spring,
And everything —
The low clouds lit
Fluorescent green by city lights;
The molten, hissing stream
Of white car lights, cooling
To red and vanishing;
The leaves,
Still running from last summer, chattering
Across the pocked concrete;
The wind in trees;
The ones and twos,
The twos and threes
Of college girls,
Each shining in the dark,
Each carrying
A book or books,
Each laughing to her friend
At such a night in fall;
The two-and-twos
Of boys and girls who lean
Together in an A and softly walk
Slowly from lamp to lamp,
Alternatively lit
And nighted; Autumn Street,
Astonishingly named, a rivulet
Of asphalt twisting up and back
To some spring out of sight — and everything

Recalls one fall
Twenty-one years ago, when I,
A freshman, opening
A green door just across the river,
Found the source
Of spring in that warm night,
Surprised the force
That sent me on my way
And set me down
Today. Tonight. Through my
Invisible new veil
Of finity, I see
November's world —
Low scud, slick street, three giggling girls —
As, oddly, not as sombre
As December,
But as green
As anything:
As spring.

Canzone: Aubade

Morning, noon, afternoon, evening, and night
Are not all seasons that we need to know;
Though we would go lamely without the night,
Recircling on itself, night after night,
Assuring us an opposite, a way
To action of a kind that honest night
Would never dream of, sibilant brief night
Could not conceive: the bitter stroke of noon.
Better that we conceive of dawn than noon,
That place where all things shift, and middle night
Sits for its portrait in half light, and still
Sits obstinately in two lights, quite still.

Though dawn is at the window, you, all still,
Take the small part of small hours of the night
And sleep away the morning, small and still,

Till my minuscule action wakes you. Still,
I cannot think that you, awaking, know
The whispered confidence of nighttime still.
Outside, the city's streets are silent still;
And morning still attempts to find a way
To say itself; and donkey's years away
Keeps hot important midday, trying still
To blandish us with talk of afternoon;
But we know now the pitilessness of noon.

I cannot think of you at all at noon
As my late lover whose long body still
I punctuate with exclamations. Noon —
The rigid, brazen, upright arm of noon —
Casts a long shadow between now and night
Where intervened the tortuous forenoon:
The twice-told tale of snaillike afternoon,
That we know better than we need to know.
What is there, after all, for us to know
That meaning clings to in the eye of noon?
Through the slow afternoon we seek a way
Of meeting evening's sullen change halfway.

Now it is middle afternoon, halfway
To evening; and, looking back on noon,
I marvel to have found some kind of way
To pass the stolid hours that guard you. Way
Off somewhere in the darkness you lie still,
Not quite recapturable, and part way
To capturing you my thought falls away
To urgencies of afternoon. All night
Your phosphorescence clarifies the night,
Makes light of darkness, indicates the way
To tunnels' ending: darling, you must know
The dead-white end of the dark road we know.

New schemes, new modes, new paradigms? We know
All of our love must go the same old way.
We must discredit learning; all I know
Is evening keeping us apart. You know
Like me that memory at noon
Springs on us all the secrets that we know

About ourselves, to try if we can know
The agony of aloneness. Lying still,
We paint ourselves all black. O lover, still
It stirs me every evening to know
We pay such court to turnings in the night;
And my thoughts take you as if day were night.

ENVOY

At last, alas! day is born out of night,
And, though our pain persists in sleeping still,
It will arise and flourish at high noon,
And furious, constant, seek to find a way
Out of our time, the only one we know.

Scattered Returns

For Howard Moss

The highest artist grapples up his art
One-handed; with the other, reaches out
To those below him on the slope above
The anonymous abyss: a grasp of love.

I

Scattered Returns

A Deathplace

Very few people know where they will die,
But I do: in a brick-faced hospital,
Divided, not unlike Caesarean Gaul,
Into three parts: the Dean Memorial
Wing, in the classic cast of 1910,
Green-grated in unglazed, Aeolian
Embrasures; the Maud Wiggin Building, which
Commemorates a dog-jawed Boston bitch
Who fought the brass down to their whipcord knees
In World War I, and won enlisted men
Some decent hospitals, and, being rich,
Donated her own granite monument;
The Mandeville Pavilion, pink-brick tent
With marble piping, flying snapping flags
Above the entry where our bloody rags
Are rolled in to be sponged and sewn again.
Today is fair; tomorrow, scourging rain
(If only my own tears) will see me in
Those jaundiced and distempered corridors
Off which the five-foot-wide doors slowly close.
White as my skimpy chiton, I will cringe
Before the pinpoint of the least syringe;
Before the buttered catheter goes in;
Before the I.V.'s lisp and drip begins
Inside my skin; before the rubber hand

Upon the lancet takes aim and descends
To lay me open, and upon its thumb
Retracts the trouble, a malignant plum;
And finally, I'll quail before the hour
When the authorities shut off the power
In that vast hospital, and in my bed
I'll feel my blood go thin, go white, the red,
The rose all leached away, and I'll go dead.
Then will the business of life resume:
The muffled trolley wheeled into my room,
The off-white blanket blanking off my face,
The stealing, secret, private, *largo* race
Down halls and elevators to the place
I'll be consigned to for transshipment, cased
In artificial air and light: the ward
That's underground; the terminal; the morgue.
Then one fine day when all the smart flags flap,
A booted man in black with a peaked cap
Will call for me and troll me down the hall
And slot me into his black car. That's all.

The Harvest, State Street

Higgledy-piggledy, Spartan Titans made
Their barren nests, like pack rats, in the eaves
And cellars of these towers. Eternal shade
Attended their brusque bringing in of sheaves

And laying up of promissory notes,
Parcels of empty earth, dry ledger leaves,
Seemingly worthless stocks, tie-breaking votes
Cast like first stones as these men, sinless, bade.

Scattered Returns:

Three Derivative Poems

(To Peter Davison, a close contemporary
who knows how it is to be young and old)

I. A CROWD FLOWED OVER BOYLSTON STREET,
   SO MANY

Old women thin as new moons, and as veiled
In lavender, step lively to the show
Windows of proper shops, stemming the flow
Of companies of broad-faced businessmen
Bound west to barter, and their color guard,
Curt-skirted clericals in parrot tones.
Teen armies send patrols: a rebel scout
Winds by upon his Honda, trailing curls
And staring down the hollow squares staked out,
In thin grey trainees' uniforms, before
The glass expanse of IBM's front door.
A matron and her mother matron strut
Between the lines in clothes of classic cut
And faces of timeless unloveliness
To shop at Peck & Peck and peck away .
The shell of hours around another day
That stands between them and repose. A short,
Hoarse newsboy, sixty, curses two short, hoarse
Newsboys, both ten. Badge-bearing engineers,
Fresh out of sessions, earnestly converse
Over their settlement of the universe.
Executives bend barward on the stroke
Of noon (succeeded by an out-of-tune
Electric carillon), fixed on the first
Martini of the day, on the first joke
To break the ice of isolation, fear,
And blank routine in blinding sheets and floes.
Bums rifle baskets for the morning line;
Teachers lead straggling classes to the field;
Brokers define the poles of growth and yield

In their rich storefronts; and just then one fine-
Faced man calls, "Edwards! You remember me.
Stetson. The freshman crew in '43."
"Of course. What's new?" "Same thing as ever. You?"
"Same thing. Your family?" "Fine. And yours?" "Just fine."
"One grandchild now." "That's great. Will you be at
The Twenty-fifth?" "The Twenty-fifth? Of course.
I wouldn't miss it. There's so much that's new
To talk about, so much under the bridge."
"That's true." "Must run." "Me, too." "So long." "See you."

II. COMING UP FOR AIR

The other day I drove through Binfield, Mass.,
And stopped: the first time since the year of drab,
Since 1944, when I and Mab
Made common cause against the town, the school,
The war (not ours), the weak, relenting rule
Of old fools over us. In Binfield then,
There was no place to go after the Bowl
For sodas, after movies at the Bin
(Where Mrs. Miniver braved on and on),
Except the Common, open to the eye
Of the town cop and every passerby;
Except the long, entangling open fields
Beyond the single street's last light, where we
Flindered our reputations in the grass.

All that time vanished, I, a conservator
Now of real money and real property,
With a new generation to excise
And tax with my displeasure, to suppress
Under the fiat of my years' success,
Drove into Binfield, Mass., and stopped beyond
The new transistor plant, where a long row
Of women's clothing stores, all clapboarded
In white aluminum, all roofed in grey
Shingles of vinyl, stood across the way
From where the Perkins Block had tumbled down
To make space for the busy Town 'n' Gown
Motel, home of the charming Common Room.

Beyond the parking meters, row on row,
I saw new acroliths: the multiplied
Endowments of alumnae who had died
And been rebodied in the shape of Art
And Science, in the form of Freshman Halls,
Squat Cages, oblong Libraries, and gaunt
Administration Buildings. My poor Mab,
Wherever you may be, dead or alive,
I hope that you do not revisit this
Scene of our innocence, whose innocence
Has been so sedulously vandalized,
Defaced, deflowered by the likes of us.

III. GARE DU MIDI

South Station. Late, the N.E. States arrives
With no great hissing, but a Diesel hum
And fume under the train shed. I return
To Boston after absence in New York,
Rearmed by my unanonymity.
Down there, beyond the hotel register,
My name was nominal; my printless hand,
Beyond its signature, could grasp but one
Lever of power: the bullying currency
Cached in my wallet. Three days nameless but
For Sir (and I no knight) or Mister, three
Days impotent, unrecognized, and I
Became a fugitive from my unsought self.
The train was refuge; from the pricking plush
In the stale parlor car I got my first
Reintimation of existence, soon
Confirmed by my sweet seatmate, once a prince
Of bores among time salesmen, now a king
Who called me by my right and simple style,
Told dirty jokes for many a measured mile,
And quite restored me to myself, along
With a drab Radcliffe girl who knew I wrote
And whom I helped into her fur-trimmed coat
At Back Bay Station. Clutching my Peal case,
I disembark now one stop down the line
And walk out through the Terminal, a place

Well named for its impending death, and staffed
By proper supernumeraries — two
Young drunken sailors, one whole porter who
Truckles one bag on his vast trolley, one
Sleep-sweeper, who, somnambulistical,
Cleans creepily down acres of the hall —
To Dewey Square, where I come face to face
With my place and my power where I belong,
Am known, hold down a job, command respect
For unclear reasons, order other lives,
Own action and invest it, shape, decide.
Unmet, unwelcomed, undeterred by pity,
I walk out briskly to infect my city.

Sonatina: Hospital

In God's hotel, the nuns in white
And royal blue refract the dawn
From each sharp, soft prune-prism face;
Their habits, dark, absorb the night
Until the aube's-egg blue is gone
And level red rays take its place,
Brazing the stiff coifs with their bright
Chasing on cotton, muslin, lawn:
Gold, silver, then the gray of base
Metals. The nuns in God's hotel
Move forward through the waves of day;
Marine times of a matins bell
Govern their visits to each bay
Of sickness, to each sound of pain,
To each discrete part of the main.

Patrick Kavanagh:

An Annotated Exequy

Well, Kavanagh, you've gone and done it, died
They way you said you would, propped up with pride
And penury in a dim nursing home
In Dublin, not in Monaghan. The morn-
Ing newspapers[1] said what you said they would,[2]
Not mourning, so it's nice and tidy. Good.
But wait. I'm here to say a thing or two
About a lovely man I never knew
Who lived in lodgings next door to despair,
And caught the winter light in Gibson Square,[3]
And walked alone in crumbling Islington,
And saw the setting of the Irish sun
On the potato fields of Monaghan
Across the ocean wild and wide, a home
To be escaped from and returned to, where
Calves called for his deft hands, and up the stair
The mother lay in her bare, crucified
Chamber, as old and constant as the tide
In rising and receding to and from
The complicated presence of a son,
Or else his absence. Absent in a slum
Of Dublin or of London, he conveyed
His country to the city, which he made
New with his patient peasant heart and hand

---

[1] The morning newspapers and the radio
Announced his death in a few horrid words:
— A man of talent who lacked the little more
That makes the difference
Between success and failure.
— "Portrait of the Artist"

[2] Reputation for Eccentricity
Said to Have Overshadowed
Talents as a Writer
— Obituary in the *Times*

[3] I'll show you a holier aisle —
The length of Gibson Square
Caught in November's stare
That would set you to prayer.
— "News Item"

And urbane horn-rimmed head. Of course he'd stand —
And be stood — too much drink in darkling bars
And wake up to the anthem of the cars
And lorries of the morning. But he got
On with the serious business of what
An artist is to do with his rucksack
Of gift, the deadweight that deforms his back
And drives him on to prodigies of thought
And anguishes of execution, bought
At all cost of respectability
And all expense of nice society,
Until, alone, he faces homely him,
The only other tenant of his room,
And finds the world well lost.[4] Well, Kavanagh,
Possession being nine points of the law,
I find you guilty of possession of
The mortal spirit of unstinted love
For all things animate and otherwise,
And of the fatal talent to devise
Live poems expressing it, transcending all
Obituaries which record your fall.[5]

---

[4]   And I also found some crucial
Documents of sad evil that may yet
For all their ugliness and vacuous leers
Fuel the fires of comedy. The main thing is to continue,
To walk Parnassus right into the sunset
Detached in love where pygmies cannot pin you
To the ground like Gulliver. So good luck and cheers.
          — "Dear Folks"

[5] He's finished and that's definitely.
          — "The Same Again"

An Unknown Western-Union Boy

Fifteen years in this down-at-heel arcade,
Your face has crossed mine like a concave blade,
The new moon's arm cocked on the old, a scythe
Reaping a field of people, a long horn
That holds one worn note constantly, although,
Boy, now your head sustains a fall of snow,
And your cheeks deepen with erosion, lose
Their fertile topsoil, carried down by days,
A Mississippi, to your delta mouth.
Your glasses flash a message still; your neat
And backhand figure prints on serif feet
Communication's progress; your bent hand
Grips on its quiver yellow arrows of
Desire, dismissal, supplication, love,
As ever. Best regards. Please expedite.
Order today. Tomorrow is the night.

Lüchow's and After

Dinner at Lüchow's. The invisible man —
Replete, clean-shaven, in a quiet tan
Dacron-and-worsted suit — pays up, gets up,
Walks out, dodging a junkie and a drunk
Disintegrating on the sidewalk, and
Heads south to haunt old haunts, a fattening,
Unlikely ghost of his emaciate
Old self. Unriotous Fifth Avenue —
Asleep in almost as profound a sleep
As in its teens, that mammoth cave of mens-
Wear basted in black silk and lined with blue
Star-pattern Bemberg — peels back from my eyes
In skeins of years: Macmillan's, Sixty-Eight,
The church in its iron close, the Grosvenor,
The other church, the old Fifth Avenue,

Apartments unremembered, Number One —
A cut-rate *gratte-ciel* — the gash of Eighth
Street bleeding neon, the streetlight-white Arch,
The Square alive with songs and arguing,
The gloomy Reggio, the tough tenderloin
Beyond it: the mean streets of immigrant-
Less tenements now turned to kinky bars,
Tout-fronted supper clubs for out-of-town
Explorers, cafés packed with solid sound
By small groups with big amps, long poster shops,
Wildcat theatres seating sixty-two,
Diggers' free stores, and *boîtes* that promise blue,
Or, rather, experimental, movies by
Great underground directors. Nothing new
About all this, except for the degree
Of license on display; what worries me
Is the parade of faces down these streets:
Young as the morning, white as inky sheets
Of the *East Village Other* smugly fixed
On the next vein of pleasure to be tapped
(Pill, body, bottle, music, pain, or speed)
At unencumbered will, at instant need;
Soft chins and baby cheeks taped tightly up
In a glazed mask of not-quite-cruel, not-
Quite-irresponsible all-knowingness,
Which spits on you and me, or would if it
Troubled to notice us. Not that our aims
Differ so much from theirs, but that our peers —
Doubles and brothers, classmates and colleagues, friends —
Anxious and thoughtless, put into their hands,
Paternally, the lethal weapon of
The gift of things and not the gift of love.

Small Space

I

MEN PAST 40
GET UP NIGHTS
And look out at
City lights,
Wondering where they
Made the wrong
Turn, and why life
Is so long.

II

WOMAN NEARLY
ITCHED TO DEATH
As her body,
Filled with breath,
Tortured her with
Womanly
Longing, wholly
Humanly.

III

MAKE THESE THREE
MISTAKES IN SPEECH?
Hear them mermaids
On the beach
Singing real low
Each to each?
Had I ought to
Eat a peach?

The Veterans: A Dream

On this green plain, their ennial caravans
Recur each summer, ripe with veterans
Who age and winter in each later year
That strings them out to tendons, fleshes their
Midcontinents with one more ring of fat,
And dims the bare rheums of their eagle eyes.
They come. A gliding through the moteless air,
A thrill of unheard wheels, and the vast barn-
Red hulls of vehicles as large as arks
Now nose and graze the meadows. In the first,
A grand march of mute couples — men in dress-
Blue uniforms, women in white ball gowns —
Marches in place, in silence, toward the bow
Under a boxcar-colored canopy.
The second is low-sided; it contains,
Above its freeboard, a long row of blue-
Black locomotives — rather, old-time trucks
Got up like locomotives — prinked with brass,
Abuzz with bells and whistles, manned by men
In Sam Browne belts and flat French officers'
(Or possibly conductors') saucepan hats.
The wheels rotate upon a treadmill track,
The men command, cajole, gesticulate,
Pump whistle lanyards, squeeze the ultimate
Speed out of throttles, slap their cabs, and cheer.
The third float, gross as any Zeppelin —
Its sides chased with sign-painters' renderings
Of Spads in combat and crude lettering,
"Tim Hodgins' Flying Circus" — makes a hum
Faint as a honeybee. The men inside
Sit fossil fighters, choker-collared, scarved,
Gloved, goggled, tunicate, in petrified
Stringers and longerons. The old V-8
Hispano-Suizas swing the hickory screws
So slowly you can see them, like the fans
On soda-parlor ceilings. Castrol smoke
Curls blue around exhaust stubs. Ailerons

And elevators wag and nothing moves.

Here is the great parade of the veterans
To their ententment on the old camp ground
That all of us will cover: rictic grins
Confining shining dentures, gentian eyes
Pinned under magnifying glass and lapped
In welt-edged pockets of machine-seamed skin,
Knurled chins programmed to haver, sparse hair gone
To thin-sun yellow, all surmounted and
Suborned by ornament and uniform:
Legions of ribbons of the Croix de Guerre,
Vineyards of Concord-Purple Hearts, a whole
Necropolis of crosses on the slopes
Of human breastbones marching as to war.
Not so, though; these inveterate corporals,
And, ah, their wives, their wives in half sizes
Besprent with tucks and gussets, pleats and bows,
Peplums and scallops, and a velvet rose
Stuck up beside their S. S. Kresge pearls,
Step on, linked, to the grassy bivouac
Where hope springs back and forward to retrieve
Some sense from time of having started and
Concluded private wars of pride and lust,
And — even such is time, which takes in trust
Our service and discharges us in dust —
Of going absent with official leave.

Bathing Song

A bath in steep perspective occupies almost the entire right half of the composition: it is cut off sharply at the lower edge of the canvas and only the legs of the woman in the bath are visible. . . . the painter's vision seems to be focussed on an area to the left of the bath . . . containing a decorated bath-mat and beyond it a piece of furniture smothered by discarded garments and beyond that a window curtain cut off by the top edge of the canvas. . . . One's eye is drawn first to the vertical strip containing the bath-mat, then shifts to take in the bath. . . . quite suddenly one perceives that a blue strip of paint running halfway down the left side of the canvas is part of a dressing-gown. Then part of a leg and a slippered foot emerge and one realises with a distinct shock that someone else is in the room. . . .

— Robert Melville in *The New Statesman*

I.

The prologues and postludes of half our lives
Are played out in this narrow arm of steam,
Tame water, sweat condensing on cool tile,
Nickel and crockery, consuming towels,
The suck of wastes washed down, sweet airs and foul,
Where one emerges like a bluff from all
The onionskins of fog and sees him plain,
Bare, shriven in the misty mirror on
The shifting wall of mist, none other than
Himself made new, none but the lonely heart
Cracked and cemented up with scented soap,
Hot water, razor blades, clean clothes, and hope.

II.

This bourgeois engine honoring Hygiene
Was thus, we thought, a vestibule between
One stage set and another, a mere chamber
Conjoining "to expect" and "to remember."
Bonnard persuades us wholly otherwise:
Besides foreshortened and truncated thighs
Embroiled in their bathwater, and the mat
Beside the tub, and the seat where she sat
To take those underclothes off which obscure
The nature of that piece of furniture
Beneath the window, something else resides

In the far marches of the picture, hides
In a blue strip dissembling a collage.
It stirs. And momentarily the mirage
Materializes as a figure who
Steals on the scene to make a *pas de deux*
Out of a monologue and blaze a path
Of forces from the window to the bath,
From him to her: a proton stream whose price
Encompasses the end of paradise.

Elegy: Evelyn Waugh

Ah, comic officer and gentleman,
Kneeling on stone and falling through the air
In R.M. battledress, sitting a horse,
Marrying gentry, getting a divorce,
Rushing the Season up to Town, and then
Reclusing it in Zomerzet again,
Rising above your station, taking train
From it to the interior of the brain,
Sending up slyly your establishers,
Turning the world off with a click, a curse
From your stark armory of bolted words,
Mimicking to the life, the death, the fools
Through whose void headpieces Britannia rules
Her residue, impersonating an
Irascible, irrational old man
Full of black humors and still darker flights
Beyond aphotic shores on jetty nights
To madness real or bogus, telling all
To a confessor in a grated stall
And stepping shriven, bent, and arrogant
From holy mutter into worldly cant,
Embracing traces of the English past
In all their fossil arbitrariness,

Embodying Highgate's mezzo sentiment
And Mayfair's sopranino *ton,* and yet,
As well, the ground bass of Commercial Street,
You wrote us, first and last, in permanent
Ink and perduring words, a testament
Of how it was in our uneven years:
Laughter in bed, our long index of fears,
Bad manners, time killed callously, a war
Always impending, love abandoned for
Short-term investments, and at long terms' end
Aloneness' monolith on every hand.

Ironic officer and gentleman,
We say goodbye with a slight tear perhaps
Ironic in intent also, although
As clear and serious at heart as you.

Visiting Chaos

No matter how awful it is to be sitting in this
Terrible magazine office, and talking to this
Circular-saw-voiced West Side girl in a dirt-
Stiff Marimekko and lavender glasses, and this
Cake-bearded boy in short-rise Levi's, and hearing
The drip and rasp of their tones on the softening
Stone of my brain, and losing
The thread of their circular words, and looking
Out through their faces and soot on the window to
Winter in University Place, where a blue-
Faced man, made of rags and old newspapers, faces
A horrible grill, looking in at the food and the faces
It disappears into, and feeling,
Perhaps, for the first time in days, a hunger instead
Of a thirst; where two young girls in peacoats and hair
As long as your arm and snow-sanded sandals

Proceed to their hideout, a festering cold-water flat
Animated by roaches, where their lovers, loafing in wait
To warm and be warmed by brainless caresses,
Stake out a state
Of suspension; and where a black Cadillac 75
Stands by the curb to collect a collector of rents,
Its owner, the owner of numberless tenement flats;
And swivelling back
To the editorial pad
Of *Chaos,* a quarter-old quarterly of the arts,
And its brotherly, sisterly staff, told hardly apart
In their listlessly colorless sackcloth, their ash-colored skins,
Their resisterly sullenness, I suddenly think
That no matter how awful it is, it's better than it
Would be to be dead. But who can be sure about that?

Upon Finding *Dying:*
An Introduction, by L. E.
Sissman, Remaindered at 1s.

I wandered lonely as a cloud in Foyles
Of incandescent, tight-knit air, when I
Spied a remainder counter, pied as a
Meadow in autumn with the relicts of
A foisonous summer: novels all the Réage
Short weeks ago, now smutched with rusts and rots
Upon their colored calyces; memoirs
Of august personages laid to rest
As early as October; ghosts of Mod
Nonce-figures, once in, now as dead as God;
And there, a snip under a blackleg sign,
"These books reduced to 1s.," there is mine,
Dying: An Introduction. Well, if you
Preach about dying, you must practice, too.

The 20th Armored:

A Recurrent Dream

Ah, sinners who have not to Ossining
Gone in the rank inconsequence of spring,
Hear a returning traveller: you cannot know
What — past that sickening old apple bough —
Magnificence flares forth, like shook Reynolds Wrap,
From that think tank atop the liberty cap
Of Overkill, Dutch sabot of a hill
Above the obsolescent rocks and rills
Of the outmoded Hudson. Turn, instead,
To our greater-than-Arlington factory of dead
Americans, where quick machines give birth
To the ultimate inheritor of the earth:
A cortex of shelved, tabled facts, a core
Of memory. My classmate, Major Hoare —
A 20th Tanker all of his natural-born,
Mechanically corrected days since horn
Of Roland stirred him in the passages
Of A. MacLeish, shows me the messages
Out-printed by the printout where the in-
Put of the thinkers comes full circle, and
Elicits answers from thermistors; where,
Short years ago, the warren of the hare,
The nest of pheasants, the rough shoot of owls
Made way for war rooms in the balmy bowels
Of Overkill, where G-6 officers
(The Hardware Corps, all hardened sophisters)
Now hold forth and hold out until the day
When miracle machines will have their way
And sweep us all, even their armorers,
Under the land, like Housman characters,
Under the beetling forelock of the hill
Once known to men in Dutch as Overkill.

The Cinematographers,
West Cedar Street

(For Michael Roemer)

There is a lion in the streets as I
Run from the travelling camera framing me
In its long eye. Under a sulphur sky
I lead my flight from men I cannot see:

The chase to be shot later. Quarrying
Down through crevasses in the baking brick,
I register a maze. The scurrying
Perspectives shuttle at the double quick

To vanishing points in chattering culs-de-sac.
Winded, I put my back to the brick wall,
The toes of my white bucks toward the pack
Baying my trail with a fearfully close call

Around the corner of the labyrinth.
Nothing can stop their tantara now but
A death. I climb up on the dinky plinth
Of a stone urn and wait to face them. Cut.

Take two. Take ten. At Sally Sayward's house
In the cool shoulder of West Cedar Street,
We seize iced Moxie from the set tubs, douse
Our heads with water, and sweat out the heat

Till Leo calls us back. The afternoon
Throws a long shadow into Louisburg Square,
Leading me on to evening as I run
Away again from the long lenses' glare.

Clever Women

Clever women live and die on our attention.
They make us feel that we are their invention.
Perhaps we are. They scale us like a tower,
Hand over hand, their eyebeams locked on ours,
Until they overrun our slower brains.
Then what confusion, what cerebral pains!
We drown in borrowed wit and rented reading,
Tags, quotes, allusions, maxims, special pleading,
Polemics, set pieces, and syllogisms
Designed to tax us for our sins and schisms
In spurning each one of those nobly sexed
And fashionably gownèd intellects
Who wear the Empress's new clothes. Alas,
We can't accommodate their weight on us,
Who weighed on them until at length we sprang,
Relieved, to life, and joined the shabby gang
Of men, our dumb, companionable brothers,
Leaving behind those weeping, waving mothers,
Who now, refleshed as a small-breasted race
Of long-haired daughters, press their aching case
Against our flabby front at every arty
Show, opening, dance, happening, and party.

Edward Teshmaker Busk
Obiit Aet. 28, 5 Nov. 1914

(After an account by Constance Babington-Smith)

Today he is fifty-five imperial years dead,
And his round, small-boy's head
(With its irrelevant real-man's mustache)
Is, we must reason, wax, mush, humus, bone
Now where he lives alone.
Fresh from his Cambridge First,
And from amusing, we read, Rupert Brooke,
Upon his infant boffin's motor bike,
He came to Farnborough
To learn to fly.
"Whatever happens NEVER TELL A LIE,"
He'd written his young brother from the heights
Of Harrow-on-the-Hill.
Now, higher still,
He mapped with Pitot tubes the body of
Science, his only love;
In midair took to bed a wife,
Science, his life;
Crashed with the Secretary of State for War
Aboard, and did not die in the flash fire,
Which, inexplicably, did not ignite;
In the last light
Of 5 November, printed on the sight
Of Geoffrey de Havilland (who knew,
Of course, about the hand pump which
Dripped excess fuel upon the cockpit floor),
He single-handed held off a whole night
For several seconds as a meteor,
And lit in Laffan's Plain.
Of course we won't look on his like again;
That's not the issue. What are we, so rich
In contradictory experience, so dim
In our élan, to make of him?

Safety at Forty:
or, An Abecedarian
Takes a Walk

Alfa is nice. Her Roman eye
Is outlined in an O of dark
Experience. She's thirty-nine.
Would it not be kind of fine
To take her quite aback, affront
Her forward manner, take her up
On it? Echo: of course it would.

Betta is nice. Her Aquiline
Nose prowly marches out between
Two raven wings of black sateen
Just touched, at thirty-five, with gray.
What if I riled her quiet mien
With an indecent, subterrene
Proposal? She might like me to.

Gemma is nice. Her Modenese
Zagato body, sprung on knees
As supple as steel coils, shocks
Me into plotting to acquire
The keys to her. She's twenty-nine.
Might I aspire to such a fine
Consort in middle age? Could be.

Della is nice. Calabrian
Suns engineered the sultry tan
Over (I'm guessing) all of her long
And filly frame. She's twenty-one.
Should I consider that she might
Look kindly on my graying hairs
And my too-youthful suit? Why not?

O Megan, all-American
Wife waiting by the hearth at home,
As handsome still at forty-five

As any temptress now alive,
Must I confess my weariness
At facing stringent mistresses
And head for haven? Here I come.

Solo, Head Tide

Far up the Sheepscot, where the tide goes out
And leaves the river water free of salt
And free to foster tame freshwater life
Far from the sea's tall terror, wave on wave
And tooth on tooth in the bone-handled jaws
Which ultramariners use as their laws,
I spy the first footprint of Robinson.
Though his birthplace gives little to go on,
He is implicit in the inward town
Where not a soul steps out of doors at noon
And no one stirs behind twelve-over-twelve
Panes in the windows. Walk uphill yourself
And stand before the shuttered clapboard church
Signed "1830" by its year of birth;
Look down through ash boughs on the whited town
Where they say he and his love slept alone
Under one roof for life, and where his moon
Singled him out, awake, each moonlight night
That spring tides steered upriver with their salt
And broke in these backwaters; feel his pulse
Still in the riverside and his strait house.

Pepy's Bar, West Forty-eighth Street, 8 a.m.

(For Maeve Brennan)

Up and betimes across the asphalt water,
Misted with morning, to where daytime presses
The fortune of these failing buildings harder
Than we would credit, and turns evening dresses
Sodden and draggled on each dancing daughter
Returning to the Bristol with her tresses
Dishevelled, past the grating at whose center
An iron spider waits for his successes.

With Dr. Donothing at Farney End

(To E. A. Muir)

> God gave thy soul brave wings; put not those feathers
> Into a bed, to sleep out all ill weathers.
> — George Herbert

What a vacation! Gullish windlasses
Creak on an endless belt of air, and neap
Tides ebb and spring upon the thunder rocks,
Noisomely reassuring, while the sun
Traverses daytime, and the Farney Light
Beams seaward, neatly taking care of night,
And meals are laid on at the End Hotel,
And Mrs. Dr. fills the night watch well,
And reading chinks the interstitial hours
As we put down the burden of our powers
And coast along the coast. How hard it is,

As we become more broadly doctoral,
More prominent (both senses), and more rich
In all associations, to detach
The woof (east-west) from warp (north-south), and both
From the surrounding, sounding seas of cloth
Which opt in all directions from our web
And loom atlantic, unpacific, up
Over others' futures. To admit
Complicity is but the start of it:
In a misanthropology of sins,
The self-indicting skip-tracing begins,
And leads insequently to skeletons
In coffins, closets, rivers, beds, and brains;
Pain turns on moralists who take such pains.

Verso, it is no wiser to withdraw
And hide in robes that say we are the law,
Though we may be, by virtue of the powers
Vested in us by the accreted hours
We climbed up here on: the warm boy we were,
Full of bluff speeches and the leveller
Of dizzy social superstructures, fire,
Would turn in the cold grave of our late fat
And tell us we can't get away with that.

Until that not unwanted other grave —
The real one — opens like a breaking wave
At Farney End, we'll sit beside the sea
At Farney End, beside ourselves with free-
Dom's implications, Donothing and me.

Lettermen

(To Justin Kaplan and Anne Bernays)

I. THE CRITIC ON THE HEARTH

When Wallaby would come to call on me,
He'd cock his little paws into a prance
Arrested in thin air, and take a stance
(Not easy, when in session by my hob
And rapt in the ignition of his cob)
As one who waters the green seedling young
With wisdom's outfall, the thick ramping sum
Of many tributary years, now come
To a grey head and splurged to purchase new
Shoots, blooms, shucks, fruit, and finally seeds, too.
But when his voice came out of leonine
Dewlaps, it was a fluted, epicene
Column of footnotes, all italicized,
That rose and rose until capitalized
By an ornate Corinthian device
Framed in the hypersonic tones of mice.
Well, that was Conrad Wallaby, the great
Tweed-bearing critic, piped and ungulate
In Pannish season, otherwise well shod
In the high-button shoes of the hard god
Of our feared fathers, ordinately fond
Of donnish wit deliberately donned,
Of shag and tepid tankards of brown ale,
Of company preponderantly male,
Of oolong tea, cress sandwiches, and pale
Dry sherry, port and nuts, dear Major Grey's,
Of good long reads in Doyle on rainy days,
Of a small income herited like genes,
Of living just beyond his patrons' means,
Of loving Art and Beauty and the stones
Of Venice and the venerated bones
Enclosèd here, of quips and cranks and wiles
Arch and archaic, nods and becks and smiles,
Of passion and expression sweetly linked.
Thank God the silly bastard is extinct.

II. DER ROMANKAVALIER

That conic head.
I'd know it anywhere.
Up the close and down the stair
Goes Birkin Hare, the body man,
Who steals, on an original plan,
Man. And woman, too.
Hot bodies dripping juices glue
Themselves under his every arm
As he pelts back
To the body farm
In U. S. Keds with silencers
On every sole. Ah, such a knack-
Er's art is his:
To charm
Life out of his retorts and in-
To them again. His Smith-
Corona shines and steams,
Ingesting reams
Of Eagle-A Rag-Content Bond,
And spitting out
A tissue of
Lives in a bone-
White manuscript,
Steamrollering their souls into
A novel, nouveau, neo, new
Roman, short
Schrift. Say, Mort,
Where those cadavers go?

Now that we know the body man,
Ask not for whom
That brazen tongue
Tolls, bell-like, in his cony head:
You known damn well
It tolls for real,
It tolls for dead,
For characters
Like Bea and Dee,
Like Jay and Kay
Like El and Em,
Like you and me.

Nocturne, Central Park South

Put a rocket up the man, in the moon
And send an astronaut to oust all stars.
No trespass! Bolts of night are ours
At an incredible bargain; bales of noon.

It is amazing how the heart locks out
All interference and clear-channels galaxies
Into one-chambered worlds. Doubt
Is the house dick and time whistles taxis.

The Village: The Seasons

(To Saul Touster)

I. JANUARY 22, 1932

Could a four-year-old look out of a square sedan
(A Studebaker Six in currency green
With wooden artillery wheels) and see a scene
Of snow, light lavender, landing on deepening blue
Buildings built out of red-violet bricks, and black
Passersby passing by over the widening white
Streets darkening blue, under a thickening white
Sky suddenly undergoing sheer twilight,
And the yellow but whitening streetlights coming on,
And remember it now, though the likelihood is gone
That it ever happened at all, and the Village is gone
That it ever could happen in? Memory, guttering out,
Apparently, finally flares up and banishes doubt.

II. MAY 29, 1941

Tring. Bells
On grocers' boys' bicycles ring,
Followed, on cue,
By the jaunty one-note of prayers at two
Near churches; taxi horns, a-hunt,
Come in for treble; next, the tickety bass
Of chain-driven Diamond T's, gone elephantine
And stove-enamelled conifer green
Down Greenwich Avenue.
Out of the Earle
I issue at half-past thirteen,
Struck, like a floral clock,
By seasonal
Manifestations: unreasonable
N.Y.U. girls out in their bobby socks
And rayon blouses; meek boys with their books
Who have already moulted mackinaws;
Desarrolimiento of
New chrome-green leaves; a rose,
Got, blooming, out of bed; and Mrs. Roos-
Evelt and Sarah Delano
Descending the front stoop of a Jamesian
House facing south against the Square, the sun —
Who, curveting, his half course not yet run,
Infects the earth with crescence;
And the presence
Of process, seen in un-top-hatted,
Un-frock-coated burghers and their sons
And daughters, taking over
All title, right, and interest soever
In this, now their
Property, Washington Square.

III. DECEMBER 29, 1949

The Hotel Storia ascends
Above me and my new wife; ends
Eight stories of decline, despair,
Iron beds and hand-washed underwear

Above us and our leatherette
Chattels, still grounded on the wet
Grey tessellated lobby floor.
Soon, through a dingy, numbered door,
We'll enter into our new home,
Provincials in Imperial Rome
To seek their fortune, or, at least,
To find a job. The wedding feast,
Digested and metabolized,
Diminishes in idealized
Group photographs, and hard today
Shunts us together and at bay.
Outside the soot-webbed window, sleet
Scourges the vista of Eighth Street;
Inside, the radiators clack
And talk and tell us to go back
Where we came from. A lone pecan
Falls from our lunch, a sticky bun,
And bounces on the trampoline
Of the torn bedspread. In the mean
Distance of winter, a man sighs,
A bedstead creaks, a woman cries.

IV.   JULY 14, 1951

A summer lull arrives in the West Village,
Transmuting houses into silent salvage
Of the last century, streets into wreckage
Uncalled-for by do-gooders who police
The moderniqueness of our ways, patrol
The sanitation of our urban soul.
What I mean is, devoid of people, all
Our dwellings freeze and rust in desuetude,
Fur over with untenancy, glaze grey
With summer's dust and incivility,
With lack of language and engagement, while
Their occupants sport, mutate, and transform
Themselves, play at dissembling the god Norm
From forward bases at Fire Island. But —
Exception proving rules, dissolving doubt —
Young Gordon Walker, fledgling editor,

My daylong colleague in the corridors
Of Power & Leicht, the trade-book publishers,
Is at home to the residue in his
Acute apartment in an angle of
Abingdon Square. And they're all there, the rear-
Guard of the garrison of Fort New York:
The skeleton defense of skinny girls
Who tap the typewriters of summertime;
The pale male workers who know no time off
Because too recently employed; the old
Manhattan hands, in patched and gin-stained tweeds;
The writers (Walker's one), who see in their
City as desert an oasis of
Silence and time to execute their plots
Against the state of things, but fall a prey
To day succeeding day alone, and call
A party to restore themselves to all
The inside jokes of winter, in whose caul
People click, kiss like billiard balls, and fall,
Insensible, into odd pockets. Dense
As gander-feather winter snow, intense
As inextinguishable summer sun
At five o'clock (which it now is), the noise
Of Walker's congeries of girls and boys
Foregathered in their gabbling gratitude
Strikes down the stairwell from the altitude
Of his wide-open walk-up, beckoning
Me, solo, wife gone north, to sickening
Top-story heat and talk jackhammering
Upon the anvils of all ears. "Christ, Lou, you're here,"
Whoops Walker, topping up a jelly jar
("Crabapple," says the label, still stuck on)
With gin and tonic, a blue liquid smoke
That seeks its level in my unexplored
Interior, and sends back a sonar ping
To echo in my head. Two more blue gins.
The sweat that mists my glasses interdicts
My sizing up my interlocutor,
Who is, I think, the girl who lives next door,
A long-necked, fiddleheaded, celliform
Girl cellist propped on an improbably
Slim leg. Gin pings are now continuous.

The room swings in its gimbals. In the bath
Is silence, blessed, relative, untorn
By the cool drizzle of the bathtub tap,
A clear and present invitation. Like
A climber conquering K.28,
I clamber over the white porcelain
Rock face, through whitish veils of rubberized
Shower curtain, and at length, full-dressed, recline
In the encaustic crater, where a fine
Thread of cold water irrigates my feet,
To sleep, perchance to dream of winter in
The Village, fat with its full complement
Of refugees returned to their own turf —
Unspringy as it is — in a strong surf
Of retrogressing lemmings, faces fixed
On the unlovely birthplace of their mixed
Emotions, marriages, media, and met-
Aphors. Lord God of hosts, be with them yet.

II

A War Requiem

(To Jonathan Peale Bishop and John Cooke Dowd, Jr.)

On vit; on vit infâme. Eh bien? Il fallut l'être;
  L'infâme après tout mange et dort.
Ici même, en ses parcs, où la mort nous fait paître,
  Où la hache nous tire au sort,
Beaux poulets sont écrits; maris, amants sont dupes;
  Caquetage, intrigues de sots.
On y chante; on y joue; on y lève des jupes;
  On y fait chansons et bons mots. . . .
Et sur les gonds de fer soudain les portes crient.
  Des juges tigres nos seigneurs
Le pourvoyeur paraît. Quelle sera la proie
  Que la hache appelle aujourd'hui?
Chacun frissonne, écoute; et chacun avec joie
  Voit que ce n'est pas encore lui. . . .
  — André Chénier

I. FALL PLANTING

1. New York, 1929

When Hartley Wintney went out on the town —
Immaculate conception in a brown
Twill suit from Rivers Brothers, over which
His Arrow Collar face appeared in rich
And manful tones, surmounted by his blond
Coif and a Herbert Johnson pinch-front hat —
He fared forth like a newborn bearer bond
Engrossed with promise. Think of him in that
Half-grown Manhattan, shouldering cornerstones
Aside, reflecting on old firms' brass plaques,
Damning the fluvium of limousines
In fording Madison, deflecting cabs
And westbound walkers, courting judgment from
The dumb irons of green omnibuses come
Up out of quarries of intense twilight
Between flat shafts of sun. Now picture him
Far east, as forceless early lights come on
And catch and lose the white moth of his hat.
Brownstones cringe under blue-lit windows where
Electrotypers cast out on the air
An alphabet of clatters; sewers leak
A peevish smell of garbage, a sure mark
Of early summer coming in New York.
Down brown steps he addresses a peephole,
Is recognized, and passes into Rynne's.

Four hours draw circles on the Biltmore clock.
On Forty-eighth, near Rynne's, you cannot hear
The fight inside or guess at its extent
Until a man, out cold, is dumped out in
The areaway. His hat is gone and his
Collar has been detached. One sleeve hangs off
His hundred-dollar suit. One garter shows
Up one prone leg, and claret stains his shirt.
Possessed, he rises up and walks back west
And comes upon his destination at
Almost the hour of two, according to
His father's half-case hunter watch, still in

His right-hand waistcoat pocket; comes upon
The sleeping Princeton Club, his sometime home,
And startles the night porter. "Here, you can't
Come in like that. My God, it's Mr. Wint — "
And dies there in the foyer, in the arms
Of Mr. Murtha, far from Grosse Pointe Farms.

2. *New York, 1932*

Shot with the huge, crude Graflexes of the period:
Sun on the stone of the baggy trouser legs
Of the men in line, on their outsize cloth caps
And hollow, woodworked faces, overexposed
To the emulsion and the elements;
Shade on the shelter, with its hasty sign,
"Soup Kitchen," in the small, prehensile loops
And stilted, stork-footed ascenders of
An old signman who learned his ornate trade
In the last flowery century; and shade
In the sharp shadows of petitioners
Longer than their slight, short significance
In history, and on the evening street
Of cast-iron mercantile establishments,
All underexposed. The line, frozen in time
And on the negative, stalls in Cooper Square.
Turn the roto page and Paul Whiteman is there.

3. *Cross Corners, Mich., 1935*

The bank owned half the county when it failed.
The second crop of hay, uncut, unbaled,
Stands sentry to a country town in shock.
Greenbottles buzz and bumble on the stock
In the Nyal Drug Store window, backed by pink,
Sun-faded sunbursts of crêpe paper; linked
Rings signify the vacant Odd Fellows
Hall overhead; next door, the Corner Store
Moves precious little of its short supply
Of Dubble Bubble Gum and green Nehi;
Across the street, R. Brown Purina Chows

Caters to few blue, cut-down Dodge sedans
With dangling tags; the droning standard fans
Drown out no cross talk in the Owl Café;
The sun sits regent in the boundless day.
Down by the P.M. tracks, a man in Finck's
Bib Overalls (Wears Like a Pig's Nose) thinks
Of someplace else, where, with a stunning sound
Of terrene thunder, the Express is bound.

4. Thomas Jefferson Henderson, 1937

At dinner in his modest palace on
Chicago Boulevard, Mr. Henderson,
The General Manager of the Frontenac
Motor Division, cuts his New York steak
Fine, finer, finest; chews mechanical
Bites into particles while listening
To Amos 'n' Andy on the glistening
Green-eyed mahogany dining-room radio,
And muses on his Southern origins,
Transcending Snopeses in the cotton gins,
And northering through his four good years at Tech
And his not happenstantial close connec-
Tions with the Chairman of the Board, Red Clay,
Whom he long served as duteous protégé,
Joker, and Georgian co-religionist,
And swarmed like lightning up the terraced list
Of top executives to Everest:
Alliance Motors' Aztec tower suite
Aloof from the contentions of the street,
Which now begins — the news comes on — to mass
Its voices and be heard through the high glass.

Drive east on Jefferson Avenue: beyond
The billboards for the All-New Fronty Eight
For '37, price $695
And up, a white four-stacker reaches up
To tie its smoke up to the smutty sky
Above the great white word, fifteen yards high,
That spells out Frontenac across the sound
Of foundry work, across the belt of smells —

Meltmetal, ozone, stove gas — that surrounds,
In clouds of visibility, the core
Of all the purposes this city's for.

Drive east and see no smoke, for once, and hear
No presses pressing on, and smell no scent
Of tractable materials being bent
To shape our ends; instead, all silence hangs
Instead of smoke up in the unmarked air;
The chain-link gates are locked, and over there
A line of lictors in blue dungarees
Bears notice of its grievance. In such peace
Lies a delusion: nightly, plant police,
Recruited on their records, deputized
For the duration, leave their paralyzed,
Emasculated, blind antagonists
For dead or worse in ditches, where the rays
Of sunrise will not interrupt their rest.

5. *La Lutte Finale, 1937*

Progressive Bookshop: International
Publishers' titles lap dot-eyed old men
Who scan a Spanish war map. Out of the Blue
Network, a messenger of unities,
The battle claims all ears. *Heimat ist weit:*
Mitteleuropa, clouded by the black,
Descendent shape, calls to her sons, *Freiheit!*
Meanwhile, Alpini move on Teruel,
Savoias bomb Bilbao, Falangist troops
With Schmeissers decimate the volunteers
Who post themselves — selections of the Left
Book Club — to wars they never made. A stir,
A surge to the front door: a winded old
Dispatch rider descends his bicycle
And leans, straight-armed, against the open door.
News from the front, as soon as he can speak.
"It's Jack. Jack. Jack — " A long saw-stroke of breath.
" 'S dead. Jack Sharfman's dead. The telegram
Came 8 A.M. Outside Madrid. A bomb."
A son, the potency of all of them,

Lies in the bosom of the Abraham
Lincoln Battalion, mourned by all good men.

6. Rosedale Theatre, 1938

Feet on the parapet of the balcony,
We cup free sacks of penny candy, gum,
And unshelled peanuts, all included in
Our dime admission to the Saturday
Kids' matinée, and see the *Bounty* heave
And creak in every block and halyard. Waves
Of raw sensation break upon each white
Face that reflects the action, and our ears
Eavesdrop upon the commerce of a more
Real world than ours. The first big feature ends;
We trade reactions and gumballs with friends
Above the marching feet of Movietone,
Which now give way to a twin-engine plane
That lands as we half watch, and Chamberlain
Steps out, in his teeth, Homburg, and mustache,
A figure of some fun. We laugh and miss
His little speech. After the Michigan-
Ohio game, Buck Rogers will come on.

7. Athens, Ohio, 1939

"ATHENIA TORPEDOED," says today's
Press in the tourist guesthouse. "WAR IMPENDS."
Out back in the black meadow, among friends —
Some summer bugs contending, timothy's
Familiar dip and scratch behind bare knees,
The duty pool of stars — I can't believe
In such disaster being broadcast, such
Mere alien, unpermitted anarchy
Loosed on an ordered world that features me.

II. WINTERTIME AND SPRING

8. *The Regiment, 1940*

"The battle of liberty may one day be
Won on these playing fields of Birmingham
University School, where only last year we
Beat Grosse Pointe Country Day eighteen to three,"
Says Mr. Dunn, our stout form master, to
Our weedy rows of raw recruits — aged ten
To seventeen — in ample khaki suits.
"The regiment," he tells our understrength
Headquarters company, already whipped
By bigger winds than we are, eyes tear-gassed
By cutting gusts of late-November air,
"The regiment will serve its country well
If the day comes, and [words drowned out] the school."
The Mauser on my shoulder galls the bone.
Fat Pringle, on my left, gives a long groan.
Wan Lundy, on my right, bends in the breeze.
I snuffle and unlock my shaky knees.
"Now Captain Strong will drill the regiment
In the manual of arms before — uh — mess.
Let's show him [unintelligible phrase]
The dedication that is B.U.S."

9. *Washington, 1941*

The solid geometry of Washington
Goes soft and butter-edged in the solvent sun
Of May. Dark men in frogs with jingling trays
Light-foot it down the humid corridors
Of the old Willard, where the spelling-bee
Contenders — having muffed "chrysanthemum,"
"Dehiscent," "hautbois," "phthisic," lost and won
The ordeal in the auditorium —
Now wait to meet the President, each head
Stuffed with a recent residue of dead
Euclidean theorems: dome hemispheres,
Spire cones, room cubes, and pillar cylinders.

Our cicerone, a spare newspaperman,
Has news for us at breakfast: due to the
Tense impasse over lend-lease, we will not
Be introduced to Mr. Roosevelt,
Who sends sincere regrets. Instead, we will
Tour more of hot, awaking Capitol Hill,
Whose shuttered faces turn toward the pull
Of transatlantic gravity, whose will
Annihilates the longueurs of the sea.

10. Detroit, 1943

In memory of the nineteenth century,
The hobby shop I run in summertime
Observes a day of silence; opening
Up in the morning, I walk into a
Wall of still must just scented with faint thyme;
The regulator clock paces a slow
And steady measure all alone; the pressed-
Tin ceiling whimpers in the heat; and no
Small Negro boys, as beautiful as dolls,
Come for instruction in the mystery
Of modelling: a wing rib pinned down here,
Between the leading and the trailing edges, on
Wax paper, which protects the plan, and glued.
Later, the delicate stretching of the blue
Tissue over the structure, to include
It in the empyrean, and a coat
Of dark-blue dope for tautness. No black boys
Appear by noon. On my way home to lunch,
I see the smoke down Woodward Avenue
And hear a dull sea far away, where black
Is East and white is West, who fight
For lone possession of the street behind
The barricades of burning cars. My shop
Stays shut all afternoon. At dusk I hear —
Above the yawps of nighthawks diving on
Their customary roofs — the treadmill beat
Of half-tracks manned and gunned by helmeted
Troopers detailed to clear the Avenue
Of riot and its grisly residue.

11. A Day Coach, 1944

A pond of vomit in the vestibule;
Fat barracks bags to fall on in the aisle;
A scrim of smoke and sweat; shive sandwiches
In fingerprinted paper and a shrill
Orange drink, drunk lukewarm with a sodden straw;
Their hawker, barely able to support
His corporation through the teeming train;
Long sailors cocked up anyhow, asleep
In the deep waters of the empty pint
Across their knees; a soldier and a WAC
Involved in one quite indivisible
Vestment of khaki; out the window, miles.

12. The Liberal Union, 1944

Election Night. The house in Holyoke Street
Blazes with hundred-watters. Light leaks out —
Despite the brownout — to define the shape
Of things to come: a crowded, derelict,
Condemned, consensual body politic,
Gone down to ashes under the rubric
Fuel of progress; down with the republic.
Under the mansard, a long drawing room
Is stacked with shiny freshmen, one week out
From home, from under mother, and with pale
And weighty bottles of cold Pickwick Ale.
A radio reports the vote; tall Tex and Tim,
Hatching with blood-red crayons, color in
Each Democratic duchy on the map
Above the mantel, to the tramping rap
Of bottles on the floor and tenor cheers.
Off on the left, some hothead and his pal
Strike up a flaccid "Internationale."

13. April 12, 1945

Behind the A.M.E. Church, the first fierce
Green grass springs on the dank and disused earth

Of littered yards with mutual surprise;
The colored kid I tutor has no eyes
For algebra, but only for the boys
Who vamp a pepper game in the play yard
Outside our grated window. Steps are heard.
It's Mr. Justice, leader of the Youth
Group Program, who looks grave and calls me out
Into the vestry and tells me, in neat
Jamaican tones, "I don't know how to say
This to you, Mr. Edwards, but they say
The President is dead." "Dead?" "Yes, today.
Come with me to Mass. Avenue and have
A drink with me to him." At noon, the long
Arm of the bar is nearly empty but
For barkeep, cabbies, and the radio.
"Two Myers Rum," calls Mr. Justice, who
Explains to me, aside, "An Island drink."
The dark rum comes. With infinite courtesy,
He turns and lifts his heavy glass to me,
And says, "To the memory of your President."

14. The '46s, 1945

Alliance Motors Tower. On the ground floor
Of the postwar, six shiny Frontenacs
Rotate on turntables beneath the bright
Eyes of a bank of baby spots. Away
Back in the corners stand the surpluses,
Unlit, unsung, of the late war: a tank,
A jeep, a twenty-millimetre gun,
A cutaway of an X-24
Glycol-cooled airplane engine. On the floor
Under the lights, crowds sniff the fruits of peace:
New rubber, lacquer, leather, a perfume
Four years abeyed but unforgotten; still
A year away from the sweet people's will.

15. East Cambridge, 1949

Behind the stacked extent of Kendall Square
There is a little slum; I'll take you there,

Laden with my black brush-filled salesman's case,
Perhaps a mop or two, and, on my face,
The first sweat of the day. This is the place
We start: a neat tan toy house, gingerbread
Proud of its peaky eaves. The lady's in.
She's German, tiny, old, respectable,
Not buying anything. Next door, a tall
Blue tenement hangs open. In its hall,
The fumes of urine and the fractured wall
Don't augur well for brush men. That's all wrong.
Up the length — gaslit, railless — of the long
And aging stairwell live star customers:
Draggled and pregnant girls who fumble coins
Among contending children; pensioners,
Dressed in a skeletal state of readiness,
Who welcome all intruders bearing news
Of the last act of the world; lone, stubbled young
Men who change babies while the wife's at work.
I write the orders in my little book,
Take a deposit, promise delivery
A week from Saturday. At noon I lunch
On tonic and a Hostess Apple Pie
At Aly's Spa in Portland Street. At night,
I leave the last room with a Sacred Heart
And Kroehler furniture for my rendezvous
With Jonathan, a breath of Harvard Square
In his black '36 Ford coupe, his bare
Feet on the pedals. We abscond from there.

16. *The Publisher, 1951*

"Now get me Captain Alice Coddington,
The General's aide. No, she's in Washington,
For Christ's sake. O.K., try the Pentagon."
The handset hits the cradle like a gun.
Burt Seltzer lifts a large, low-calorie
Elastic band to his abnormally
Small mouth — a hotel slit for razor blades —
And chews with relish. His long fingers, which,
At first glance, seem to have an extra joint,
Play lancers with a pencil, whose sharp point

Riddles a Webster's Second Unabridged,
Open to "Minotaur." A crapulent
Bar of the best band brass bursts in the win-
Dow, and — except for Burt — we crowd around
To see the source of that preëmptive sound.
A small parade, beleaguered by a gale
Of paper snow, pursued by biped wolves
With cameras, traverses the bare, pale
Hot tundra of Fifth Avenue. Behind
The army band, a fancy phaeton
With the top down, a glittering '41
Chrysler Imperial, daunting as the sun,
Cradles the recalled General, recalled
Just as he is today, in suntan hat,
From his long and all-promising career
Halfway around our curve-ball-spinning sphere,
Halfway from earth to heaven, lit by love
Of his high mission and laid low by Jove.
"Elaine, you stupid bastard, where's my call?
Don't give me that crap. I can't wait at all.
Yeah, put me through now." Pause. A brief reprise
Of masticated rubber. "Alice? How
You doing, darling? I mean with the book?
I know it, sweetie. Sure, he just went by.
Listen — don't worry. Just remember we
Need the whole manuscript September the —
Right. O.K., honey. See you. *Ciao.* Goodbye."

III. HIGH SUMMER

17. The Candidate, 1952

Archaic Boston, a splayed hand of squat
Brick business buildings laced with shire-town smells —
Roast coffee, fresh fish, lettuce, tanneries —
Cools into fall and warmly welcomes back
Its horse-faced grandees, panama'd, in black
Alpaca jackets, posting down State Street
To their renumeration on the high
Chairs of their countinghouses. Close at hand,

On Batterymarch, a plan they would deplore
Takes shape as six signmen affix a long
Hand-lettered banner to an empty store.
"O'Kane's O.K. with Massachusetts," it
Declares in characters some four feet high,
Pointedly pointed with a union bug.
Inside, I meet his campaign manager,
White-headed, red Lucretius Gallagher,
Late editor of the set Boston *Sun,*
And set to work to make a senator
At an old upright Royal in a room
Quite like a city room, and on the run
To many contacts: first, the mother of
Us all, Maureen O'Kane, the matriarch;
Next, Kath O'Kane, the sister, a thin, shrewd,
And shining foil with Niccolonian
Schemes to bring down the arch-Republican
Incumbent, Adams, on his own Palladian
Home ground; last, Kevin, the calm candidate,
Halfway between his person and the shape
Of a great figure, in the pupal stage
Of statecraft, now half-metamorphosed from
A moody, willful, and mercuric young
Man to the measured senator to come.
In his high, prosperous cell, the prisoner
Seems easy in his bonds, under the dour
And time-releasing sedative of power.

   18. Brynfan Tyddyn, 1955

In the horse latitudes, there is a farm
Upon a hill in Pennsylvania.
Young men in irons pursue a mania
For motion there, surrounded by becalmed
Blood brothers in an age of stasis. Out
Of Wilkes, across the river, up the bluff
Of Forty Fort, and into the snow roll
Of ridges, we emerge upon a road
Where racing cars blur by, and consequent
Dust settles on the rye. We ease our red
A.C. down off the flatbed; John gets in

And comes back dirty from his practice laps.
The grid forms up for our heat — under two
Litres — the green flag falls, a rush-hour mass
Of cars howls off and dwindles. Silence. Smoke.
Two minutes, and a faint whine-grunt precedes
The field into the chute before the straight.
An A6 Maserati leads a light-
Blue 1.5 Osca in a scratch duet
For loud soprano six and tenor four;
John comes through third but first in class, ahead
Of sundry Bristols, and bangs on his door —
A spoof on Nuvolari — for more speed.
The standings hold for three more laps. Then John
Loses his right-rear in the pit-straight chute
And slews off down the dirt escape road, no
Power or brakes to stop him, to a stop
Deep in a stubble field, while his wild wheel
Smashes a sheriff's windshield. We retrieve
The car and load it, limp with our reprieve,
And drink our luck in tepid Stegmaier beer.

    19. Cahiers du Cinéma, 1956

Dissolve from a proscenium arch of "L"
In Flushing to a matching arch of mike
Booms, light stands, Fearless dollies, blimps inside
The building in its shade, where thirty-two
Souls stiffen at the sound of "Speed!" and clap
Of clapsticks clapping on the set. In dream,
A blond wife ambulates across a room
Built out of flats, her back lit by a Con
Edison evening sun. She's carrying
An insubstantial crown of peach ice cream
To her peach-featured, immaterial
Young holy family. She muffs a line.
Cut. Take two. Outside, by the Optimo
Cigar Store, a live, dirty, dying man
Dives for the *Daily News* in a trash can.

20. Claremont, 1957

It's a long, long way from the Park-Lex
Building up to that institutional
Ridge-running street between hot Harlem and
The lion Hudson. High Edwardian
Doors wrought, or wreaked, in iron let me in
To a tall, cool, dim, dull mosaic hall
Equipped with one wee elevator. On
The fifth, my friends come creeping out to greet
Me and my gift, a gift-wrapped fifth of Fitz.
Within, with Steve, the meek Chicagoan,
Escaped, by luck and struggle, from a slum,
And Ren, short for Renata, his bird-wife,
We talk a little about him: his course
In letters at Columbia, his plans —
Ten years old and still twining out in new
Directions — for his first novel, about
Writers and bookies in Chicago. And
We talk a little about me: my five-
Year plan not to write anything at all.
But mainly we discuss the threats — Bomb,
The State, Mass Media, the Thought Police —
That freeze us in our ruts and stay our hands
Upon our keys and brushes, staves and pens.

21. A Marriage, 1958

November russets flush the last of green
Out of its summer coverts; mist and frost
Condense and crystallize on lignified
Black twigs; red berries shrivel; a sad light
Undistances horizons, setting dense
Swatches of nothingness beyond the fence
In non-objective umber. We arise
At seven in our tiny country house —
The center of November, and the point
Of no return to cities, with their sour
Remarks on ruinous first marriages —
Eat eggs, dress in dark clothes, get in our black

Jaguar roadster, and in dusting snow —
The season's first, greasing the roads — we go
Across the line to Nashua, where, in
A blank room of dun office furniture,
We say our vows before a registrar
In rimless glasses, and, as witnesses,
Flower girls, trainbearers, maids of honor, two
Gum-chewing, French-accented typists, who
Congratulate us gravely when the ring
Has been slid on, when the deal-sealing kiss
Has been exchanged. Stiff handshakes all around;
A chorus of farewells; we're homeward bound
On now quite icy roads, to lunch alone
In a decrepit tearoom; to come home
To a new, mutual aloneness in
Our little house as winter enters in.

22. Writing, 1963

For years he was cross-eyed, the right eye turning in
Shyly, and he, shyly ducking his head
To hide the inturning, failed to notice the eyes
Of all the others, also in hiding from
The eyes of others, as in a painting of
The subway by Charles Harbutt. Self-denying
Can get you something if, behind the blank,
Unwindowed wall, you don't become a blank,
Unfurnished person. He was lucky. In
The dark of those bare rooms to let, there stirred
Something: a tattered arras woven with
A silent motto, as Eliot said. A word
Now, in his thirty-sixth summer, surfaces, leading
A train of thought, a manifest freight, up to
The metalled road of light — for the first time
In ten disused, interior years — along
The rusted, weed-flagged lines. And so the raid
On the inarticulate, as Eliot said,
Begins again. Square-bashing awkward squads
Of words turn right about under the sun,
Form ragged quatrains in the quiet room

Under the eaves, where his pen cuts its first
Orders in ages, and the detail moves off
The page, not quite in step, to anywhere.

23. *Cambridge, 1963*

A wake, without the whiskey or the words
Of eulogy, before the one blue eye
Of television in the deepening
November evening. When, earlier,
My secretary said she'd heard that he
Had just been shot, we gaped in nervous pre-
Lapsarian unbelief. Now it is not
More real but we are less so, and the scream
Calls us to places in a doomsday scene
Of national disjuncture from a show
By Wells or Welles. Lear's "never," a hoarse crow
Of omen, takes wing to the rooky wood
Of early terrors suddenly grown up,
Grown old in one weekend. A catafalque
On wagon wheels rolls, powered by muffled drums,
Down the vast desert street to which we come,
Clutching our wives and wallets, to assist
In turning nature art; in the night mist
Behind the White House, two linked silhouettes —
A great *Life* picture — cut across the lawn
To leave the sound stage and to be alone.

IV.   HARVEST HOME

24. *A Walk in Roxbury, 1964*

A sense of last times. On Columbus Ave.,
A hot May day. A sky of mother-of-pearl
Brings leaves on the few trees and people on
The many front stoops out. Home-painted signs —
"The KING's," "Jack's Sharp Store," "Marnie's Bar-B-Coop,"
"Hell Fire Redeemer Church" — illuminate
Exhausted brownstone streets, the hand-me-downs

Of cold-roast Boston in Victorian
Days of white hope and glory, whose new voice,
Litigious, rich, impoverished, mocking, coarse,
And fine, hangs heavily on the alien air
Above the grunt of traffic, rising where
A printed sign points out the Peppermint
Lounge Sip-In. I adjust my Nikons and
Begin to photograph a happy crowd
Preparing for an outing. They do not
Protest or even notice me, though they
And I both know that this year is the last
Of truce and toleration, and the line
Between us broadens as I zoom the lens
Back to wide-angle. I still have the print
Here. How far off those smiling holiday
Faces and their stopped laughter are today.

25. *Talking Union, 1964*

The liberator of the laboring
Classes is interviewed on "Meet the Press."
The ruffian who led the Frontenac
Sit-down is missing; his aged surrogate
Is a stout statesman, silver-polled and -tongued,
And silver-tied over a white-on-white
Dress shirt under a trig, if Portly, suit
Tailored by Weatherill. His priestly, bluff
Face with its large pores dryly swallows up
All pointed questions; his brown coin-purse mouth
Doles out small change wrapped in the florid scrip
Of Federalese: "parameters," "key gains,"
"Judgmentally," "negated," "targeting,"
"So, gentlemen, you see." So gentlemen
Are made, not born, with infinite labor pains.

26. *Rockville, Illinois, 1965*

Above the corn, the vanes of Rockville gleam,
Aloof, an island in the severed stream

Of Illinois, which feeds a landlocked lake
And never goes to sea. Here in the heart-
Land, I am right where I came in: the in-
Termitting thirty years of prosperous
Accretions have glossed over the plat, plain
Life of the plain people; have made them rich
In dollars, acres, air conditioning
Against the prairie heat, but largely not
In spirit. Still, their hospitality
Comes easy, and the chairman of the board
Of the Rockville National is open as
The barefoot farm boy with a string of mud
Cat he once was, or, rather, thinks that he
Once was and permanently ought to be.
But touch a nerve of doubt, and property
Is ringed with tense defenders: hollow squares
Of fattening Minute Men leap from their shares
To raise their automatic arms against
The roll of interlopers, black and red,
The union agitators and the fed-
Eral animal, sow and juggernaut,
That suckles at their wallets and will squat
On their rights soon. Tornado clouds of fear
Raise sickles over Rockville, tier on tier.

27. An Estrangement, 1966

Webb Beatty, having drunk too much at lunch
In some dark dive where food is only served
To justify attendance, tells me his
Troubles: how Penny, his long-standing wife
Is nipping sherry all day long and rye
All evening; how the hard goods of her ends —
"A Kelvinator, Christ's sake, with a dec-
Orated door, and that old Cadillac" —
Foul up his airy, ivory ideal
Of how to live, and blight his middle age
With bills and sorrows; how Lucinda Fry,
A junior buyer with a jocund eye
And small but gold-filled charms, has solaced him

In the broad daylight of her little room
At lunchtime, making him a feast of sheets
And steam fresh from her shower; how he may throw
His dead-end life up, and may even go
Away alone to a far shore to start
A new one, packing only shirts and heart
In his light luggage; how, in that sunset,
He and Lucinda will find all content,
And paint and write in concert as Bach plays
Behind them all their minuends of days.
His words slur now; his face slips out of shape
And into neutral; white wings of escape
Beat at his ears. He reaches for the check
And misses it. I pick it up and tell
Him nothing but the truth: I wish him well.

28. New York, 1967

Eyes flick blades out from under low lids, and
Turn down again to fasten on the sparks
Struck by the sidewalk. My eyes meet that tide
Halfway: the same aloofness, the same stab
Of quick cognition, the same lowering
Of sights to shoe lane, having sized them up
And put them down for good. The girls require
A little longer for each dancing breast
And mincing leg. Only the mannequins
In Bonwit's windows render me a straight,
Blank stare, which I return in kind. The Pan
Am Building, in its jointed corridors,
Affords relief: acquaintances are cut
Off neatly by their bends, and nearer friends
Truncated, disembodied, guillotined
By abstract passages and unseen doors
In a new social contract of surreal
Withdrawal and avoidance, an absurd
Theatre without end and without word.

29. Two Candidates, 1968

A private conversation in a room
Rife with the public and the press. Amid
White sheets of flashlight, the hot, desperate
Advance men poised to seize the candidate
And whisk him to his next engagement, late
As ever, he lets fall a casual
Comment upon the state of poetry;
Laughs lightly over an egregious lie
Expounded by an arch-opponent; cites
The over-erudite allusions of
Another rival to the ancient Greek.
"That's Aeschylation in political
Quotation," he remarks in a slow, calm
Voice at the middle of the maelstrom.
The other office seeker occupies
A lidded bed under the gritty eyes
Of gleaming notabilities, a guard
Of honor changed at each night hour; the eyes
Of those unknowns who, in a double line,
Reach backward out the great church doors, around
The block behind the buttresses; the eyes
Of early watchers high up in the sun-
Struck monolith across the street, who see,
At length, a coffin carried out; the eyes
Of mourners at the stops along a route
Just the reverse of Lincoln's; the dry eyes
Of the most high and lowly in the long,
Decayed, redounding concourse of the Un-
Ion Station; late, the eyes of Washington.

30. New York, 1968

The surf of traffic in the arteries
Of evening inundates all ears; in crosstown streets,
It is occluded by occasional
Yells, ash cans falling, Sanitation trucks
Regurgitating garbage, witching cries,
A crystalline lone footstep with a limp,
And Robinson's phone ringing in his flat.

Still, sometimes our small noise and voice are heard
Above the melancholy, long, advancing roar
Of transit reaching up the beach of our
Old ananthropocentric island, to
The bass of the night wind, and we come true
To one another, till the rising town's
Unhuman voices wake us, and we drown.

31. Thirty Thousand Gone, 1968

In CONUS, whence all blessings flow, I drive
To Ayer for beer. On our road, amber flares
Ripen like grapefruit in a grove of air
Fast growing dark. Down in the valley, small-
Calibre guns begin long, gibbering
Dialogues out beyond the mock Perfume
River, really the smelly Nashua.
Tank engines ululate. In Vietnam
Village, street fighters infiltrate the set
Of simulated buildings, while fléchette
Canisters fired by 105's protect
The point with sheets of tissue-shredding darts.
The heavies enter. Flashes shatter night
And impacts puncture my unruffled drum-
Roll of exhaust. In Ayer, the archetype
Of post towns, with its scruffy yellow-brick
Two-story business blocks, shut shops, bright bars,
It's pay night. In the orchid neon light
Shed by the Little Klub, a herd of ponycars
Grazes an asphalt pasture. Feat M.P.'s
Snuff out a flash fight at the Hotel Linc.
A Charge burns a little rubber to
Arrest two ready, wary, cruising girls
Whose buttocks counter-rotate down Main Street.
'Nam veterans in troop boots and a chest
Awash with medal ribbons stare down knots
Of new recruits, high on Colt 45.
The Package Store is all decorum. Men
In black bow ties wait coolly on the boys,
Their guns and clubs prudentially concealed
Behind the counter. With my six-pack, I

Leave town, passing an Army ambulance
With beacon on and siren winnowing
The road ahead. A yellow GTO
Has flipped atop the railroad bridge, and bare-
Armed viewers with mauve cheeks, purpureal
Eyes, lavender-green lips in mercury-
Vapor-lamp light look on in ecstasy
At others' errors. From the overpass
On the road back, I see a divisional
Convoy bound westward, double strands of lights
Strung clear back to the third ridge, coming on
Slowly, preserving prescribed intervals,
Diminishing the other way in one
Long red ellipsis, going, going, gone
Into the red crack that still separates
The blue-black air from blue-black earth: the gates
At the world's end. The battle on our hill
Still rants and tatters nighttime till a red
Flare, like a larger Mars, can supervene
And make a false arrest of everything.
The last burst dies; the battlefield goes dark;
Cicadas sizzle; towns away, dogs bark.

V. IN THE NEW YEAR

32. Twelfth Night, 1969

Snowbound on Twelfth Night, in the interact
Of winter, in the white from green to green,
I warm myself in isolation. In
The aura of the fire of applewood
With its faint scent of McIntoshes, in
The disappearing act of the low sun,
A marginally yellow medallion
Behind the white snow sky, under the in-
Undation of sharp snowdrifts like the fins
Of sharks astride our windowsills, I hide
Out in my hideout from the memory
Of our unlovely recent history,
And of those fresh divisions just gone west.
A sharp sound brings me back: perhaps a tree

Cleft by the cold, but likelier the crack
Of a gun down at Devens. Snow begins
To lance against the window, and I see,
By luck, a leisurely and murderous
Shadow detach itself with a marine
Grace from an apple tree. A snowy owl,
Cinereous, nearly invisible,
Planes down its glide path to surprise a vole.

Pursuit of Honor

For my mother and father

Notes on *Pursuit of Honor*

It's pretty presumptuous for a writer to annotate his own work, but I'm told that the allusions in some of these poems require a clue. Hence:

"An American in Evans Country." Kingsley Amis and, latterly, Robert Conquest have been having fun with a series of poems about a rat with women called Dai Evans, who operates in a section of Wales his creators denominate Evans Country. In this poem, I was spoofing the rather infantile and gleeful sexual rapacity displayed by the Evans sequence.

"The New York Woman" was the headline and protagonist of a series of ads for the Chemical Corn Exchange (as it then was) Bank. Their lady was impossibly svelte; mine is, I hope, more life-like.

"Pursuit of Honor" contains, as you'd suspected, a good deal of Tarot-pack and Grail-legend symbolism, though it is not arranged in any precisely parallel or sequential way. The children at the Thalia are watching a re-run of *Grand Illusion*.

"Excuse for an Italian Sonnet" expresses a middle-aged writer's dismay at being obscured and superseded by young writers who condemn his methods and his values.

"J.J.'s Levée." Under another alias, J.J. is also the inspiration for an important character in a series of celebrated Irish-American novels. ". . . and later die" is an adaptation of a line from W. C. Fields. "The Order of the W.C. with Chain" was an ironic and imaginary decoration invented, I believe, by the R.A.F. in World War II.

The Big Rock-Candy Mountain

(To the memory of my half brother, Winfield
Shannon, itinerant farm worker, 1909–1969)

> A mason times his mallet
> to a lark's twitter . . .
> till the stone spells a name
> naming none,
> a man abolished.
> — *Basil Bunting*

I. "ON A SUMMER'S DAY IN THE MONTH OF MAY,
   A JOCKER COME A-HIKING
   DOWN A SHADY LANE IN THE SUGAR CANE,
   A-LOOKING FOR HIS LIKING. . . ."

The land was theirs after we were the land's,
The visionaries with prehensile hands —
The Wobblies, Okies, wetbacks — driven and drawn
To cross the land and see it, to select
A tree to lie out under: a Pound Sweet,
A Cox's Orange Pippin, a pecan,
Persimmon, Bartlett, quince, Bing, freestone, fig,
Grapefruit, Valencia. The trundling trains
That took their supercargo free are gone,
And so are they; a thousand circling camps
Down by the freight yards are dispersed, watchfires
Burnt out, inhabitants transshipped
To death or terminal respectability
In cold wards of the state, where their last rites
Are levied on the people, ritual
Gravediggers of the past, ratepayers for
A lot in potter's field. Old Gravensteins,
Bedight with morbid branches, shelter no
Transients at length. Our suburbs saw them go.

II. "AS HE ROAMED ALONG, HE SANG A SONG
   OF THE LAND OF MILK AND HONEY,
   WHERE A BUM CAN STAY FOR MANY A DAY
   AND HE WON'T NEED ANY MONEY. . . ."

Uninterest in progress was their crime,
Short-circuited ambition. They came out
On a Traverse County hilltop one late-May
Morning and gave an involuntary shout
At those square miles of cherry blossom on
The slopes above the lake; exclaimed at wheat,
Fat in the ear and staggered in the wind,
In Hillsdale County; up in Washtenaw,
Spoke to the plough mules and the meadowlark
A little after dawn; in Lenawee,
Laughed at a foal's first grounding in the art
Of standing in the grass. Too tentative,
Too deferent to put down roots beside
Us in our towns, outcast, outcaste, they rode
Out of our sight into the sheltering storm
Of their irrelevant reality:
Those leagues of fields out there beyond the pale
Fretting of cities, where, in prison clothes,
We cultivate our gardens for the rose
Of self redoubled, for the florid green
Of money succulent as cabbage leaves.
They have gone out to pasture. No one grieves.

III. "OH, THE BUZZING OF THE BEES IN THE
    CIGARETTE TREES,
   THE SODA-WATER FOUNTAIN,
   THE LEMONADE SPRINGS WHERE THE BLUEBIRD
    SINGS
   ON THE BIG ROCK-CANDY MOUNTAIN. . . ."

A young man on a Harley-Davidson
(An old one painted olive drab, with long-
Horn handlebars and a slab-sided tank),
You pushed your blond hair back one-handed when
You stopped and lit a Camel cigarette.

You laughed and showed white teeth; you had a blond
Mustache; wore cardigans and knickerbockers; wowed
The farm-town girls; drank beer; drew gracefully;
Fell, frothing at the mouth, in a grand mal
Seizure from time to time. In your small room
In Grandpa's house, you kept your goods: pastels,
A sketching block, a superheterodyne
Kit radio, a tin can full of parts,
A stack of *Popular Mechanics,* three
Kaywoodie pipes, an old Antonio
Y Cleopatra box for letters and
Receipts, a Rexall calendar with fat
Full moons controlling 1933.

IV. "OH, THE FARMER AND HIS SON, THEY
          WERE ON THE RUN,
      TO THE HAYFIELD THEY WERE BOUNDING.
      SAID THE BUM TO THE SON, 'WHY DON'T
          YOU COME
      TO THAT BIG ROCK-CANDY MOUNTAIN?' . . ."

When Grandpa died and your employer died,
And the widow sold off his tax-loss horse farm
(Those Morgans being auctioned, going meek
To new grooms less deft-handed than you were,
To new frame stables and new riding rings),
You hit the road at fifty and alone
Struck out cross country lamely, too damned old
To keep up with the kids or keep out cold
Except with whiskey, cheap and strong. Too long
You hiked from job to picking job, and when
Snow plastered stubble laths, you holed up in
The Mapes Hotel for winter; did odd jobs
To keep in nips of Richmond Rye; dozed through
The night till spring; fared forward once again
To summer's manufactory, a mill
Of insect tickings on a field of gold,
And fall's great remnant store. Last winter, you
Spent your last winter in a coffining
Dead room on Third Street in Ann Arbor, where

Only the landlady climbed up your stair
And passed your unknocked door in sateen mules.

V. "SO THE VERY NEXT DAY THEY HIKED AWAY;
   THE MILEPOSTS THEY KEPT COUNTING,
   BUT THEY NEVER ARRIVED AT THE LEMONADE
      TIDE
   ON THE BIG ROCK-CANDY MOUNTAIN. . . ."

In Goebel's Funeral Home, where row on row
Of coffins lie at anchor, burning dark
Hulls — walnut, rosewood — on a light-blue tide
Of broadloom, we select Economy —
Grey fibreglass with a white-rayon shroud
And mainsheets — and stand out into the street,
Becalmed already in the April heat
That conjures greenness out of earthen fields,
Tips black twigs pink on trees, starts habit's sweat
Out of Midwestern brows. In Winfield's room,
A cave of unstirred air kept in the dark
By pinholed shades, we shift his transient
Things in a foredoomed hunt for permanent
Memorials. No photograph, no ring,
No watch, no diary, no effects. Nothing —
Beyond a mildewed pile of mackinaws
(On top) and boots (precipitated out) —
Except the lone cigar box. On its lid
A rampant Antony advances on
Bare-breasted Cleopatra, areoles
Red as lit panatelas, but inside,
Only a heap of fingered rent receipts,
On pale-green check stock, weights a linen pad
Of Woolworth letter paper. Here begins
Winfield's last letter, in a corn-grain-round,
School-Palmer-Method hand riven by age,
Drink, sickness: "April 17. Dear Folks —
The weather has warmed up some but I don't"
No more. The hospital bed intervened.
Peritonitis. Coma. Peaceful death.
In truth it is. In Goebel's viewing room
The guest has been laid out, now neat, now dressed —
In shirt, tie, jacket — as if for a feast.

It is not over-stressed. He looks his age
(Not brotherly at all; avuncular,
Judicious, a thought sallow, robbed of the
Brilliance of his two straight and sky-blue eyes)
And takes his silent part upon the stage
Miming repose, an unemotional
Exit dictated by the prompter's page.
Later, in the three-car processional
To the old graveyard, we ride just behind
His Stygian Superior hearse, a Cadillac.
The grave has been dug under tamaracks;
The young Episcopalian minister
Dispassionately, as he should for one unknown
To him, says the set words designed to send
The dead off; soon the open grave will close,
The mason test his chisel and begin,
Tabula rasa, to cut that name in-
To his blank slab of granite, much as that
Void grave will take the imprint of his weight,
And all his travels will be at an end.

ENVOY

But, prince that fortune turned into a toad,
Instead I see you — camped beside a road
Between old fruit trees in full bloom in May —
Lie out under an agèd Pound Sweet and
Sleep soundly on the last night of your way
Out of a rifled and abandoned land.

An E-Type on the Interstate

(For A. P. Klauer)

White needles wipe around their black-faced clock
Faces in unison. Ninety. The tach
Trembles on forty. Forty, I take stock
Of the houseful of time behind my back —
The scruffy luggage on the luggage rack,
Stuffed full of tears and sweatshirts, held by locks
Both temporal and spiritual, packed
To go to ground with — and am glad, ticktock,
To have outdistanced it. The road ahead
Is straight and empty, but a curled raccoon,
Unmarked, unmasked, caught in the wheels of noon,
Recalls tonight's appointment with the dead;
And I, rejoicing in the practiced aim
Of middle age, make haste toward the same.

Among Schoolchildren

> . . . For Dockery a son, for me nothing,
> Nothing with all a son's harsh patronage.
> — *Philip Larkin*
>
> I have no daughter. I desire none.
> — *Weldon Kees*

I. ALTON B. PARKER SCHOOL: THE SENIOR MULTI-SERVICE CENTER

If forty is a perilous age, if it
Is knife and tightrope, watershed between
The steeps of early and late ages, it
Is still a coign of vantage, still a prime
Viewpoint to fall from. In the green-limed room
Under the Parker School, old people come

To get their lunch for fifty cents, the same
Hot sandwich, canned peas, milk, stale gingerbread
The children have just eaten. Suited in
Their bare respectability, they weave
With laden trays toward a greener room
Where chairs and tables are; are overhauled
By a long, giggling pigtail of small girls
En route to gym, who do not look at them
Or get looked back at. The old ones pursue
Their way to table, shed coats, sit and eat,
Secreting extra bread and milk in bags
For future reference. With honor and
The inner man both satisfied, they break
Sharply and jarringly with discipline,
And, to a piano deftly out of tune
And passably well-played by one of them,
Sing shamelessly old songs: "Smiles," "Over There,"
"Give My Regards to Broadway," "Tea for Two,"
And send one hour of a blue afternoon
To where all hours are, even those when tunes
Like those were new, and they were schoolchildren.

II.   WITH MASTERS AT THE RITZ

Punched in, puffed out, snowed on, embodied heads
From a class yearbook — shy of boyish lips
And shorn of down — bob shockingly up in
Rod Masters' narrow room and hand around
Their damp hands to be shaken, raise their damp,
Perspiring glasses high in tentative
Salutes to tenuous remembrances.
On a loud ground of voices, classmates change
Subjects and partners in a crabwise dance
In search of old acceptances, now void.
The women come in three kinds: stumpy, square
Careerist mothers lost in middle age
And not to be recalled as wives, beside
Their shining husbands most like firstborn sons;
The brittle girls of forty who fight rear-
Guard actions to retain each tooth and nail
Intact, and though succeeding in detail,

Immediately stake and lose it all
On one harsh giggle, a hysterical
Reaction to their striking torturer,
The steeple clock in Arlington Street Church;
The second wives, bland, smashing showpieces,
All under twenty-five, on whom it dawns
Now, if not earlier, that they will be
Conspicuously consumed by the proud, sad,
Bald men who ransomed them and their half-mad,
Half-envious coevals. Masters takes
My elbow like my schoolfellow; his feat
Thumb-finger pressure thrills my funnybone.
His old child face, ascending like the moon
On these our revels, sunders in a grin
Of head-coach desperation at the load
Of youth we shoulder up the hill of old
Appearances — a smile of failing rage.

III.   A SEMINAR AT HILL

Tatnuck is set on seven hills, like Rome,
But differs otherwise. Its Capitoline,
For instance, is presided over by
A city hall in grafted Romanesque
Above the bare-bone granite skeletons
Of handsome, dead mill buildings whose last stand-
Still fell some forty years ago, above
Mechanic Street, where three-deckers surround
The small Hill campus, where old Tupper leads
Me out to meet inquisitors in beads,
Boots, beards, jeans, granny glasses. They sit in
Defensive order in four far-off rows;
I stand behind a holy podium
Above the groundlings and am introduced
And opened up to questions. None arrive.
No ex-cathedra judgments inspissate
The air from me to them. Impasse. I shunt
My stool out to the pit and sit in front
Of my non-interlocutors. Poor Tupper primes
The pump with his thin questions. Then one kid
Requires my views on Rod McKuen, which melt

Right in my mouth. I see Bob Dylan and
Paul Simon trembling on the tips of tongues
Like spring guns set to send me up. My own
Tongue's thick in transports of translation: strange
Terms — "like" as a conjunction, "bag," and "thing,"
In their nonce senses — seek to close the range
Between us, while a sobering sea change
Informs my questioners, appending "sir"
To phrases that increasingly grow square
As time wears on. Through no interpreter,
We speak each other's language to avoid
A confrontation, a concession, an
Exchange of terms across the bargaining
Table inside the truce tent. Met halfway,
And reassured our meeting is without
Result (that's how we said it would come out),
We go our several, vindicated ways.

Cock Robbins Opens in New York

Cock Robbins opens in New York: an amp
Big as the Empire State and a reverb
Vast as an echo up the Hudson make
Him and his downy nestlings known, if non-
Grata to citizens who swarm and hive
In marble halls beclouded by the fads
Of our days, stammered, tense, sensational,
Chameleonic, inescapable.
These ruffian boys late out of Eastcheap, in
Buffoonish finery, dundrearies, grins
That mock our laws of gravity, repeal
The compacts that compound our commonweal,
Try our rough justice and convict it of
Malfeasance, beat on every town-house door
In inquisition on our small hours, prove
Our age and majesty a legal fraud,

Pull down our high estate and kid our god,
Commence to play on the great stage of our
Most ornate music hall. The young arise
By rote with undiscriminating cries
To greet them; we retain our costly seats
And look on, exiled, as the music beats
Its way into our hearts, and the loud words
Reduce us to the pygmy status of
Outlanders in the land we sprang out of,
Unearthly excommunicants of love.

An American in Evans Country

(A garland of limp stamens for K.A. and R.C.)

Great men are big boys now; in retrograde
How sad steps they lead down the little girls
In fantasy to bed behind the shade

Of evening on the shingle, where the blade
Of night cuts off the vision of their pearls.
Great men are big boys now in retrograde:

Alone in regal rooms, beyond first aid,
They take their alter egos, lapt in curls,
In fantasy to bed behind the shade.

When dawn begins its daily, brazen raid,
Their godhead his pink forehead re-unfurls:
Great men are big boys now in retrograde.

Philanderers are reborn, but never made
By human hands, except the hand that hurls
A fantasy to bed behind the shade

Of age approaching, appetite turned jade,

Desire digested in the maelstrom's whorls.
Great men are big boys now in retrograde,
In fantasy, in bed behind the shade.

First N.Y. Showing

Think of those homosexuals at the Park-Bryant, think of them
At the All-Male Film Festival, Continuous 9:45 A.M.
To Midnite. Think of them in a transport of being received
By their kith, their kind, in being invited to
A show of their own, a show of their flag; of being deceived
By the tempter, the pander, the spectacled speculant who
Bids on, at lost-property auctions, the shape of their self —
Their only shape, really, preoccupation with self —
In brown-paper wrappings and ticketed, there on that shelf.

Manchester: Night

The cars spit past beside the Merrimack.
In Unk's Fine Foods & Liquors, a dim tank
Swimming with emptiness, strip-lit by night's
Dead shades, a dying waitress waits for me
In cancer's yellow livery. She stands
In silent service, messmates, till I call
For beer and Red-Hot Chile (sic). "A bowl!"
She cries across the waste of pastel booths,
And goes away as I plug in a dime
To play "Blue Tango" on the jukebox. Time

Resumes for three loud minutes and then stops.
Two women's voices fifty feet away
Trade August compliments like katydids,
Contesting who will pay. My supper comes
On wings of the stone angel from the hills —
The Uncanoonucs westward — where old graves
Still rear her likenesses incised in slate
Now losing its flyleaves. This stuff is hot,
As advertised. I sip my beer and eat,
Maintaining life in this void house of night,
Whose high green vault is battered by a moth.
Nine-thirty. My car must be ready now.
The waitress-mask takes shape beside me, worn
As currency, withdrawn, all but the form
Of flesh on bones, from life. Alas, farewell:
I leave a tip and pay the tart cashier
A dollar-sixty — chili and a beer —
And issue into Second Street, where cars
Full of the young idea ramp and roar
In social circulation on their strip,
Their clearing in the forest of the night
Made habitable by the humane light
Of Merit Gas, Zayre Stores, Ho-Jo's, and Unk's.

The New York Woman

The assistant editor of *Crewel World*
(The Needleworker's Helper, ABC
Paid circulation, 1-1-68,
1,007,773)
Heads home to lunch. In the diffusing lens
Of distance, her long face is pretty, young,
Unfingermarked; close up, it's pretty young,
But hatched with all the crosses of New York:
Divorce, childbearing, wishing, failing, work.
Beside her blue side, her small hand hangs on
To an enormous, tatty orange man's
Briefcase replete with fancyworkers' dreams:
Patterns, instructions, yarn lists, letters, schemes
Of art-struck readers to diffuse their cause
Across the country in a crewel crusade
To mend a ravelled world they never made.
Obliquely, Sarah stares into the dark
Inside her letter box and sees the light-
Er darkness of a letter. Hell, a bill.
Up marble treads she trudges, up until
A skylight drops a halo on her blond,
Untidy head. Palming a porcupine
Of bristling keys, she punctuates the stale
Air of the landing with a yielding Yale-
Lock cluck, and enters into 2½
Rms, rec redec, with fp, kit, and bth.
Her sad son's photo stares, reproaching her,
From Grandma's farm above the gas-log fire;
The kitten, claws locked in an afghan, sleeps;
Her pink Picasso juggler mirrors her
Tight lines around the lips. She sighs and goes
To her Rollator-Top GE, which holds
Cat food, pork chops, a wizened chicken leg.
She eats the chicken cold and sips a cup
Of Instant Yuban. Hope, proceeding up
From her warm belly, lodges in her throat
And complicates her swallowing. She tries
A smile extravagantly on for size

And prudently forgoes it. The doorbell
We all sit tight for, powered by a dry cell,
Gives a cracked rattle, and she buzzes in
Her visitor, the editor of *Man,*
Not, as you might suppose, a sword in tan
And turtleneck, but quite instead a pale,
High-foreheaded, mild, intellectual-
Appearing, troubled mother's son named John.
And, judging from his step, he's drunk again.
He swoops in on the door — got it in one —
And espaliers her upon the whitewashed wall
In a facsimile of an embrace
Remembered from bad movies. Find her face,
John, and you'll be home free. Shook up, she smiles —
For real this time, like a Madonna does —
And softly scores him for his naughtiness.
He's all for bed; she's all for holding him
Off at arm's length, in her apartment's power,
And owning him with her eyes for an hour,
Until he charges out or falls asleep
On the rag rug beside the kitten's dish.
He falls asleep, as advertised by his
Stertorous radamacues. She gets her wish:
To skip her office afternoon and sit
In silence with another whose needs fit
Her pitiful and unsolicited
Gifts: doglike love, unlimited belief
In journeys' endings, tolerance for grief,
An aptitude for mothering, an art
As painstaking as any crewel heart.

Mouth-Organ Tunes:

The American Lost and Found

I. IN A HO-JO'S BY THE RIVER

This mouse-grey man with currant-black eyes stealing
Around the edges of his rimless glasses, stealing
Out of the restaurant behind his wife's grey raglan
Back and permanent-framed face — revealing
A world of middle tones suspent in mildness,
The lipless grey moue of the long-gone childless,
A rosebud button nose, the wild blue flaglets
Of March-air eyes impugned by reddish lashes,
The streambeds down each cheek in gouged meanders —
Now sidles past my elbow in lost motion,
All hesitant and tremblant, to the Flanders
Fields of parked cars to which a rootless nation
Repairs for movement and repose on Sundays.

II. AND DID THOSE FEET IN ANCIENT TIME
     WALK ON NEW ENGLAND'S MOUNTAINS
     GREEN?

Spring and an empty house and an empty spring-
House over the spring. A millstone for a door-
Step. Wind in slattern shutters. A thin green
Sheen in the dead grass ringlets, and a squill
Blowing beside the door, blue, blue. No paint since when.
The swayback barn — shed, really — open to
All comers. Hames inside. The pasture fence
Squandering stones on fields. The kitchen is
Savage: enamel coffeepot, a pile
Of yellow *Union-Leader*s, overalls
Stiff on a hook, cracked plates in the dry sink,
Bagged bluebottles in webs, an empty quart
Of Carling's and a Black Flag ant trap on
The pantry shelf. When purple lilacs last
In the dooryard bloomed, and Sirius early drooped

In the western sky in the night, Myles died.
This spring I mourn his unreturning pride.

III.   LIEDER EINES FAHRENDEN GESELLEN

Jesus, is Schimmer a flaky son of a bitch.
Listen what happened Friday. This is rich.
Friday he threw a party in his pent-
House. East End Avenue. Invitations went
Out one month early. All embossed, addressed
By secretaries, with — get this — a crest —
His monogram, for Christ's sake — on the flap.
Maida and I, we put on all this crap —
A costume party, *you* know. I was Gen-
Ghis Khan, she was the fair Maid Marian
In a green doublet slashed right down the front.
You should of seen it. Anyway, we went.
Got there right on the tick. Big hullaballoo
Already under way. Celebs. Champagne.
An eight-piece folk-rock combo. At least two
Bars in each room, pouring booze like rain.
And right in the sunken conversation pit
In the living room, there was this thing, floodlit
From up above: a funk-art statue of
A cop in a crash hat, standing above
A dead kid tangled in his motorbike,
All one side blood. I never seen the like,
It was so real. So still. It shook us up.
But we got over it and had a cup
Of Schimmer's punch and looked at his Jim Dines.
All of a sudden hell broke loose. At nine,
The dead-kid statue suddenly stood up,
Climbed on his bike and started it. The cop
Whipped out his gun and fired it as the kid
Took off out through the foyer. Panic! Did
That party ever come to a sudden stop!
Of course, it was a put-on. Schimmer hired
A couple actors. The bullets the cop fired
Were blanks. The blood was phony, too. What some
Wise bastards won't do just to have some fun.

IV. GOOD INDIANS

When Radiation Therapy fills up
With grey lay figures, walking-stick insects
Pulsating feebly in the new blue chairs
And staring at the hangings, to the tune
Of gallows Muzak, then I know the big
Machine behind the lead doors, and the still
More powerful machine this whole thing is
Are working at capacity to take
The overflow from the end of the trail
And ferry it across the Little Big
Horn to the land of Nembutal, where sleep
Comes easy to such specimens as these.
Come, Mrs. Karsh, come, Mr. Bailet, let's
Put on our bathrobes and put down our bets
On a sure thing — the god in the machine —
Who will wish us away from this sad scene
And carry our spirits over the narrow seas.

The Dump: A Dream Come True

When Mrs. Finnan died, aged eighty-one,
In brave Brick Bottom, Somerville, her son
Did right by her: he called Kennealley in —
The funeral director — and had him
Take care of everything. (And so he did:
At the closed-coffin wake, he begged that Jim —
Who had his generation's taste — take just
One peek at her, to show Kennealley gave
Full value, even with a dear one whose
Face never would be seen. Jim did; a whore's
Pink-painted cheek shone out at him; "There!" said

Kennealley. "Wha'd I tell you? Hundred per cent.")
After the wake, Jim cleaned out her junk —
She was a pack rat — and took it to the dump
In his Ford wagon, cluttered to the eaves
With the sort of truck no one who ever grieves
Wants to hang on to: corsets, letters, lamps,
Black hats, bent saucepans, pie tins, cancelled stamps
From Eire, medicines, a heating pad.
At the town dump in Milton, Jim drove in
Through skeins of smoke and stopped beneath the rim
Of a semicircle of junkhills, on whose
Heights men emerged and, high and giant, strode
Down them to meet him. Close to, they were not
So formidable: half a dozen drunks,
Or winos, rather, each with his day's beard,
Each keeping back respectfully as Jim
Unlocked the tailgate and unloosed on them
His mother's treasure. As he worked, one man
Touched his brown cap and asked, "Is it a death?"
"Yes," Jim said. "It's a death." "A death. A death,"
The men around him echoed, and a grave
Smile lit their faces at a picker's dream.
Still they stood still. Jim emptied out the last
String-tied suitcases, souvenirs of Rye
Beach, bottles of elixir, Spanish combs.
He shut the tailgate. As he drove away,
His rear-view mirror showed him how the men,
No longer decent, static, claimed the piles
Of pickings for their own; how fortune smiles
On someone as the obverse of her frown.

Tears at Korvette's

Inevitably, in Fifth Avenue
The past comes up to strike me like a rake
Stepped on in innocence: before my eyes,
Stung by the brusque repeal of fifteen years,
My old friend-enemy Gerson appears
To me in perigee, orbiting near
My earth for the first time in many moons
At undiminished speed, looking the same
At forty as at twenty, full of blame
And waste and numinosity and flame.
But now, he indicates, the tide is caught
At full and harnessed to his errant art,
Filling, last summer, a bare gallery
In Boothbay with a lone epiphany,
A one-man manifestation, a late show.
Soon, maybe, Hirschl, Adler, Perls will cast
Their tender shadows in his way at last —
"But come on in with me. I got to shop
For toys. My daughter's birthday." In Korvette's,
Talking impasto and Cézanne and reds,
Wearing a single paint spot of gamboge
For buttonhole on his blue blazer, badge
Of art in action, Gerson picks his toys —
Plush Mr. Rabbit (up to seven years),
A Dolly Tea Set and Miss Tiny Tears —
And pays with big bills scattered from his hand,
And leaves with bundles cumbering each arm,
And says goodbye with a sad flash of charm,
And leaves, a divorcé, for his hotel
And Nancy's birthday party, held among
Those canvases which were not for so long.

The Time in Venezuela

Caracas roads: the wind blows out to sea,
Reminding us that cross roads really cross
And go their ways unsensible of loss,
Just as, one numbered day, you must cross me.

And then I must stand out to sea and turn
Which way wind favors into other ports.
Enormous item in the heart's thick torts:
The dead-slow passage out of haven, when we learn.

Learn the crook backs of dock cranes, mile on mile;
The bitter pills of storage tanks; the fat
Flames of waste gases; the grand, greasy *jatte*
Of Venezuela. And unlearn your smile.

Letter from Coast to Coast

Alone and lately loitering beside
The margin of our Old Swan Swamp, between
Cattails' exclams and periodic green
Sleeves of slack water dotted with wood duck,
I hear a joyous and archaic noise
As you plane down and drop your PBY,
Still rocking, at my feet, and clamber out,
Still twenty-four, in ensign's whites and white
Limp cap bereft of wire, to share your pint
(Green River) with me. Since it is not so,
It never happened, and instead you go,
At forty-three, a lost alumnus, to
The wildwood of Los Angeles to take
A new, maybe a false, identity,
Why then I'll reconstrue you from the start

In hopes of finding you yourself again.
Scene One: interior: a vaulted, bare
Chicago armory; in middle air,
The film-winged monoplane which you have built
Outflies all opposition, hangs aloft
Far longer than the others, and you win.
Scene Two: exterior: night: playing fields
At an Ohio college, '39.
You, freshman rebel against discipline's
Old sanctions, scourge of upperclassmen, rash
Defender of the innocents, are pursued
By armies of your enemies as you run,
Buck-naked, through the end zone and across
Dim yard lines up the field. (You said you thought
That you were flying then; but you were caught
And, laughing, dunked in gallons of deck paint
To make a coat of many colors.) Three:
Interior: Iowa City: Primary
School husbands yellow Stearmans in the ag-
Ricultural college of the corn for miles
Around, around the Hawkeye Hotel room
Where you, on liberty, set up your house
Of love, your folding, falling portable
Cardhouse, your desert tent, your home, with a
Slight girl who knew the words straight off the farm
(A waitress at the Maquoketa Grille),
Whose mouth spoke all unmade-up words, whose warm
Recipience built a mansion house among
The suffering furnishings, a house raised up
On Friday night, pulled down by Monday noon,
Where you would not in lordship walk again.
Four: Whidbey Island. Unforetold cascades
Of fog shield real Cascades, a point of not
Just passing interest to the flying boat
Between the sun, a soft-edged sovereign,
And the hard water, aqua regia,
Which solves all foreign bodiments which fall
Into its see, its jurisdiction. Full
Speed ahead, you climb to overtop
Putative mountains, sketch a new approach
Miles westward of the unseen beach, and turn
Into the wind, into a drunken dream

Of flight you wake from in Scene Five, upon
A couch in the Corpus Christi Officers' Club,
Where a mad captain damns your disarray,
Disgracing your gilt stripe, gilt star, gilt arm
Of service, and your gilded, grounded wings.
 Six: war's message ends; over and out, you ride
A Harley's pillion seat down dawn's Midway
Behind a fellow section man, who, rapt
In rye, noise, and discovery of hap,
Yells, "Even the weathervanes are pointing at
Us!" Seven: exterior, years after. New
England engrails in green the blue car you
Drive, laying down a screen of oil smoke,
On your appointive rounds as leader of
Bookish discussions, led for learning's love
(And earning's gold, exiguously prized
Out of the firm foundation's flinty side
To keep your children in some penury).
Those children — Eight: interior — a scene
In your old house in Boston; your wife sits
In a chair out at elbows while she knits
Over her belly for the occupant,
And you withdraw to paper and descant
A poem on her state, about to bear,
Open and secret, far away and there.
Again — in our hotchpotic office, shared
In irony and raddled by disdain —
I see you lay aside your work and write
In verse, in longhand, on your own; your right
And dutied (ah, too heavily) mystery,
Too seldom exercised. Your history
Could end here, fashionably out of date
And indeterminate, but a new start,
Embarking on your grand emprise. You write
Of life in space, in aerospace, beyond
Brakes, sprags, and clutches of our antique, fond
Twenties and thirties. I cannot pursue
Mastery that way; between me and you
The gap, once only continental, grows
Spatial and universal; in the prose
Of your curt letters I read new-wave verse
In a galactic Morse I cannot break.

I must retreat (cf. Scene One) and take
You as I found you, or I thought I did;
In the Still River swamp, my motives hid
By noble nature, I await the plane
Which, nonexistent, will not ever come.

SCENE TWELVE: INTERIOR: ENVOY

Prince of infortune, you come back to me
On our green terms by a black happenstance.
The phone rings in my study Sunday night.
It's you, clear clear across a continent
And crying. Your most sympathetic son —
Already paying on the note of his
Grave promise at sixteen — drove north last night
With a school buddy to inaugurate
The fishing season in the high rivers
With a first cast for trout; the singing line,
The Silver Doctor riding, diving under
The downbound water, registering a strike.
No plane came. Earlier, their station wagon —
Shooting the lacets of a Sierra highway —
Devolved upon an intermountain truck
U-turning, straddling the whole road, and struck
It broadside. Both were killed. Now, with your former
Wife, you maintain a mortifying vigil
Over the past and all its presents. Move
As you will in time and station, chance above
All designates your place. I sign this love.

New Year's, 1948

(Boston: Washington and Dover Streets)

ELEVEN

"I'm looking over a four-leaf clover
That I overlooked before," reiterates
The jukebox in the bar downstairs, which baits
Ladies with "Ladies Invited," but attracts
Thin seers nighted by their cataracts,
Snow-shovellers between white-collar jobs,
Purple-nosed punchers with ring-bounded brains,
And connoisseurs of California wines.
Up here we hear each clover leaflet fall
Between bouts with the El, whose braking wheels
Loose bob and treble bob and grandsire peals
In honor of the infant year, which springs
Out of this artless gallery of things
That we walk in, inspect, join, grasp, and leave,
Like the old year, with mourning on our sleeve.

TWELVE

For auld lang syne we take a tot of rum
And drain it toasting our hosts, Blanche and Slim,
And all our progeny, the days ahead,
Which, born in ice, swell into summer's bed
And dwindle into fall and ice again.
We toast discontinuity of pain;
The likelihood of trials recessed; the sense
Of living lightly in the present tense;
The touch of girls; the trenchant teeth of pens
Set loose on paper; the steep sum of men's
Expectance. With one toy hand, tiny Slim
Encinctures Blanche's high, wide, handsome bum;
With the unknowing other, he unveils
Arcana of the axillary tail

Of his erst mistress, Ardra Pease, and calls
For one more bumper to salute the wails
For a year dead and from a one newborn,
Whose daybooks our rude doings will adorn.

ONE

Beneath the aiguillettes and *fourragères*
Of the tall, leaning, browning Christmas tree
Sits a skin-covered birthday gift for me:
Bright Sally Sayward, once and again to be,
Perhaps, my stringent bedfellow, but now,
In intermission, the beloved of
The base recorder-maker, Jason Love,
Who flirts across the fogbound room with Nan
Milton, the playwright and remittance man,
The double agent whose much misprized name —
Hernando, actually — brought him Fame
In drag on his arm at the Beaux Arts Ball.
A noise of voices through the thin-skinned wall
Reminds us that the Linds are also here:
The zeta-shaped Greek scholar in a vest,
His woolly wife who would have won the West
One-handed, and her feminine friend, Tink,
Who now grows tipsy on a tiny drink
Of Mr. Boston gin and speaks in low
New Orleans tones, though she was born in Stowe.

TWO

"Well, happy birthday," Sally Sayward says,
Enduing me invisibly with bays,
Each leaf to mark a year. "Now, go away,"
She tells me, twenty, but, near-man, I stay
To press my case with passive rhetoric
Where deeds are needed. Nonetheless, her quick
Rejection is retracted. By degrees,
I talk my way down to my bony knees
And kneel and squat and sit beside her, where

My drinkless hand can infiltrate her hair
And fathom her resistance. Soon her square
Mouth may traverse to meet my mouth, and then,
Our crossed stars nodding, we'll be off again.

THREE

Drink drives my doze as, bedded, I embrace
An overcoat called Sally, and awake
With a harsh cry of fraud. She's gone. I rise
And steer, dead-reckoned, by the beam of noise
That issues from next door. But she's not there —
In the loud night, out of my borrowed bed,
Sally, my quarry, with her Love has fled,
And left me odd among these couples who
Now settle down till morning in the blue
Shadows and crannies of each other, while
I hunt the yellow bathroom down the hall.
Wind shakes that jaundiced box like dice: the glass
Skylight screams, hums, and hisses in the first
Blast of the first squall of the baby year;
The bare bulb curvets on its furry chain;
Chill takes my ruddy knees; a dust sifts down,
Which turns out to be snow; I stand and head
Back to my horizontal cloakroom, bed.

FOUR

I'm taking Sally Sayward out to lunch.
Inside the Union — say, this place has changed
Since I last ate here; look at all those wild
Magenta murals on the walls — all eyes
Lock onto us, the hunter and his prey
Brought back alive, if only for a day,
A date, a lunch, a showing-up of all
The bucks and stags stuffed in that musty hall.
We march abreast, my hand dressed on her arm,
My eyes right on her onionskin disdain,
Toward the serving line, where old colleens
Stand and deliver soup, slaw, salad greens,

Lamb patties, peas, beets, coffee, brick ice cream.
This round room has changed, too; it's lavender,
Sashed with long draperies in jungle green.
Look — there's a blood-red change booth with a brass
Wicket enclosing money and a man.
We step up to get nickels. The change man
Becomes my father. Recognition. Up
Goes the gold wicket, bang!, and out he shouts —
Face lit with flame, no doubt a trick of the
Sensational décor — "No, no, no, no!"
Dream ends. Escapement of small hours resumes.

FIVE

Doze, wake, and entertain those sawed-off dreams
That spring on you at morning, when all things
Distort and shiver; men on stilted legs
Mutate into short blobs, and blots explode
Into thin alphabets of wiry stars;
Simples turn double, petals form whole heads
Of leaves like cabbages, perspectives go
Back to beginnings like a Chirico,
And you fall down the fun-house chute of sleep,
And land, awake, in trouble, on the street
Of dreams, where every door turns you away
To face the undeclared but actual day.

SIX

To tiptoe through the tulip shapes of coats
Flung down upon and under snorters in
The clover-overlookers' den, the long
Coach corridor of their thin railroad flat,
Is difficult when hung, re-drunk on cold
Flat water, bearded, shod in dirty socks,
Laden with leaden shoes. I snap the locks
Back thunderously, fire myself out through
The door with a grand slam, and gravitate
Down to the vestibule to don my shoes.
The street is infinitely sinister:

A lamp ticks like a clock; the wind harps on
The stanchions of the El; a taxicab
Creeps, cruising, up on me; a sewer fumes.
I walk quite quick. In leeward doorways, eyes
Of derelicts move with me, and the lees
Of their bare bottles glint in ricochets
Of public power and light. At Berkeley Street,
Brick rooming houses stop. Ahead, the bulk
Of the John Hancock, lately dried and signed,
Inscribed across the top with Christmas lights,
Picks itself out in density against
The slightest lightening of sky. It's cold.
I trot, borne on a heavy wave of air,
Down St. James Street and into angular
Park Square, where, halfway home to Pinckney Street,
I stop for coffee at the Waldorf Lunch
And sit in solace with the morning bunch
Of regulars — red cop, green grandmother
With three bags full, brown lavatory boy,
White rummy with a tie, black counterman,
Pocked yellow cook presiding over fire —
All busy keeping an ice age away
From their cold hearts while waiting for the day
To break and bring in a gilt-edged new year.

Dying: A Resurrection, 1969

When ambient death came in out of the cold
And laid a glove on me in our rematch,
I covered in a trice the rest of the road
Before me, and at the end of the steel pier
I walked the final board feet of the plank,
Lapped in injustice like St. Elmo's fire.
Abridged, I burned with moral purpose, seethed
With fever to persist, sang angry songs
Of vengeful, mutinous futility,
Slowed my halt feet to a dead march, prolonged
The bittersweetness of each breath, paroled
Myself with garlands of last words. The day,
Freckled with birds in grasses, ripe with life,
Infinitesimal and infinite,
Hung on the hinge of me; the night, mooning
Over its lover, soon to be lost at sea,
Reproached me darkly in its waning hours.
When, purged of anything but regret, I fell
Into the ocean's arms, a curling swell
Swept me back safe ashore to wake ashamed
Of such dramatics, such forebodings, such
World-girdling ego. Sheepish revenant,
I crept back into life as into much
Too large a pair of trousers. Evident-
Ly even desperation leads a charmed
Life, valetudinarians go unharmed
At times, self-sorrow often sobs in vain,
And morrows rob us of our mortal pain.

Pursuit of Honor, 1946

(To Anthony Hecht)

> The King of Hearts a broadsword bears,
>   The Queen of Hearts, a rose —
> Though why, not every gambler cares
>   Or cartomancer knows.
>
> Be beauty yours, be honour mine,
>   Yet sword and rose are one:
> Great emblems that in love combine
>   Until the dealing's done. . . .
>   — *Robert Graves*

I. PROLEGOMENON

Fired out of Cambridge with a flat report
Above the cheering heads of friends, I fly —
Like any cannon-fathered aeronaut —
Out of the circus maximus where I
Made such a spectacle that I was shot
As an example. Figuratively, of course.
Now I skim south with sandbags of remorse
To ballast my high spirits as I hop
The hedges of Rowayton, Greenwich, Rye,
The merchant fleets of Westchester, the top
Of Bronx gasometers, and soon the high
Tors of Manhattan, which is where I stop.
Its streets spread hard arms into which I fall,
Another outlander who heard their call
Of anonymity and a new start
Among exponents of a single one
Pursued by corollary zeroes, part
Of everyman's megalopolitan
Birthright of passage. At the concrete heart
Of our discrete cosmogony, I light,
Fresh out of Eden on my maiden flight.

II.   A TABLE DOWN AT CRONIN'S

In the beginning, at the Pentecost,
We five survivals sit down in the lost —
Whitsunday pinxit — distance where the crossed
Oars shine down on full fifty empty booths
Abandoned by their aestivating youths,
Except for us, Art, Nathan, Joe, Lou, Perce,
Their rearguard, now more than a drop the worse
For celibation and for acid ale.
Reading the *Summer News,* I blanch a pale
Fishbelly under my weak week-old beard
At seeing Honor's picture over *"Weird
Sisters* Shows a Profit,'' an account
Of the quite satisfactory amount
Her Radcliffe literary magazine
Rang up in blackmailed advertising. "Keen
On that one?'' reading my struck look, divines
Sir Percival, my newfound British friend.
"Yeh, gone,'' interpolates sad Joe, my round,
Unworldly roommate. "Lessee that,'' says Nate,
Our blue-jawed, eremitic, Lincolnesque
Assyrian scholar. "That's a handsome head.
Where's she this summer?'' "Home. New York.'' "Well, hell.
Why not go chase her? You can't let her cool
All summer. My advice is board your horse.''
"You know, Lou,'' Art, our curate, our vicar-
Ious confessor ruminates, "he's right.
You should head down there posthaste and take up
Where you left off.'' "You'd all like that.'' "We would.''
"Voyeurs!'' "Uh-hunh. Just keep us posted.'' "What
A horny bunch by proxy.'' "Yes, indeed.''
"Well, I give up. O.K., I'll go. Who'll come
Along? You, Perce?'' "Why not? I can't complete
My education till I've seen New York.''
A feeling of well-being at a goal
In common, the electric brass-spice smell
Of a new round of brews, the sweat and *Nuit
D'Amour* of Mae, our waitress, the dimmed light
Of last-call warning, prologue to the night:

Thus the grand compact, sealed in Croft Cream Ale
At Whitsuntide, whereof I may not fail.

III.   EVENTS IN TRAIN

What is so rare as a journey in jejune
Anticipation of flat train fare, which
Teases the topless tower of ileum
With insubstantial visions of a rich,
Repletive borborygmogenesis?
None but a rough suspension of intent
Over the roadbed of the marshalling
Yard at the junction where beginnings shunt
And couple up to undistributed
Middles — mixed goods — bound for bad ends upon
Wrong roads. The waybill transitively joins
Our names up in its long petition for
A change of venue. In the hours of trial
Before our trials resume, Sir Percival
And I play gin, eat Butterfinger bars,
Read *Cue* for what's to come, and speculate,
Inside and out, en saga, on our great
Assault on the great world, which goes pitch dark,
Precociously, at 99th and Park.

IV.   ANSONIANA

A changing of the guard in Verdi Square:
Down, down through stratus strata of the air
Of evening, pink, hatched by flat plates of grey,
Sink, singing, emblems of an age that is
An Orphean underground now, in the dark
As to the names of archaeologers
Whose digs will bring it back to light in an
Age that awaits before. The armies of
The occupying hour patrol the shells
Of space and splendor, topped with turreted
Saltshakers, railed with Beardsley rays inked in
In India-inklines, undried, aglint
With the sunk sun's farewell-performance tint

Of spark and ash. The beetling night watch heaves
Wide shoulders by, leading diminished legs
To timelier, if less immediate,
Haunts and resorts. The morbid discharge of
All arms of service, incongruent, skulks
Through unranked crowds of indeterminate
Station — brusque doubled-breasted men, isosceles
Girls tapering to ankles from the eaves
Of padded jackets, duodecimo
Editions known as children — to a strange
Place, home. My generation of the just-
Too-young to serve, the knowing connoisseurs
Of ration points, home-firers far behind
The unimagined fluid, bloody lines,
Are, on the other hand, at home at home
In six years' cumulus of dinginess,
Where best-dressed back and side go slightly thread-
Bare, paint peels down to primer, rust erupts
In small pocks on dim chrome. We take our way
West to the Hotel Henryk, a blasé
Trail through the shabby, civil wilderness
Of buildings whose great age has passed away.

V. HONOR PERCEIVED

Pu we, to wit: a spring of throstle stops
Plashes unheard, implied, about the side-
Walk Café de la Paix, né Rumpelmayer's,
Beside the St. Moritz, a short trot from
The maidens' castle called the Barbizon,
Off-bounds to errant boys. The sun's sixth sense
Of increase on the first hot day of peace
Invests June's filles at tiny tables with
The mantle of mère earth, the mystery
Of all man manufacture. Sisterly
In their like cotton dirndls, poised to spring
Upon the season and to seize the day
And pick and press a leaf for memory,
They bat their fritillary eyes. A leap
Beneath my third shirt button indicates
That one of them is Honor. I present

My person, trussed in thongs of awkwardness,
To the blue justice of her unmoved eyes.
Her long mouth parts. A word falls out. A smile
Just liminally crosses the threshold
Of her thin lips and disappears. "Sit down."
I fold up like a shelter half. I'm in.

VI.   33 W. 58

In digs at dusk. A woman in the Wynd-
Ham semaphores toward us with a gin-
And-tonic in each hand. We sink back in-
To our apartment, much more populous
Than Perce and I account for: sumptuous
Brown bodies lean on walls, recline in chairs,
And even loiter on the pair of stairs
Up to the toilet. They are — just our luck —
Not jet nubilities, but instruments
Formed by a greater hand than ours to shape
Ephemeral, undying song: in short,
A grave consort of cellos and bass viols,
Left in our keeping by the sublessors
To shame and humble our indiscipline.
The radio's partita, filling in
Our chamber silence, coruscates with two
Spadassins' strokes, accelerando to
A bloody quick conclusion, and a mince
Voice comes on to report the upshot of
The first test at Bikini. A long boom
Takes several centuries to fill the room.

VII.   DR. FISHER

Perce peels off east to pick up fair Elaine —
Dark Honor's late Miss Massey's Classes chum —
At a Park West address where mercury,
Hermetically limed in glass, burns night
Out on the heights of Siamese-twin towers
With bleak and minatory faces. I
Lope loosely northward on my two-gait feet,

A little overdue for Honor, through
Manhattan's second growth of tapestry-
Brick residence hotels and uniform
Apartment doormen fronting for the brass
Plates of professionals, the renting class
That God made doormen for, toward the door
(Brass, bet you anything, and manned) of her
Father's apartment house. That must be it:
The Corbin Arms, illuminated by
Three ravens statant noir upon a bend
Azure; in chief, a cor argent; below,
Natedna Realty Management. The boy
In his tight elevator and outsize
Cap braided "C" returns my skeptic look
And flies us slowly up to 12, where I'm
Expected or abandoned. The small brass
Knocker made like an anchor swings away
From my pursuing hand until I find
My fist just touching the low nose of an
Eccentric little man in evening dress —
White tie, top hat, and tails. The butler? "I —"
"You're Honor's friend. You're late." No servant, he.
"Come in, come in." So, Dr. Fisher, we
Are face to face at last. But not for long.
"Dear, I must run." Her dark face, conjured up
Out of a far room, makes a blandishing
Mock moue of disappointment. "Daddy, not
So soon. Why, Lou just got here." "Can't help that.
M-merlins won't forgive me if I'm late.
K-kiss." He scoops up Honor in one arm,
A Boston bag, apparently of tricks,
In his free hand, and kisses her upon
The parted lips, to my surprise. " 'Bye, love."
" 'Bye, Daddy. Hurry back." "Again," to me.
Door slams. "I'm sorry Daddy couldn't stay.
You'd love him. But tonight's his magic show."
"Magic?" "Yes. At the Merlin Society.
He's Warlock this year, so he does the show."
"He ever saw you in half?" "Lou, you're a pill.
Of course not. Daddy's eaten, but I saved
You some." Under a mounted swordfish once
Subdued by Dr. Fisher in Key West,

According to the plaque, I eat a steak
Now rather cool and well, while Honor serves
My needs with half a heart and sands my nerves
With sidelights on her old man and the sea.

VIII.   A GAME OF CARDS

The chair she sits in, like a Spanish throne —
A steal on sale at W. & J. Sloane —
Glows on the table, a waxed looking glass
Reflecting the divine diviner in
Reverse, muting her purple dress between
Two muted pillars of the alcove where
She now prepares to read my future. Her
Already dark hair shades to filaments
Of black laced with blue lights across the grain
Of the smug tabletop; behind her, there,
A tapestry of palms and pomegranates
Minutely wavers in the whistling air
Sent by a baby-blue electric fan
To promulgate her strong, invisible
Perfume among my senses and eclipse
The tune of flutes and obbligato oars:
The *Water Music* on the Vic. Oh, rare
For me, her Querent, that she now takes up
The pack and picks the King of Pentacles —
The glum professor with the money sign
Upon his orb — as my significator.
She shuffles, cuts three times, and lays the First
Card, muttering, "This covers him," upon
The King. It is the Queen of Wands, reversed:
An influence of opposition in
My inquiry. "This crosses him," she says,
Placing the Second Card across the First
To show my obstacles. It is the great
Magician, upside down, who threatens me
With a physician, madness, or disgrace.
"This crowns him." The High Priestess in her chair
Between two pillars represents the fair
One whom I sue for, object of my quest.

"This is beneath him." The Lovers, reversed,
Suggest foolish designs and failure as
The weak heart of the matter. The Fifth Card,
"This is behind him," is the Five of Swords,
A recent thrust against my fortune. Six —
"This is before him" — Knight of Pentacles,
Reversed, who signifies a brave man out
Of work. Touché. The Seventh Card. "Himself,"
Is me. Zero, The Fool, turns up, about
To step right off a cliff in his bêtise.
Eight is "His House," the tendencies at work
Upon the matter. Six of Pentacles:
The present can't be counted on. "His Hopes
And Fears" is Nine. The Four of Cups predicts
More contrarieties. At last the Tenth:
"What Is to Come." Her facile hand turns up
The King of Cups, who warns me to beware
Of ill will from a man of standing, and
Hypocrisy disguised as help. The lock
Clicks back and Dr. Fisher lets himself
Back into his demesne. "But won't you stay
L-long enough to have a stirrup cup?"
"Sorry. Must run, sir." Peace. The charm's wound up.

IX.   UP IN CENTRAL PARK

When Olmsted rested on the seventh day
And saw that it was good, he went away
To new commissions and abandoned his
Green Eden to such old pols as Parrott
(Who, in his civil goodness, framed and bought
Full many a journeyman in Albany)
And such new lovers as Perce and Elaine,
Soon to be scouted out of paradise
By a paterfamilial sergeant of police
To shelter in the cities of the plain
For having eaten of the knowing fruit,
The peach of each to each, which wasn't nice.
It wasn't quite like that, though, Perce reports
To me upon his prodigal return

At two or so a.m. "You can't conceive
How ludicrous it was. There lay Elaine,
Dying to shuffle off her moral coil,
And there stood I, embarrassed, pants in hand,
Couéing mightily to get a stand,
Suppressing laughter at the sight of her
Too bogus portrait of a succubus,
An *âme damnée,* poor strapping, pure Elaine.
I'd just commenced to button up my fly —
She was half-sitting with her dress awry
And looking furious, of course — when that
Great chuntering policeman shone his torch
Bang on my button-hand and then on her."
"You get run in?" "Arrested? No, just warned."
"It's over with Elaine, though?" "Not at all.
For some odd reason, my great chastity
Simply increased her ardor. We shall try
Conclusions again Sunday, she and I."

X. E. 86

Kiss, kiss: a badminton of lips. We serve
Each other right on a banquette in back
Of the Carrara corridor of her
Aunt's old and elegant apartment house
Not too far from the Park. In the near-dark
Of one bronze flambeau flamed with a flame-shaped
Rose bulb of maybe twenty watts, we twine
Together, high on the new-pressed May wine
Of mouth and breath on ours, of breast to breast,
Soft license on inevitable bone.
Impromptu bowers are not secure; this one
Exposes us to elevator-waiters, all
The passengers in transit of the hall,
Alighters from, embarkers into cabs
And Cadillacs drawn up to and away
From the bronze doorway: *poules* with poodles on
Short leads, old, corporated Homburgers,
School-capped small boys with nurses, overdressed
Shoppers of fifty with antiqued, distressed

Visages under teased, tormented hair,
All seen in silhouette. The kissing stops:
The lack of setting for a second act
Halts our rehearsal on the verge of some
Unmanning pit of swelling, lickerish
Orchestral *tutti,* and sense brings us back,
Disheveled, breathless, to the leather bench
Where Honor murmured, *"Je vous aime,"* in French.

XI. LATE NEWS

Elaine, brought back by Perce as evidence
Of triumph just in time to interrupt
The midnight news with her own bulletins
Bespeaking siege and fall — what mangonels
Must have unhinged the wellsprings of her eyes
When Maybelline, once run, once smudged, now dries;
What catapults laid low those Parian
Pillars of Hercules, her two-stone thighs;
And what ballista cut the tethering string
That moored her tongue, which, linguimitted, flies —
And fills my ears with ancient histories
Of Honor and her father. "Don't you know
The story of his stammering?" "Well, no."
"Well, first of all, his wife was Vivien
Valenti, the Poughkeepsie poetess —"
"Um, 'What lads saddled me and rode away —' "
" 'In the odd hours I do not know.' Yeah. She
Married Roy Fisher when he was still a kid,
Just back from Old Vienna, starting out
As — what was it they called it — oh, an al-
Ienist. Seduced him, maybe. Anyway,
She died of languish or whatever all
Pale lady poets die of — drowned herself,
They say, in Lake Sebago — and left him
Alone with Honor. You can figure out
What happened after. Sure, Electra. First,
He had himself an ever-loving fling
With every lady patient he could join

On his official couch; but pretty soon
He realized there was no substitute
For his late wife. Except, of course, his own
Daughter, aged seventeen. That summer, we —
Honor and I and Maribel Cohane —
Went skinny-dipping mornings off the float
Back of the Fishers' camp. One morning, we
Felt we were being spied on. Sure enough,
The cattails parted, Dr. Fisher rose
To his full five-foot-two between them, and
Boomed out in his best voice (you know that cove
Can echo like a canyon), 'Honor, come
Back here this instant and put on your suit.
How dare you go in swimming in the muff?'
Those echoes. Silence. Laughter. I'm afraid
We tittered him back through the rushes. And
He's stammered ever since, at least with us.''
The fisherman who lost his circumflex
And waded waist-deep in the stream of sex,
Casting his flies at any likely trout,
Was thus at last by his own line caught out.

XII.   THE TOURNAMENT

Broadway, way in to too many tissue
Sections to count — the scruffy, canyonesque
Desertion of the fifties, the mock-swank
Ziggurats overlooking the poor mouse-
Brown brownstones tailing off down Fifty-ninth,
The crazed-white, glazed-brick, ex-Locomobile,
White, Marmon, Mercer, Pierce, Simplex showrooms
Divided by blank, mangy warehouses
(One sporting a half-scale Miss Liberty),
And the bombé façades of down-at-heel
Hotels still capped with clouds of verdigris —
Still boasts, a constant in all neighborhoods
And climes whatever, a bright, glorious bar,
Crawling with living colors, on each hand.
In each of these along the course of our

Up-Broadway walking tour to Honor's house,
Perce and I square off, face up, take a stand,
And down our ten-cent Rupperts, chug-a-lug.
Broadway, already skewed, comes more undone
And levitates at the periphery
Of vision as we doggedly slog on.
A draw: at Honor's street we calculate
Each has consumed an easy twenty-three
Glasses in transit. Oddly, Honor's not
That glad to see us; Dr. Fisher seems
Less cordial, if that's possible, than last
Time I came calling. Well, we know where we
Aren't wanted. Let us go then, you and me.

XIII.   GONE AWAY

"Lou dear, I hate this place so much I can't
Describe it to you. Veddy-veddy beach
Club, strictly from 'So Little Time.' All my
Relations naturally belong — the ones
That Dad won't speak to. All the women (12
To 70) in unbecomingly
Brief bathing suits, and all the older men
In paunches and Coronas. They play gin
For high stakes steadily and keep one eye
Peeled for peeled ladies. All the younger ones —
My uncles, born with sterling-silver spoons —
Wear polo shirts with little college crests,
Play golf, and are weak characters. My aunts —
The worst of all — are beautifully groomed
And talk exclusively about 1) clothes,
2) other people's troubles, 3) their trials
With their domestics, *viz.*, 'They're always no-
Good anyway and think they're just as good
As anyone. Such children!' Speaking of
That — children — theirs, my cousins, are all dressed
And polished beautifully, not spoken to
Except commandingly, and *never* played
With. Lou, it's hell, and I'm so desperate

For the real world — or is it the other way
Around? — that I wish you'd sling me a rope
From that gaunt tower of yours. Nothing worthwhile
Till I come back to you. Miss me a lit-
Tle. Till New Hampshire, all my love, my own."

XIV. NORTH

A day coach made of barge boards, with a stove
Dead center. Musty plush. A clerestory
Of sooty lozenges, lunettes of blind-
Ing black. Moth-wing-white mantles of a Pintsch
Compressed-gas lighting system. Ricky-tick
Conductor jointed like a walking-stick
Insect, with silver glasses, silver punch,
And silver seat in his sere serge. A Pen-
Guin in my lap, I swot up Overshot
And Undershaft as the impoverished
Saltboxes tethered to the littered yards
Of marginal New Hampshire stage a fly-
Past and escape beyond the picture frame
Where Concord now spells out its static name.

XV. HONOR REPRIEVED

While Mim and Arthur, eager councillors,
Go at it hot and heavy in the Hawk
Hotel, or so we fantasize, we walk,
Moist hand in hand, up Main Street to the top
Of town, where we fall into a copse
Hard by the railroad tracks, and fall to fool-
Ing in the gloaming, testing Honor's rule.
Inviolable music of her spheres
Appearing serially — Saturn's moons —
Incites my astronomic eye, and I
Prepare to telescope myself into
Its promised land of origin, when O!
A bolt of cramp flung by retributive
Gods on Olympus or Chocorua
Hits me amidships, interdicts my fire,

And interjects me far into the mire
Of a green-rimmed dump-swamp, there to relieve
The thumbscrew pain. For Honor, a reprieve.

XVI. S.S. GASPÉ

"Lou, darling, it's more fun aboard the ship
Than I'd expected, though at night I miss
You more than I'd expected. Last night we —
Daddy and I — waltzed off, quite literal-
Ly, with the first prize at the Captain's dance:
A crude brass statuette of dancers on
A plastic plinth. Some handsome surgeon's son —
Columbia Presbyterian — 's making eyes
And overtures, but I've been cool. Miss me.
Must dash — late for the Captain's table. See
You in Cambridge, love, in twenty-three,
No, twenty-two days, or eternity."

XVII. LES ENFANTS DE THALIA

At summer's end, Colditz or Wintersborn
Flies its Oflag from icy battlements
Above the stifling balcony where Perce
And I, a farewell party, watch alone
And early one hot matin, the dead march
Of Rauffenstein, de Boeldieu, Maréchal,
And Rosenthal through black night and white day
In search of honor and/or freedom, pure
In word and deed as only the pre-war
Was. They don't make them like that any more.
Especially not Perce and I as we,
Shortened and shadowed by the midday sun,
Say terse adieux aboard Pier 83.

XVIII. HONOR PRESERVED

Light up the sky, Commander, where the west
Flares up, dies down, and deepens into one

Untinted, wind-bearing continuum;
Light up with the reflections of your red
Neonic name the shape of Honor's room;
And light the shape upon her single bed
Of our reunion. But the practiced key
Cannot, at last, unloose her private locks,
Unclasp her dots and hooks and eyes and stays,
Unveil her lunar marbles, lit by not
Blood from within, but neon from without.
No, no. "No, Lou, I've promised Daddy not
To do a thing both of us might regret.
I'm sorry, but it simply isn't right."
Right. Heart in hand, I nimbly say goodnight
And go out gently into that good night.

XIX.   THE PASSING OF THE CUP

So, in the upshot, on St. Cyprian's
Feast day, hind-driven by the western wind,
I come to Cronin's, errant, seeking for
Old comrades, and find Joe already there,
Alone as I am, swigging Harvard Beer.
Some bragging on the summer's conquests; some
Shorthand dismissals of the girls of spring;
Silence and comfort, each of us knowing
The other has failed equally, New York
And Pittsburgh being equal in the eyes
Of the flint paymaster who doles girls' thighs
Out barely to the infantry of boys
Who mass about his wicket. We preserve
Our solidarity, virginity,
Hope dashed and risen, eagerness, and nerve.
Joe hands his mug fraternally to me.

XX.   LA TROMPE FINALE, 1969

Three-foot-high kings, queens, knaves with black-and-white
Photograph faces pasted in adorn

La Trompe's rude Breton walls: each king and queen
Of hearts is a romantic lead; each knave,
A juvenile. The diamonds are all
Industrial-financial types and wives;
The clubs are entertainers; and the spades
Are black celebrities. The maitre d'
Steers for my table, bringing, in his train,
Honor in Pucci, Guccis, and Sassoon
Hair-do, a little younger-looking than
I saw her last at twenty. " 'Lo, Lou." Face
Presented, seamless, for a glancing kiss;
Hair black and silver. Editor of *Grace,*
Glass of all fashion, arbitrix of form,
Tyrant whose imprimatur is the norm
For millions of fleeced sheep in their Dubuques,
Proposer and disposer of boutiques,
Hair men, hat men, shoe men, photographers,
Danseurs and dancers and biographers
Of taste, I bid you welcome to a taste
Of past en croûte: my ugly, aging face,
My parlor games with words, my petty pace —
An inch a day — toward obscurity.
Will that unman you? I'd not reckoned with
Your thoroughness, dear Honor. None could doubt
The realness of your interest, the thought
Behind your frown, the putting me at ease,
Except in context of the aim to please
And conquer. Ah, then, Honor, you have power —
The broadsword, not the red rose, in your bower —
But I hold honor, a weak, withered flower
In my pale, uncommanding, and free hand
As I ride out upon my bicycle,
In joker's silks, across the laughing land.

In Bardbury

(For John Malcolm Brinnin)

"This ere is what," says Mr. Carpenter,
The coffin foreman, in a herringbone
Waistcoat and gold-rimmed spectacles obtained
On the National Health, no doubt, "This ere is what —"
And points one digit to a neatly joined
And midget casket, just, to judge from the
Miasma of acetone, neatly cellulosed
In a suitable baby white, "This ere is what
We buried the remains of Mr. Eliot
In out there," pointing to the churchyard of
St. Muse. "And shockin little of im there was:
Two little volumes not ardly bigger than the
Basingstoke telephone book." With which he shook
His ploughshare nose and a colorless drop fell off.
"Now look at this ere": a rod-long oak box,
Full fathom wide, wood dark as blackbeetles.
"This ere size is the one we ad to use
To plant the Poet Laureate, if you'll excuse
My French. More books than a ole libary."
Thanks, Mr. Carpenter, for the florin tour
Of Plume & Sons' back room. I point my broad-
Stub nose toward the moist, unpainted air
And pad out past the bone booths in their rows
To the green-grown, grey-pocked graveyard right out there,
Patrolled by stick-straight Mr. Sacrister
In his green-grown grey cerement.
"Two new memorials of special note
You'll wish to look at, sir," he says, by rote,
And courteously conducts my crofted arm
To one small marble marker, two by two,
Charged with her arms and "By Appointment to
H. M. the Queen her Poet Laureate."
The tumulus extends five yards in front of it.
A pause. Mist drips from lindens. My guide clears
His throat, discreet. "On this side, sir, we ave
The other monument." A minute's walk.
Above the tiny mound, a tall Trajan's

Column materializes out of moist
And pearl-grey air. A cool Ionic plinth
Incised with one chaste E. A fluted shaft
As great in girth as any tree, which shades
Up into thickening mist and disappears.
"Massive but tasteful, sir, I'd say." The yews
Drizzle in silence on St. Muse.

Convenient to Victoria

One night's stop at the Prince Consort Hotel
Is quite enough to entertain grim dreams
Long afterward of dissolute empires
Cracked, checked, and crazed amid the dusty plush
Of Ottomans in the tall drawing room;
Consumed in the ill-simulated flames
Of the electric fire; flushed down the puce
Throat of the toilet on the dais in
The vast and draughty ballroom-shaped bathroom;
Palpated, medicated, doctored, dead
In the sprung, ruptured king-and-queen-size bed.

An Arundel Footnote

(For P.L.)

"All that survives of us is love." Maybe
Not even that, it seems. Rising above
The glass case housing shilling relics of
This agèd and advanced church — art postcards,
Piper's pied altar duly reproduced,
Wide-eyed and side-whiskered accounts of how
The great spire toppled in a storm of wind —
There stands a rack of cheap guides. One depicts
The earl and countess supine on their tomb
And holding hands in perpetuity.
Alas, the facing text gives them away:
"Though many visitors to Chichester,"
It says, "are touched by this unique display
Of marital devotion, it is thought
That a Victorian mason rearranged
Their marble hands, once crossed upon each breast,
To meet and intertwine." Good night, sweet Fitz-
Alan, trapped in the prettifying power
Of a hypocoristic century
By its unloved assigns. All that survives
Of us and of our petrifying wives
For certain is a lying effigy.

A Life in Alabaster Street

His mad nurse pops pink bubble gum, and chews
On in deep beats — a metronome — to news
And rock on her transistor past all hours.
Far cars near, squealing, bent on merciless
Night errands, and redistance their dark powers
Up Brattle Street. Insane boys cackle by,
Incising their graffiti on the sky
In unknown tongues and accents. Wives next door
Beshrew lapsarian husbands, in the wrong
From the first fall of marriage. Down the long
Sword-arch of elms a party shatters out,
In tittering components, to the street.
Miles off, putrescent cities of the plain
Ignore the generous closing hours of pain
And violate the air with a cold green
Glow: worms and serpents. Dr. Wilmerdene
Moves, millimetrically, his light head
And faint eyes to the clock beside the bed
In his frame house in Alabaster Street,
Encouraged by false dawn. A.B., A.M.,
Ph.D., Litt.D. (hon., from U. of M. —
What a commencement *that* was), Wilmerdene
Decides to live till morning, meet one more
Sun in his father's window in his street
Besieged and stormed by madmen, who will not
Take him alive, however.
                              Phoebus, rise,
Precurred by sea-born Venus; regularize
A regulate life begun in unsurprise
And ended in confounding. But not quite:
Sun, dawn and touch his shutting eyes with light.

A Loss of Largess; Its Recapture
(And Point After)

(For John Updike)

Where are the belles of yestere'en, when Harkness
Reared Gothathletic pinnacles on darkness,
Where sate their dim dams in effasive, noctious
Harmonic bombazines, at least an octave
Over the battle? Where are those dames, dangled
On stringlings above mantels lit with bangled
Epergnes and lustres, ordering with mingled
Parade-ground basses and restraint-enstrangled
Triangle tingles of politesse their embalmy
Crack cakewalk waxwork corps d'élite of calmly
Extinguishing retainers going dark?
Today we have the proceeds in the park
Of their harbinging; in the standard carks
Conveyed by every face in every car
That laterals across from bar to bar,
Completed in the end zone of the high
Sixties; in the infirm plasticity
Of talltale fictions in the plastic city
Sent up, shot down (short life, short art) by those
Gallinulistic whooping cranes that raze
All parallelepipeds here below in G's
Good time, the sucaryllic by and by;
In how sad steps the dancers from the dance
At yon new discothèque take home, their pens-
Eroso tragic masks replaced to fie
Upon the desert teatray of the sky
And the uneasy vacuum of the street
Diminuendo to a dusty point
Of vanishing; in preternatural taints
Of outlandish unlikeness on each lass-
Itudinous pale pancake female face
Sub specie aeternitatis, less
Real than ideal in the race
For surety and demonstrata, damned
To disaffection and unravelling

In our unspacious, curt time-travelling.
Las! Las! Those belles wring out our witchèd larmes
Of lamentation for passé, accomp-
Li, done and done in in the niche of pomp
In progress ruckwards in the new-moon stone
Of night. Lick, lick, light, at the eastern hem
Of rich ink arrases, whose only son
Is born anew and dries our eyes with his
Frank, pink, unfaceable first sight; his light
Breeze dawns on us and islands us in calm,
Slow-moated selffulness. A fiddler crab
Crawls cancrizantally across the slab
Of pine to pencils, handsels one upright,
And imperceptively begins to write
On the blued goldfields of a legal pad —
Past Karnak, Babylon, Larissa, Rome,
Londinium, Firenze, Washington,
And the last sad daguerreotype of home
That the late holocaust consumed and curled —
The next line in the last act of the world.

Excuse for an Italian Sonnet

KLAIUS:
. . . I that was once the musique of these vallies,
So darkened am, that all my day is evening.
STREPHON:
. . . Me seemes I heare in these ill-changed forrests,
The nightingales doo learne of Owles their musique. . . .
— *Sidney*

This wretched mode, a huddle of untrue
Positions reminiscent of the way
Our generation stood, obscuring you,
Grown in the gathering evening of our day,
Who now rise to eclipse our withering view
Of perfect, present, future, and who may
Outlast us and accumulate our due
Deserts and honors, is a cell of clay

Confining us in our mortality,
A constant wailing wall to which we go
For counsel in insensibility,
A leaden treasury of what was so,
And may, in changefulness, no longer be:
A rectitudinal yes nearing no.

J.J.'s Levée, 1946

Awaking way up in the eaves of Lowell House,
Facing the East, where trouble always starts,
Opening his one blue eye to meet the sun's
One red one, J.J. crooks his back and farts.

His hand feels for the glass on the nightstand,
Ticking the empty glass of muscatel,
Finally finding the one with the blue glass
Eye rolling gently in the tiny swell.

Into its squirming socket with a suck
Just like a kiss his bogus eyeball goes;
Up he now sits and strips his T-shirt off
And picks black putty from between his toes.

Weighing one hundred ten pounds soaking wet
And standing five feet, seven inches tall,
With a pigeonhole in his chest big as your fist,
J.J. sings in his shower, ''Bless 'em all.''

He maps a life: first east from Central Square
(His point of origin), bachelor of arts
And master too, wit, rake, and bon viveur
And gift to every girl of foreign parts.

Then to get grey and great at the big feet
Of pundits, learning hard new A, B, C

(The secret one that spells out man his fate),
In kindergarten to the Nth degree.

Now in his forty-dollar flannel suit
One size too big, and his one-dollar tie
One inch too wide, J.J. picks up his books
And goes right out to live and later die.

J.J.'S ENVOY

"All bleeding men and women ought to get
A bloody great gold medal for their pain
And duty in the face of certain death:
The Order of the W.C. with Chain."

In Baltimore—Why Baltimore?—
Did Kahn

A grisly torture dome decree, where Alf
Kahn made incisions in his secret self
Under the attic eaves. At work all day,
He'd bundle groceries down at the A
& P, hating such servitude; each night,
Up in his attic, by a ten-watt light,
He'd write, in anguish, ten more pained lines of
His monstrous opus "Succubus," his love,
His mother, wife, and children, youth, old age,
Past fury, present anger, permarage.
Stuprate, he rent his fabric with each kiss.
His pieces kissed again. No end to this.

Inflation

(For Alison Lurie)

I.

With a black manifesto of pistons, David became
Goliath: the small boy from English High
Grew giant and arched over neighborhoods
Of cheering followers, the president-
To-be of boroughs of new consciousness
Of his all-potent role. Time was when he
Licked fictions into shape at an unknown
Address, humbly petitioned publishers,
Modestly took his kudos when it came,
Tapped diffidently down the hall of fame
To meet his laurellers, and, amply crowned
And seated firstly on his dais, frowned.
But not for long: the conscience of a king
Is a quite different and distant thing
From that of an unknown; his majesty
Is self-propelling into grander spheres
That are undreamt-of in a commoner
Philosophy; the silver band of stars,
The brass choir of the sun, accompany
And herald his arrival at the throne,
Where a new paradigm of royalty
And secondary rights, created from
Unpromising materials — a coat
Upon a singing stick — holds sudden sway
Over the aerials of his old world.

II.

It is not easy, though, to wear that suit
Of lights, all heavy bullion and brocade,
Or to support that pointed two-edged sword
Stiff in its scabbard hard against one's side
Or to sustain the tiers of worshippers
Who people the arena with their cries.
One grows to fit the emperor's new clothes

In height, in girth, in lightning from the eyes;
Becomes a sort of grown-man's Santa Claus
For every season, flourishing his gifts
Eternally before the studio
Audience and his legion fans at home.

III.

Now no behavior is unknown to him:
On Cambridge Common, he exhorts the scum
Who turn a field of daisy faces up
To his rough sun and rain to follow him
To the moral ends of the earth in a dead march
Against our fathers' errors; later, comes
Home hung and splits his wife's lip with his fist
And drinks her blood in bed; at parties, cuts
Out wide-eyed girls from herds and topples them
On beds piled high with coats; runs, as a joke,
Or not a joke, for Congress, on a plank
Of endless drugs and love; records the moon
Shot as a phallic conquest of his own;
Transcends his old self at the Remington
Portable in his dirty furnished room
Not far from Fenway Park. From his town house
He looks down on the night lights of the land
He rose above, true to his promise, and,
Ah, like a comet through flame he moves entranced,
Wrapt in his music no bird song nor bough
Breaking with honey buds shall ever equal,
To us a legend, to himself a law.

Empson Lieder

(For his sixty-fourth birthday)

I. LAW SONG

> Law makes long spokes of the short stakes of men.
> — "Legal Fiction"

We're all on different time scales. This clipboard
Will easily outlive me, given luck.
This house will, barring fire. The deep-set rock
Ledge that it rests on will no doubt endure
To the hundredth generation of our pure-
Eyed sons, if any. Only we are such
Short-timers, really, re-upped for a hitch
Indefinite in length, but not too long.
You will therefore please forgive my haunting song
Of awe at walking on the very bridge
Where Joe C., sporting his First Army badge,
Took taxi for the war in '44;
Of *frissons* at last sitting on the bench
Where Sally and I shared a Wursthaus lunch
Not too long after; of astonishment
At finding that the same key, pitted, bent,
Unlocks the same strongbox my father spent
The thirties filling with strange stamps; of love
At learning that the niches just above
The main floor of the library are still
Unstatued and available to fill
With our imaginings. Thereof my song,
Interior, quite tuneless, and unlong.

II. EVEN SONG

> Not to have fire is to be a skin that shrills.
> The complete fire is death. From partial fires
> The waste remains, the waste remains and kills.
> — "Missing Dates"

My unburnt hydrocarbons having made
A pall of killing smog, eftsoons I died
And came to Heaven. Sitting at the side

Of the great War Lord (a Brahms with sabre scars
Upon his temples and the porches of
His gun-deaf ears), I saw my residue
Coil mortally down there, a mustard gas,
Around the throats I'd failed to cut of those
Who'd cant incredibly through a half life,
Who'd twist on valiantly for penny gains,
Who'd trade you in on something more *courant,*
Who'd flee from those whom sometime they did seek,
Who'd go blind in the glitter of their rank
And brag that they had only them to thank
For such preferment, such an unctuous
Deathbed on shock absorbers, who'd find fault .
With their subordinates for their results,
Who'd hang blame, like the shrike, upon a thorn,
Who'd lose touch with the urgencies of dawn,
Of leaf bud and leaf fall, of the small sun
Of February, the large moon of March,
The redwinged blackbird in the dying arch
Of elm, the great horned owl in the live pine.
A thunderstone, a bolt from the light black
Of my position high in Father's firm,
Struck them as lightning fingers of my late
Waste, left behind below. They died, of course.
Up here I heard the fat tires of the hearse
Fizz on the icy streets without remorse.

III. GIRL SONG

> And now she cleans her teeth into the lake.
>   — "Camping Out"

> Project her no projectile, plan nor man it.
>   — "To an Old Lady"

The heavenly body we once pointed for
In our near nonage — seen across a cyc
Of contrarieties in indigo,
An outer vast of obstacles whose fields
Of gravity press-ganged us into their
Cool marbles spinning in a gallery
And only barely let us go — is now
An older Merlin's lame familiar

Shorn of the charm of distance, bound to serve
Her homely, well-worn purpose, passion spent.
But yet, but now, a new low music moves
Her parts and person in a unison
Not heretofore perceived. "And now she cleans
Her teeth into the lake." That morning comes
When aching, groaning, feeling hateful from
Last night's exchanges, we turn angrily
Toward some matter-of-fact arising sound
She makes, and take a scourging wound, and see
In her shape, ground down by years of our eyes,
Our image twinned — the good we failed to do,
The bad we funked, the mediocrity
We killed our time on till it called a halt —
And love her for it, as we love ourselves.

IV.   WAR SONG

> This hint of anti-aircraft is disarmed
> And as the fleets at a shot reascend
> The eye orders their unreachable chaos
> (The stars are moving like these duck, but slower,
> Sublime, their tails absurd, their voices harsh). . . .
> — "Flighting for Duck"

Great sheets of earth are inaccessible
To sounds of war; no man on earth is. I
Walk the back meadow where I used to walk
Before all this and find the fall leaves stilled,
The partridge drumming waning, the clear bray
Of crows diminuendo far away,
The very grasshoppers conservative
Of their small violins, the piano cows
Now lowing low, the dogs sparing of bays
And distant view hallos, and the rare men
Laconically calling in the fields
Seldom or never. But it is not they
Whose voices falter; it is I whose ears
Fill up, silt up, with war, and cannot hear
The nature of the world. At not quite dusk,
Our pond ducks — blacks and mallards — circle and
Splash down and leave me staring at the first
Stars, few, unconstellated, swaddled in

Buff smog, immobilized. Before the orange
Moon shoulders up gas strata, I can hear
One bullfrog pluck his bass string. In the void
Ensuing, single combat shakes the world.

V. SWAN SONG

> Then there is this civilising love of death . . .
> — "Ignorance of Death"

The swan puts beauty in a picture frame
Of freshets, lilies, water-ratty banks,
Bullfrogs, bulrushes, and impending death
To hang upon the brain-grey walls of our
Study of consciousness. See how she glides
Down these far reaches of our state-approved,
Man-sanctioned nature, toteninsular;
How she gilds eddies by reflection; how
Her song is silent, pregnant in her throat;
How, under contract to our common-law
Employer, she must make at last her fare-
Well tour to pay the inland revenue
For all her rich, consuming idleness
Before our eyes, for all these books of hours
Burnt in the loyal service of her grace.
Then she will sing — Opus Posthumous — and
We'll be assured again, in our book-lined
Dayroom at the top story of the mind,
That easefulness unbalanced by unease
On the diurnal scale will be redressed
By night, that anesthesiologist,
In the damp draperies of his dark gown
Whence our white throats will finally pronounce
The native woodnotes of our fatal song.
It is not audible. It is not long.

A Posthumous
Collection

I

Descriptive and Satirical

Getting On: Grave Expectations

One felt that age, with his stout walking stick,
Would knock one all of a heap: a whistling stroke
Would demark youth's absconsion with one's teeth
And appetites, enounce a standing joke

That would last one for life. It was not so:
The youth's illusion of immutable
Youth soldiered on till middle middle age.
The adolescent sired a haggard double,

Equally feckless, boyishly scuffing toes
On every female's turf, tilting and drinking
Glass after glass of days, squat seven-packs
Of weeks, flat fifties of full years, and thinking

Of how tomorrow, mastered at a swallow,
Would taste going down to join the spreading coral
Atoll of spent times a man's presence is
Built on, his rootstock, leanings, roles, and moral —

That swelling anthem of live-statue motion,
All meaning swags and swashes of his gesture,
All idiosyncratic dips and curvets
Revealing someone swaddled in his posture —

And how tomorrow's morrow would dawn likewise,
To be conspicuously consumed. But somewhere
Behind the thin and letlessly repeated
Air of the arras, note of the carpet figure,

The warning bells of closing time are ringing
Ever so softly, though they will take courage
To redivide our last days into brangles
Concerning crumbs and dregs, dissolve our marriage

To our dear self, the lost boy in the burning
Building of bone — the fat being in the fire —
And post our rigid statues to the nether
Trenches of Flanders, hanging on the wire.

Spring Song

Life is so long the passage of the seasons
Blurs like a carrousel before the static
Eyes of the onlooker who, rising fifty,
Grows slow and oaklike, dying in his fashion
Of imperceptible progress to the autumn,
While grasses spring in unison from the meadows
Full-blown in seconds, lilacs bloom and blacken
In minutes, apple blossoms shuck their petals
And grow green fruit in hours, ashes open
Fistfuls of leaflets, whose light-green veins darken
To forest green, lighten to tones of copper,
And fall down in a day to usher winter
Into his complex of spare silver branches,
His winter palace, in a growing silence.
I hate, as agent for my slowly failing
Senses, my withering sinews, drying juices,
And hardening heart, these hasty evidences

Of what I'll come to in the coming season
Of reckoning, when all the green will vanish
From expectation, all anticipation
Of folly to be rectified tomorrow
Will perish, and a leafless log of body
Will be cast on the wood fire of December.

August: A Jingle Man

A ländler enters the heat-stifled land
In elfin octaves on our purpling road
Diminishing to dusk in a late haze
That has to pass for sunset where no blaze
Kindles and quenches; mountain pipes, abroad
Improbably, soon seek and take our hand

As if we were some children. Round the bend,
The tune gains strength; a monstrous music box
Rolls, Juggernaut, upon us, with the force
Of giant tinkling rooted in the source
Of infancy and plashing off the rocks
Of Eden, which we thought was at an end.

It heaves in view, materializing out
Of thickening particles of purple air:
A scarred white reefer box upon a truck
Whose dinged pink panels have seen better luck
Conducted by a kid with long, dank hair
And an expression of the sorest doubt

At having made himself a jingle man,
At having chosen our forsaken road

Where no coin-clutching children flag him down,
At having to go on to the next town
In front of his unsold and softening load
While we, behind him, hear his Dopplered tune

Go high and tinny in an eerie skirl
Of magic ravelled and the twilight rent,
As if to point at his retreating back
And question his emprise, and, jangling, mock
The simple hope of grace that must have sent
Him out, Pied Piper in a childless world.

On Picking and Smelling a Wild Violet While Wearing Driving Gloves

Eponymous violet dandled in my fingers,
A swatch of violet upon the blackness
Of the thin kangaroo skin dully shining
Where it had fixed the wheel between my fingers
For miles through lowing droves of evening traffic
Stampeded westward from the epicenter
Of meadowlessness to the greening country
On the first Monday after daylight saving,
I lift your violet petals and gold chamber
To my gross nostrils rankling with tobacco
And sniff for any fragrance. At first nothing —
Certainly not the violet of perfume —
Can penetrate the nose of civilization.
A second whiff, and then the faintest sweetness —
The finest elfin essence of distinctive,
Generic airs, the rarest violet gasses —
Comes through, as clear and tiny as a baby's
First word, and reforms my understanding.

Under the Rose:
A Granfalloon for Kurt Vonnegut, Jr.

1

Under the rose, our catchmentarians
Prevent escapement with an ad-hoc hick-
Ory stick that beats and sweeps and cleans our clocks
Of forwardness and ongoing; their neat tics
Wink publicly in congress, blink the noes,
Reëmphasize the ayes, lick venous lips,
And lickerishly launch all Helen's ships
To fill our idle hands with sheets and stays,
Amaze us with queen's gambits, and bemuse
Us, counting cloudy hours under the rose.

2

Under the rose, the canes and thorns are red
As precious blood of strawberry and haw,
Near relatives under the common law
Of relativity in garden beds,
As in our own, where under the cerise
Wamsutta foolscap of life's legal brief
We burgle others, following our nose,
Our prow, our frontispiece, our horny caw
Across our territory, over low-
Lands of despond to where our vengeance lies
Between the teeth of leaves, under the rose.

3

Under the rose and jessamine of airs
Begun with blueness, laced with nightly black,
Peppered with stars, imperforate by moon,
We walk in pairs asunder, as at noon
We walk alone asunder, as at nine

(A.M.) we walk outside ourselves. The lack
Is, though communicado, that we fare
Forth only, boldly, in despite of those
Glib lines delivered at a waning back,
A disappearing eye, under the rose.

4

Under the rose, all honor overdrawn,
We bob and dimple in a minuet
Of metronomic confrontations, whose
Lord God horologist is with us yet
When we've lost every stitch we had to lose:
All, all our sureties put out to pawn
At Uncle's, all *orgullo* up the spout,
All soft dubiety now concrete doubt
As, in the last cement of etiquette,
We curtsy to our peers under the rose.

5

Under the rose, such bombinations rise
As may soon see the world well lost, and it
Just started on its promising career
This very morning, though fulfillment lies
Back of beyond. The really tricky bit
Is the next fifteen minutes. Good King Lear
Has quite a lot, in fact, to be sorry about.
I hear recriminations interpose
Their steady drumfire under the bombs, my dear,
Under our cool last words, under the rose.

The Clearing in the Woods

Behind this cabin, children, is an oak,
The nearest of the circumstantial ring
That stands and counts its rings and keeps its score
In hundreds, children, hundreds, just beyond
The pickets of our eyes both day and night.
Look out this window at the clearing: it
Is daytime, and its space is limitless.
Look out this window, children, now that night
Has lain among us: nothing, you can see,
Spreads all around us in its unknit skeins.
Yet there are oaks, their torsos rife with rings
Begot of waiting, just beyond our ken,
Beyond the bourne of consciousness, where we
Lay down our senses on that unnamed day
When those oak sentries let one pass, and he
Comes straight across the clearing to take one
Of us back of beyond. No, it is true:
I know because my father told me so,
And one day, to insure that I believed
What he had said, and to preserve the state
Of things as they must be — the cabin, then
The clearing, then the woods — one came for him.

American Light:
A Hopper Retrospective

I. HOPPER

A man, a plan, a spandrel touched with fire,
A morning-tinted cornice, a lit spire,
A clapboard gable beetled with the brow-
Shadows of lintels, a glazed vacancy
In shut-up shopfronts, an ineffably
Beautiful emptiness of sunlight in
Bare rooms of which he was the sole inhabitant:
The morning and the evening of his life
Rotated, a lone sun, about the plinth
On which he stood in granite, limned by light
That lasted one day long and then went out.

II. ETCHINGS

The starling canyons of our cities, stone
Woodlands whose only predator — besides
The falcons falling on the pigeons — is
The shambling, scuttling, sidelong pygmy, man,
Drew him to draw them: a long figure, lit
By an arc streetlight, hurrying between
Herculean pillars of structures at whose feet
The summer awnings in tan duck await
A summer morning, to his rendezvous
With the rest of the small hours; a naked girl,
Facing, on all fours in her unmade bed,
An evening wind that bellies curtains in
And carries the last light to model her
Vanishing shape in perpetuity;
A couple in the subway, rapt in their
Portable ambiance in an empty car —
Bound, possibly, for New Lots, or for the
Ultima Thule of Dyre Avenue —
Set face to face on a longitudinal
White-wicker seat, his boater on his knee,

Her sailor straw upon her head, her long
Skirt just revealing twinkling ankles, his
Strained face confronting hers, oblivious
Of the sharp nattering of straps and blinds,
The greased, electric, artificial night
Of a supposititious tunnel, or
The parti-lighted, real, and echoing night
Of a putative trestle anchored in the air.

III. PAINTINGS

The flourishing Republic could afford
An unparalleled sky: an honorable blue,
Out of which fell a withering, cherishing light,
Pointed as knives, which whittled the world to size
And held it up for acclamation. That
World started looking west from Washington Square
Across a pride of hard-nosed chimney pots
Supported by squat rubrics of brick stacks
Relieved by ventilators and skylights
Pooled in the sun and shadow of a sharp
Midafternoon. Over — the heart leaps up —
Far over west, last barrier before
The Jersey shore and the whole hot heartland,
A single loft building on Varick Street,
A huge, hooped, staved wood water tank on top,
Stood blue-brown boundary and sentinel,
Imperishably fixed — a crag, a tower
To overawe the river — in the eye
Of its observer under the moving sun.
Also a portion-controlled pie slice of light
Falling untrammelled into the window of
A side-street cafeteria, where two
Lay figures — an American naïve
Woodcarving of a buxom girl in blue
Descended from a bowsprit, and a grave
Wood-chiselled man, down to his cigarette —
Sat fixed in amber morning, slanting on
The naked cruets on their doilies, on
The barren tables and blue-plastic chairs,
On her as she stared on her empty glass,

On him as he stared past her at the street
Of dark shops opposite: a mystery.

IV. LATER

Two last exhibits must be introduced
In evidence, if it please your honor. One,
Called "Two Comedians," painted at the end
Of Hopper's life, shows Pierrot, stage front,
Grim-lipped, in whiteface, presenting Pierrette
To an unseen audience; the figures are,
His wife said — following his death and soon
Before her own — intended to represent
The painter and his wife. Such comedy —
So high as to be cosmic — is perhaps
Played out in the second exhibit, "Sun
In an Empty Room," where the interiors
Of all his early years are fused in one
Apartment room movers have visited
With their pantechnicon of mise-en-scène,
Taking away the givens of the past —
Beds, rugs, lamps, people, papers, chiffoniers —
And leaving a sizeable memorial
To his life and to the state he lived it in:
A green tree blowing outside; streaming in
Through the two-light window, forming cream oblongs
On window wall and alcove wall and on
The bare wood floor, a shaft of morning sun
Peoples the vacuum with American light.

Model Rooms

The sound goes off, and muted, squinting legions
Proceed, in vinyl-timbered station wagons,
To where World Goods augments and gratifies
Their thingful lust to be the centerpieces
Of dried arrangements of mass-cherished items
That are entirely them. Which brings us to
The ranks of model rooms roped off with velvet:
Rock maple, fruitwood, gumwood, teakwood, Hitchcock,
Colonial, provincial, pop art, rustic,
Trig old Kentucky home sweet homes with plastic
Protectors on the chintzes, master bedrooms
With his-'n'-hers matched dressers, eat-in kitchens
With wrinkled windows in their country hutches,
And nurseries ablaze with supergraphics.
All are invitingly untenanted,
Lit through their glassless casements by a sunlight
That disobeys the patent laws of nature,
And, to the representatives of rootless
Races of movers-on across the endless
Colors of seas and countries toward the rainbow's-
Ending of home, their speckless emptiness
Speaks, in the silence, a stentorian promise.

Amazing Grace, 1974

In this night club on Fifty-second Street,
An aeon after Auden's suppressed sigh,
A singer, warming up the audience —
A congeries of critics here to judge,
A bleating herd of suckers to be fleeced —
For the top comic, lone star of the night,
Goes out, infantrywoman, to the point
Of contact with that mumbling enemy,
Her many-headed hive of auditors,
And lays her unfledged talents on the line
Between réclame and dank ignominy.
She belts out songs into the banks of smoke
Caught by the same spotlights that capture her
Innocent sequins, peach, green, peacock blue,
And innocent features, pink with makeup, white
With apprehension, peach with youth. The mob
Is plainly restive — where is their overdue
Impressionist, for whom they have endured
Hours in this noisome cellar, *prix-fixe* meals
Made out of orts of cattle, melting drinks,
And unexampled decibels of sound?
She sings on doggedly. ''Amazing Grace''
Is her next text, and, with amazing grace,
The social contract holds; she sings as if
The audience were hers to have and hold
In the perspiring hollow of her hand;
Her listeners, rising to her distress —
Theirs also, but for grace, at any turn
Of any corner, clock, or calendar —
Hush their cross talk and manfully applaud
As, on a reedy note, she finishes
And flashes her back's sequins (indigo,
Rose, rust) in a half bow that could also
Be a half sob. Applause. Amazing grace
Laves all of us who, chivvied by unchance,
Anxiety, disaster on our way
Out of the wide world, pause to clap our hands
For one who fails full in the face of us,
And goes down to defeat to our applause.

Man in the Street

There is an alien intelligence
In Boylston Street: hour after crawling hour
On these cold days a pole away from spring,
He aims the ultimatum of his eyes —
A bitter, distant blue behind the scales
Of steel-rimmed spectacles — upon the press
Of passing people: students with their girls
(A nice distinction, aided by the grant,
In many cases, of a chin tuft on
The one and not the other); pimps and hos,
In transit to or from their tricks or pads,
Their courts of either kind, in which they hold
Or are held in contempt, their metalflake
Cats with Rolls grilles and wide whites, crouched beside
The curb, bound soon with regal cargoes for
The top of the world, where all men must look up
To see their highnesses sashaying by;
Small businessmen, no longer jocular,
Lax soloists behind the counters of
Shoestores and drugstores, but worn oarsmen in
Great corporate triremes; big businessmen,
Olive, fat-sideburned, suited in extreme
Didoes of cut upon a chequy theme
And fencing with cigars; and women, waifs
At fifteen in marcescent green fatigues,
At thirty-five in beanpole business tweeds,
At fifty in an autumn haze of furs
Surrounding a still sun that has burnt out.
The watcher on the curbstone takes all this
In, into his far older, other sense
Of the way of the world, and, though nobody speaks
A word to him — only an elderly
Man with a red face, tidily dressed in
An antique double-breasted windowpane
Plaid suit and a wide-brimmed fedora hat,
Who leans upon an early Polaroid,
Its wooden tripod garlanded with snaps
In black and white (a sailor and his girl,
Two Northboro basketballers on the town,

A squat, flowered tourist couple) of the sort
He'd take of you or me to eke his hours,
In nickels, dimes, and Bickford's coffee spoons,
Out till the next check day — there can be no
Doubt (see how erect he stands) that he has seen
How far the world has moved beyond his own
Primitive civilization to the verge
Of purest nothingness. He rests content
To stand back on his curbstone and survive,
The old time-server, the last man left alive.

Work: A Sermon

(For John Normand)

Listen, my brothers and sisters: it is our office
To steel each other on the shining spindles
Of craft we chiselled from the pigs a novice
Brought — bar stock in ham hands — to bear on learning
The habit he professes, the work turning
Constantly in the chuck, where a spark kindles
Cognition of perfecting fire.

Thenceforward, you are not a hand for hire,
Primarily, but a shaper, routing form
Out of its bed of matter, a void mire
Of contents without contrast, filling space
With inchoate nougat, out of which a face
Must be extravagated to the norm
Your masters died and left behind.

To shape a pintle, if you were quite blind,
Would thus not be a working miracle,
But simply template-tracing in the mind,

Long since locked in a programmatic vise;
Beyond that, what is devious and nice
Is to launch out beyond the clerical
Into constructive intercourse —

Beyond the sexual — to found a force
Of sighted minds tapping the elephant
Bulk of the undiscovered in a Morse
That remits concrete soundings of its shape,
Subjects its untracked inwards to the tape-
Worm of learning, segmented for measurement,
And binds its listening devotees

Into an orchestra of their expertise,
Playing piano and forte on the instrument
Of their minds connected in series with an ease
No soloist commands. Work, sisters and
Brothers, not for riches or a land
Of glory, but to write our testament
Of love upon the day we seize.

An Anniversary:
A Lucubration

I.

Marriage isn't, after all, a prison;
Nor a chancery court where every decision
Goes against both the defendant and plaintiff;
Nor a plaintive
Duet in an old-fashioned birdcage whose cover
Is replaced by the owner when day is over;
Nor a long lease on a bridal suite,
Every stitch prinked in yellowing white:

The infinity of hell
In a small hotel;
Nor, unlike courtship, a paper chase
After a face
That turns out to be foolscap in the end
And goes to ground;
Nor a delighted pairing
Of the attributes we were wearing
When love struck, a gestalt
Consonant to a fault;
Nor a silent contract
Of service in the abstract,
Printed, patient, in the concrete
Earth beneath our feet;
Not a universal journey in the dark;
Not a short walk in the park;
Not a kind of unheard singing;
Not a conditioning bell ringing;
Not an exaltation;
Not a condonation;
Not, in fact, a thing
Like loving.

II.

Marriage, after all, is ordinary,
Like looking at a prairie.
The best of it
Is you get used to it.
After untold episodes of hope
And giving pearly fancies too much rope
And falling in between into despair
And finally arriving there —
The run-down, shut-up station with a lone
Baggage cart under an arc lamp and no one
To meet you and no town and your lit train
Pulling away west in the rain —
You finally realize you've arrived
At all there is to having lived.
And that's when anything that's going to happen does:
The first humane exchange of selfish lies,

The first unprogrammed anger,
The first perception that a stranger
Inhabits your present and will inherit
Your future, irrespective of her merit;
The first dispassionate
Appraisal of her person for the cash in it;
The first unexpected Doppler
Effect — like the rattle of a poplar
Hushed suddenly — of the silver of her laughter
Here now and real and still here after
It has died away;
The first real earthbound day
You two trudge out in unison
Under the pendulous arc lamp of the sun
To find your station,
However humble, in a failing nation
Where one from many has no valid voice
These days, and one from two must make a choice
To keep themselves by being ordinary;
By looking, while the light lasts, at the prairie.

The Better Half

Whither away, and wither away, and with
Yourself, arms laced around your rib cage to
Embrace yourself as if a couple, you
Wind up alone, one drop, ridiculous,
Poised, pointed downward — like an old-time bomb
In wing racks — from the red, distended wings
Of your nice nose. There, there. Blow and return
From that unfleshly, spaced-out, scary bourne
From which few detainees return. My dear
Joan, whom I really don't know, since you both
Employed a single cook to spoil your broth,
My milliards of condolences. He's gone,
That prestidigitatorissimo,
Only connector between time and place —
You upstate in apartments, you downstairs
In the cll kitchen in the antique Cape,
You suckling babies, graduating sons
From sonhood, seeing towering daughters off
To Life, where, as researchers, they will learn
The price of everything — he's gone to sleight
Another, younger, greener acolyte
More capable of faith than, doubtless, you.
With all his honors on his turtleneck,
He'll sigh no more, my lady, for the one
Who pottered round his garden and brought up,
From dragon seed, a minatory crop
Of spitting images and prodigies.
No, in the eyes of other people's sons —
A fallow field refracting his pinpoint
Face lecturing — he'll take his grace and ease
And end on a fraternal note. Applause.

And in the run-down watches of this ae
Night, in the folds of his new comforter
Under a skylight in the Factory
District, he'll start, and turn, and say, "It's me
You care about, not what I am." And she
Will turn, annoyed, and sleepily agree.

And you, past whinny-muir and the brig o'dread
This ae night, and in solitary, will
Bootlessly realize that only you
Could have made the first man that the second killed
And left in your self-seeking arms for dead,
And left forever. Christ receive his soul.

The Persistence of Innocence

A string-straight road from Ellsworth to Bar Harbor:
The town at one end, mountains at the other
As barren and serene as Contra Costa's.
Along this road (past the Gray Elf Shop) huddles,
In the rank field grass, pelage of that isthmus,
A barrow of a building, front two-storyed,
Back straggling out back in a tail of ell,
And partially encircled by gaunt cabins,
All in one pale and whitish tinge of green,
A tumbledown memorial to summer.
The answer to the color is the inn sign,
"Green Moth Motel," across the front, embellished
By a large, amateurish freehand painting
That represents, of course, a luna moth.
What was the sublunary sense of omen
That called the owners, finding the great insect,
Perhaps, upon a twig of timothy,
Flexing its purple-deckled wings like bellows,
To name their new place for it? Innocence
Persists and sanctifies such hackneyed places
With its transfusive and resurgent hope
Of better days tomorrow and tomorrow.
Though I am far from Ellsworth, I know well
The wind eroding the Green Moth Motel
Against the counterforce that keeps it going
Toward its mooring at the foot of nothing:
Breath, breath, restated past the coast of knowing.

II

Nostalgic and Narrative

A Comedy in Ruins

When Joe C., wearing his First Army patch,
'Toon sergeant's stripes, web belt, a breastlike clutch
Of hand grenades beneath his President-
Ial Unit badge, and an unclean Garand
Exclaiming at his back, walked out of spring
In Brandenburg — the small blades pressing up
In armies underfoot as in an hour
Of peace — and into no-man's season in the strings
Of dust and mist that held the city up
To ridicule, a riddled hulk that once
Swam like the *Gneisenau,* he swaggered like
An armored conqueror in Mexico,
Due, no doubt, to the pint of kümmel that
Invested the prime see of his virtu.
Bowlegged, manly, he fared down stiled streets
Paved stonily with shopfronts, dammed by walls
Descended from house walls, and led his men,
Silent, except when shouting to prove that
Life on this cratered moonface might exist,
In Indian file toward the rigid heart
Of an extinguished empire that, short days
Ago, saw coronary sunsets glow.
At last, a street of dreams, crumped only to
The second story, in which paraffin

Lamps glimmered; on the unscathed first
Floors, red lights becked benighted victors in.
Joe formed up his platoon in column of
Twos and advanced upon a sanguine door,
Rapping seigneurially, stubbled, drawn
With weeks of combat in the sudden light
The opened door conferred upon his face.
An ancient madam in a dotted-swiss
Green dress, most suitable for picnicking,
Bowed him and his formation into a
Gaunt hall confounded by a serpentine
Oak banister curved sexually up
Into uncharted regions hinting of
Musk and surcease. The whole platoon, behind
Joe now, conspiratorially playing up
To his thrasonics, square-bashed to a halt
In perfect line astern. A butterfly —
A childish, gawky skeleton in green
Chiffon, promoted through the vacancies of war
To première whore at an unripe nineteen —
Sashayed, sacheted — whiff of chypre — down
To meet Joe on his level and his terms.
Struck madcap by an undergraduate,
Unformed impulse — a saving grace — Joe bowed
With utter gravity to his lady green-
Sleeves, rose, and murmured, audibly to his men,
Who froze their laughter, "At your cervix, Ma'am;
Dilated to meet you." And went up to bed
In youth, in spring, in jest, in death, in ruins.

Love Day, 1945 *

Slowly the ancient seas,
Those black, predestined waters rise
Lisping and calm before my eyes,
And Massachusetts rises out of foam
A state of mind in which by twos
All beasts browse among barns and apple trees
As in their earliest peace, and the dove comes home.
— *Anthony Hecht*

I.   MINUS ONE

1. Averil Sayward Snow

Imprimis, in her shower in Quincy Street,
The lady vanishes and reappears,
Venusian, in an ocean spume of steam,
And stands, material, on her bathmat —
Pink, white, and twenty-three — and dries her feet.
Naked, she to her naked face applies
A thin clay skin, and to her bare green eyes
Brown underlines, which will italicize
Her ultimate impression. A mute rose
Buds on her noiseless lips, and an Arpège
Of scent spans all her octaves. Into clothes
She skin-dives skillfully, emerging whole
And foliate in a war-torn world whose leaves
Too often stem from embarkation, as
Did Charley Snow's. (Please figure to yourself
Particulars of severance in the rain
In terminal night light beside the green
Sleeper, Shoshone Falls. Enough.) Now grass,
Now flesh widow, combatant unaware
In unknown actions, Averil descends
Her meat-and-mothball-smelling stairs, which end
In many mailboxes. The glass door gives
On a dank night of Germinal, the last of March.

---

* L-Day — or Love Day, in Navy parlance — was the official
designation for the date of the Okinawa landings, April 1, 1945.

2. Marshall Schoen

Schoen, pale and flued in black, girt in a white
Bath towel, sacks his tottering chest of drawers
In search of underwear. Big books fall down:
Thick Skeat and Onions, gamy Partridge, firm
And appetizing Whiting, solid Flesch.
Once natatorially attired, he now
Dons don's apparel: a black flannel suit
From Hunter Haig, pink shirt, illicit knit
Tie bearing Pudding colors, grape-juice shoes,
And is the utter lecturer, complete
As any man can be at twenty-two.
He smokes a Raleigh standing and rereads
A hortatory letter full of grief,
Foreknowledge, and commercial wisdom, in
An old man's unskilled hand, on his old man's
Dry-cleaning letterhead from Bedford Ave.
("Spotting Our Specialty"). Immaculate,
He slams the tin door to his tutor's suite —
Lowell G-46 — and drums his steel
Taps down the steps toward the trashy scent
Of ice-out in the river, borne by drops
Of mist that frost his horny spectacles.

3. Charley Snow

Somewhere off Okinawa, a DD
Makes for her station as a picket in
The outer radar screen. The tumulous seas
Break over her forepeak as her exec.,
Lieutenant Snow, relinquishes the conn
And goes below to take a trick of sleep
In his scant cabin, peopled by a framed
Portrait by Bachrach of his Averil
In sweet-girl-graduate cashmere and pearls.
He sleeps; the *John E. Hagan* alternates
Between beam-ends; the wardroom fiddles field
The anchor-marked but errant coffee cups;
The radar's catcher's mitt revolves above.
Thus ends his Minus One, thus enters Love

Day, April Fool's, and covers Charley Snow
With darkness till the winds of morning blow
Like sirens in the rigging, and the blips
Begin to cluster on the scanner's map.

II. L-DAY

1. Marshall

Schoen, waking, files a variance of light,
And knows he is not home; recalls last night,
Embodied still in Averil at his side;
Hears hunts of bells in ancient order ride
Out to enounce an Easter rising of
A sun, a Son, a nation twenty-nine
Years earlier, and, from his lover's bed,
A newborn Schoen, who, shaken, sees the pearl
Of morning fall like hail upon his arm,
Upon the peeling windowsill, upon
The Ford-strewn street outside, upon the Yard
Diminishing away in its chaste pale
Beneath the magic realism of
Its elms and bells, upon — turn back — the arm
Of Averil outside the covers. Schoen,
Like to his western homophone, completes
His manifest destiny: to penetrate
The world and person of the earlier
Arrivistes, keepers of the general store
Of fashions, notions, drygoods, who decline —
Agèd and inbred — to elect a fine
Young newcome to entrap their daughter's hand,
Their bolts and boxes, language, life, and land.

2. Averil

Revert to Averil, on whose eyelids light
White arts of morning, on whose ears repeal
The bells, rescinding silence. Through a slim
Slit fringed with lashes, she first apprehends
The sheet her blond arm pinions to her side;

Next, the next pillow, wrinkled, vacant, void
Of its oppressor; next, the high-hung room
Alive with light in a particulate
Manner, like mica; next, cut out of black,
But deckled white on every edge, his back
Framed in the window, a flat souvenir
Of the dimensionality of night
That had at her repose, a sharp unlike
Those cutouts of her ancestors — enshrined
In cover glasses — retrogressing up
The stairs of her house in West Cedar Street.
No, this is a new silhouette for her;
A step beyond her east to a frontier
Where new men cross the customs barrier,
Home in on her flat-lit retreat, and fill
Her bed with new, kinetic night. She smiles —
Just testing, just conducting maiden trials
Of her first real commission, of her first
Deep-water venture out of the milk-white,
Cream-calm home harbor — shivers, and, awake,
Shams sleep and prays the Lord her soul to take.

III. PLUS FIVE

1. Charley

Dead in the water, her main battery
Out of commission, fire in the engine room
Making a black smoke marker two miles high,
The *Hagan* lists and settles for a lull
Between attacks. The slap of seas, the cries
Of wounded in the wardroom are subdued
Again by planes and guns (the forties sound
Like fists upon tin tables; twenties purr
Like muffled air compressors). Now Group One
Abandons ship; a hundred treading men
Watch in the water as a Zero weaves
Inside the guard of forties — a pale cowl
Blackened with oil and exhaust, two red
Roundels beneath the wingtips — and explodes
Amidships as his wingman, well alight,

Straddles the foredeck and goes up. Fire flows;
The ready-ammunition drums go off;
The weather, making up, sends a great swell
Under the ship and breaks her back. She sinks.
Men swim in the first silence in a week.
Two hours pass and an SC comes to glean
Survivors from the waters. Nearly two
Hundred are rescued, not including Snow.

2. Averil

Averil, at this selfsame moment, bends
Her dawning eyes upon a book of dawn's
Language, at least in English: an old green-
Bound Anglo-Saxon reader. Kennings swim
Before her in the whale road, and she kens
The sense of continuity: the men
Upon her husband's ship upon the sea;
The women here at home in the mead hall;
Their comforters upon that bed, asleep
After love's labors, lost to the wide world
Of search and service Charley Snows are born,
Not made, to man; the waiting game of her
Kind, womankind, Penelopes who must
Not fend off suitors in the interim
Nor stand on principle, on pain of dust.
What love she bears for that poor man who sleeps
Within her benison, beneath the deeps
Of purpose realized, desire fulfilled;
She covers him against the coming cold.

IV.   PLUS THIRTY-SEVEN

1. Marshall

Of that long, soft, and early-bearing spring
The warmest day to date comes, carrying
The rumor of the bells, too many and strong

To let the rumors of newsboys along
Mount Auburn Street be heard. The Lowell bells —
Unmatched and matchless — now take up the call
With jingling thunder in an imbecile
Outburst of joy. Outside, the sparrows in
The Fly Club hedge sing, audibly, "V-E!"
And many a passenger wears an unwilled grin
To think that that's all over. Marshall Schoen
Marches, on a more sombre errand, north,
In his most sable suit and most subdued
Knit tie, a mourning brassard almost on
The dark stuff of his sleeve. Northward to grieve —
And not as any member of the wake,
But as a rank outsider on the black
Edge of disaster's cloud of celebrants —
He goes, untempted by the blossoming
Delicatessen of a Cambridge spring,
Unleviated by the lifting of
A six-year siege, unmoved by his late love.
When he arrives at Christ Church, that slight frame
Survival of an age of easy grace
Complete with shrine — a Tory bullet hole
Preserved in the pine reliquary of
Its thin grey sides — he sees a black pigtail
Of straggling mourners disappearing in
To hear Lieutenant Snow absolved of sin
Posthumously, and coolly eulogized
In the embalming tones of Dr. Wise,
The well-loved Rector. Standing on the brick
Sidewalk outside, arms folded, chin down, Schoen
Shakes his head once and marches home again.

2. *Averil*

World's youngest widow, in R. H. Stearns weeds —
Black veil, for once across an unmarked eye,
Black tailleur on a proper figure, black
Pumps cantilevering a perfect calf —
Twines black-gloved hands as if, though not, in prayer,

Drops chin, blinks back no shadow of a tear,
Shakes her head shortly once, as if to clear
Inconsolation out of it, and dumb
To Dr. Wise's plashing words, and numb
To that small throng of ill- and well-wishers
Who drill her back with ravening, unveiled
Eyes bright with speculation, sits her mount —
An off-white pew — with ladylikeness, which
Is one thing she knows cold, and perseveres.
What they don't know, although they know a lot,
Is at the moment still her secret: what
The numerous troop of non-red-letter days
Investing her desk calendar now says,
Predictably, is sure to come. A crux
Of time forms in her mind; Love Day recedes,
All its cross-purposes self-cancelling;
Today a war and man of war both come
To their dead end; tomorrow, unremarked
For anything, will be a day at home
For Averil, beside herself with due
Bills to be honored; for the first time, too,
Possessed, perhaps, of the resources she
Will need to meet them. A recessional
Hymn strikes up in Christ Church, Episcopal.

At the Bar, 1948

McBride's. Round tables in a cellar off the Square
Give point to your intensive, angular
Embodiment. In this sub-basement of
The Tower of Babel, full of talk of love
Which glances off our faces, we conclude
Our business over stingers, each betrayed
By an embezzling partner. In whose bed
Did we commit each other's substance to
A voided contract, countersigned with no
Co-maker's name? No matter. In this place
Of love and excrement, only the face
Of one's true love is legal tender. All
The tubes and armatures behind the wall
Of superfice, red conduits and blue
Recirculation systems, all the two-
Way valves are immaterial to this
Low-lighted limbo where the random wish
Is father to the title deed of love.
Now that the glittering Indian gift we gave
Returns on ruffled waters, and we drown
Unbuoyant sorrows and ourselves go down
Below the surface of a sea of young,
Or, rather, one-year-younger lovers, long
Sea-miles behind us, and the jukebox plays
Our old song, "Kiss me once and kiss me twice,"
We leave these latitudes for the blank beach
Of singleness, beyond the utter reach
Of those warm waters. In the Brattle Cab
I realize you're drunk. Arrived, you stab
Your front door with a key and stumble in.
I help you up the steps, a stranger in
Your house and person. At the top you turn
To bar the way to me. Your kiss will burn —
Hard, acid, alcoholic — on my face
For many a measured mile, a stinging trace
Of our unfounded and spontaneous
Combustion in the desert of our dust.

The Escapists, August, 1949

(For Philip Finkelpearl)

I. BENZEDRINE

A wintry widow and her daughter, a
Wintering spinster, owners of the old
North Cambridge house my feat foot rested and
Locked on a moment in that summer of
Heat and my flight from full employment, loomed —
Those spinnerins of tart authority,
Lick-lipped Defarges — over my fecklessness
To such a point that one steamed night I chewed
The whole wad from a broken Benzedrine
Inhaler, and was soon transmogrified —
Shuddering like a glacier's cusp with cold —
Into a frozen, lone Birds Eye Green Pea,
Hurtling through interstellar corridors
In outer space for all eternity.
Next morning when I, thawed and shrivelled, woke,
I told this to the friends bent over me —
My wife B.K. and Chas — who seemed to find
It quite in keeping with that bootless time
When none of us, so full of promissory pride,
Had yet delivered on a jot of our
Self-fulgent art, so plain to all of us.

II. RENT-A-CAR

The morning's fog, washed down in veils of rain,
Shimmered and vanished in clean sun, and I,
Still manic at the apogetic high
Of the long-acting drug, proposed escape
From these four walls, from the four corners of
This town that did not recognize our powers
Nor wreathe our brows in laurel. "Let's go rent
A car and take off anywhere," I heard

My voice, on filter mike, feed back to me.
"Let's." "Let's." "Yeah, let's," I heard myself reply.
Down at the Robie place in Brattle Square,
Chas signed the docket for a rent-a-car,
Which rolled forth forthwith: a black '48
Convertible, a spanking Ford V-8,
Condign transport for three kids blowing town.

III. EN VOITURE

Where did we drive to? Chas, with his licensed skill,
Taking his steersman's trick at the taupe wheel,
Holding her steady as she went, and I,
A novice in inertial guidance of
A self-propelling vehicle, with B.-
K. wedged — enthusiastic dormouse — in between
Her two conductors? We drove to the west,
Threading the new grey graphite of Route 2
To where the earth, in undulation, reared
Huge mountains to the eyes of shore-dwellers;
And to the north, where we walked hours upon
A desert beach bestridden by the bones —
The wooden ribs and spines — of skeletons
Of perished sailing ships; and to the south,
Where, in the moteless dusk of the dead day,
Robie's reclaimed us from our pilgrim's way.

IV. SEPTENTRION

Steamed clams and Harvard Beer at Jane's Café.
And home again up Upland Road. Not quite:
In the north sky, a cold, ungodly light
In serried streamers, ranks of organ pipes,
All the world's curtains, green, red, glacier blue,
Caught our child's eye and held it in the play
Of the fall's first aurora, the far shore
Of the remote, aloof, superior,
Immortal river we had been searching for
All of our first free day, part of its night.

New York: A Summer Funeral

Our life is unwelcome, our death
Unmentioned in 'The Times.'
— *T. S. Eliot, "The Rock"*

*Memento, homo, quia pulvis es, et in
pulverem reverteris.*
— *The Liturgy*

I. EAST HARLEM

Arrivists, insightseeing, come to grips
With the ungraspable, the unforeseen
Waste laid to East One Sixteenth Street by noon:
The trappers, leg-ironed in their own steel traps,
Chew through their femurs just above the knee
And spatter red ink on the balance sheet
Drawn up about them — the hulk-cluttered street
Of steel and tissue derelicts, the by-
Blown children in the gutters, waiting their
Short turn as fodder for the glittering
Trade goods in stores whose parrot lettering
Broadcasts its hawkers' cries through pewter air,
The rusting surf of empties, pleasure spent,
Investing curbstones, the rank vacant lots
Of chicory and bedsprings, the sagged cots
Set out on fire escapes, the blurred sun bent
On murder by asphyxiation. All
These felonies are laid at our clean feet
By accident; our cab zigzagged en route
To our appointment with a funeral.

II. WEST TENTH STREET, 1871

A dance a little lamer than a waltz,
But a cappella, turns her from the glass
Surveying the Fifth Avenue and halts
Her, white in white, facing his fading face
As he completes his evolution and —
Struck hopeless in the presence of her grace —
Takes his all-broadcloth Sunday-morning stand
Upon some antique principle and says

A word of climax, swamped by the iron band
Of church bells swarming for a summer day's
Ingathering of their unruffled flocks,
Two by cool two, to justify the ways
Of man to God. A thousand steeple clocks
Now finger the eleventh hour, and these
Two walk to church, a dead march of two blocks.

III. HOTEL SPLENDIDE

"Against that sure cliff beat all hours of the night,"
I wrote in nonage twenty years ago.
Now all hours of the day also compete
In its erosion, and its honors go
To tatters on its mouldered battle flag:
The teens, a dream of peace and a parade
Receding and returning less some limbs;
The twenties, a green shoot in a green shade
That never ripened in an air of *blague*
And shrivelled in the thirties, when a plague
Of settling scores descended, murdering whims.

The forties? Ah, then I set foot upon
Its stage, a pygmy interloper in
Its shades of grand transactions come and gone
With black portmanteaux and a whiff of sin.
Fifties and sixties: then I filtered down
From bitty servants' rooms high in the eaves
To 'tween-decks suites with engine telegraphs
(Inoperative) for steam and wheat in sheaves
Of plasterwork (inedible) to crown
The ceilings (after Adam), and to drown
My cowed-youth's first gasp in a million laughs.

Now, now, the seventies. Now, now, indeed:
A queasy glaze of heat sets shivering
The buckram recto of the white façade
And sets the lobbyists to havering
As they demand their rooms from the, perhaps,
A trifle less obsequious desk clerk
Than ever wore those morning trousers when

The world was new and only after dark
Did dissolution threaten, and a lapse
In manners did not redraw all our maps
And make old ways impassable again.

IV.   501 MADISON AVENUE, 1921

The morning and the evening: what a lull
There was when, fresh from Childs, he came to work
Before the typists and sat all alone
At his scored desk of mission oak to write
The first car cards of morning in a white
Refraction of sunup upon the hull
Of the building opposite, and what a lark
To answer "Johnson" when his upright phone
Rang around nine to summon him to meet
With Silliphant, his chief, and state his views.
And what a benison when the evening
Stole in and lit his gooseneck lamp, and all
The typists dimmed and tinkled down the hall,
And double-decker buses in the street
Approached extinction, and the cries of news-
Boys dwindled, and he filled the evening
With those sharp, seven-word, new-minted saws
As kept him — after all, a novelist
In secret, a subversive, one who spied
Upon the dance of commerce — in the black;
In Tripler Norfolk jackets on his back;
In what it took to circumvent the laws
Concerning liquor; in a little list
Of worthy girls; in, well, a certain pride.

V.   BANNERMAN'S FUNERAL CHAPEL, INC.

Do you know Ben Klein in a suit so grey?
Do you know Ben Klein in a face of clay?
Do you know Ben Klein when he's far, far away
With his death in his hands in the morning?

Do you know that bitch whose tongue is death?

Do you know her last word is "success"?
Do you know Ben Klein with his last breath
Cursed them both as he died in the morning?

Yes, I knew Ben Klein and his Queenie, too,
The wife that saw his trajectory through,
From a find to a check, from a check to a view,
From a view to a death in a morning.

VI. EINE KLEINE LEICHENMUSIK

Di Lido Arms: a buff-brick, Dieselesque,
Constructivist construction in the mode
Of Emery Roth, a *schmutzig* arabesque
Reared on our gullibility, a lode
Of yearning turned to angst, a humoresque
Transmuted into horror notes that bode
Us ill. One in the elevator says,
In black, unsteady felt-tip, "Just two days
Ago one of our tenants in this car
Was robbed at knifepoint by an addict. We
Demand the management to man the door
Twenty-four hours a day with security
Guards to safeguard the endangered lives of our
Tenants. Write or phone the Finster Reality
Trust at ORegon 8-9864
Today and say we won't wait 1 day more."
A skirl of voices down the *dunkel* hall
Prefigures the existence of 9-A;
Verification comes when we see all
The mourners of the morning, quasi-gay,
Eating, commiserating in a pall
Of Tueros smoke that fills the little bay
That gives on the East River, where the gaze
Of Queenie, crying, smiling in a maze
Of contradictions, turns repeatedly,
As if to seize the reassurance of
Geography; as if, perhaps, to see
Klein cast off lines and so begin to move

Downriver with the tide toward the sea,
A civil effluent — released from love
And ducted into nature's ways — for whom
Scavenging voices populate his room.

VII.   AMELIA AT THE PLAZA, 1910–1970

She tarries at her mirror in the new,
Already grand hotel, a veil of grace
And summertime repose between her two
Blue eyes and those two coolly in the glass
Before her watching her across the space
Of sixty years ago, the morning light
Paying its usual homage to her face.
Heydays, like bodies, tarnish into night.

She dresses on the backcloth of the blue
Windows where early June is taking place,
Shrugs into her white dress, a fall of too-
Anticipatory silk and fussy lace,
With resignation and a fine grimace
At marrying a stranger at the height
Of her self-knowledge in her own embrace.
Heydays, like bodies, tarnish into night.

This morning in the Oak Room, with friends who
Recently lost a daughter, we erase
Her memory with small talk, giving due
Avoidance to her absence, keeping pace
With the dead march, a measurely footrace
Whose stragglers fall unnoticed in our flight
And vanish at our backs without a trace.
Heydays, like bodies, tarnish into night.

Princess, in your slight hand you held the ace
Of wands that obviates our kind of plight:
You lived before we found us in such case.
Heydays, like bodies, tarnish into night.

VIII. SATURDAY NIGHT AND SUNDAY MORNING

When night owls settle into wan cafés
Accounted for by night, and coffee urns
Chuckle their comments on the draggled strays
Cast into inner lightness where there burns
One grease-streaked night light, shedding on the ferns
Its yellow absolution from the need
To grow and flourish, and the waitress turns
Her dazed face to the faces she must feed,
That vanished city turns upon its deed
Of darkness, and makes up in marshalling yards
A train of consequences that will lead
To one quick dazzling shuffle of the cards.

IX. HER WEDDING JOURNEY

Leaps out of Jersey an improbable fire,
Vaults — gouts of purple, clots of sanguine — all
The intervening river, sheds on Pier
14 and its departing paddle-wheel
Steamer, the *Commonwealth,* a vascular
Aura, and on those newlyweds (who lightly leave
Niblo's, the Winter Garden, Rector's, the
New Amsterdam behind) an orchid flush
On her pelisse, a rusting stain of brown
On his black jacket with grosgrain lapels.
Steam cases, paddle boxes drum: a wake
Propels them backward out into the stream,
And then, reversing, south around the horn
Of the Standard Oil Building and its clump
Of spare contemporaries; lastly north
And east across the silence of the Sound.

Aboard, they dine off Chincoteagues, Dover
Sole (hock), endive, rare *entrecôte* (claret),
And baked Alaska. In the stateroom on
A-Deck, a little flushed, they both undress
To engine noises and unite in bed,
Not without guesswork, and sleep supervenes.
Morning. An ebbing tide slaps the blunt hull
Like a newborn as it swims, intent, upstream

To anchor at Fall River. They debark —
Trunks trundled in a truck behind — to take
The Boston boat train, in whose dining car,
Blurring the sadnesses of the swamplands
And jewelry towns with its sheer speed, they eat
Their first breakfast, agog, as man and wife.
Back in the parlor car, a slackening
Of purport brings him to his feet to smooth
Her cloak across her shoulders; at Back Bay,
They leave the train and hail a hansom cab
To traverse the one block to their hotel.

X. THE WINGS OF MAN

Hermetic in our tinsel Upmann tube,
We trundle, smoking with conation, up
Into the sallow, grey inverted air,
Tucking a raggle-taggle stratus layer
Between us and the city, which whites out
Those miles of individual circumstance
That separate the dancers from the dance —
A woman in a mirror, a dead man
Waked in a funeral chapel, a live one
Lulled by the trivialities of power,
A couple sailing, taking for her dower
The immaculate skin of inexperience,
Another, parted by a worldly doubt,
Attending church in concert, two or three
Succored by coffee in a night café,
None stirring on the bare street in the dense
Silence of Sunday, slipping in from sea —
And leave us, barren after the funeral
Of our own salad days and their venue,
To fly on singly, doubly you and I,
Across these short knots to the by and by
Of empty retrospect, toward the fall.

A Late Good Night

(For Julian Moynahan)

I. SHOP TALK

Sven Nilsson was a wizard motor mechanic.
See here: him posed, a king, in the swelling bosom
Of his poor family: fat wife, thin kids,
A suckling babe, a night-black Labrador,
A tacky cottage on the bulldozed fringe
Of an unseemly suburb. When his hands,
Passed tools by all of us in surgical
And silent pantomime, undid head studs,
Chipped, milled, and chamfered surfaces, torqued nuts
Down to the last inch-pound, slid pistons in-
To clean new bores, pressed interference fits
With strength and tact in equal measure, he
Reigned effortlessly in his mystery.

II. AFTER HOURS

When he, however, knocked off work, the black
Boyg of dark Nordics walked him down the street
To Harley's Bar, where boilermakers made
His darkness manifest. Humped on a stool,
He'd drink for hours in silence, hating what
He'd come to: a fine mind, fit for abstruse
Transactions, but unschooled and chained to a
Long, facile, crack-nailed pair of hands inlaid
With years of grease and carbon. His Munch face,
A black-fringed white wedge riven from the moon,
Would fall and fall like a storm glass until
It waned to nothing in the shadow, and he'd wake
To hump himself unsteadily back home.
Late summer, seaboard-humid: one dog night,
He took a shortcut home along the tracks,
And fell asleep beside them, where a train,
Shunting and snuffling late toward the yards,

Fell on him undefended and cut off
His good right hand. A milkman found him there,
All bloody in the muggy milk of dawn,
And drove him, servered hand and all, to the
Town hospital, where they sluiced pints of blood
Back into him and sewed his hand back on.

III.   AFTERWARD

It took, and so did life. Sven, in a sweet
Trance brought on by a taste of borrowed time,
Allowed the young Dunne brothers, his patrons
And friends, to form a cordon sanitaire
Of love about him, and to isolate
Him from his hunter, nothingness, in a
Long rataplan of small talk about cars
And books and politics. But how can you,
As Julian Moynahan says, convey your love
To one convinced of his own worthlessness?
One winter's night, just having buttoned up
His last MG-TF, and having sat
Alone at Harley's Bar until last call,
Sven headed home again along the tracks,
The new snow creaking underfoot, and slowed,
And stopped, and fell asleep, curled on the rail.
A train cut him in two. He marked his last
Position with iced blood upon the snow.

IV.   NOW

Could anyone have done what we could not?
I doubt it very much. Some stars are born
Out of our context, and proceed alone
Upon their rounds to some far rendezvous
Dictated by their hue and magnitude,
And, to our joy and terror, flare and die.

Going Back: A Word with Leslie Vandam in New York

Time warps and weaves invisible parallels
Into a monofilament of gross
Sensations, rolling on time's web-fed press,
Into the window out of Gramercy Park,
Through the good, gracious living room where talk
Too frank offends the old-guard furniture;
Out the small, frosted window of the pink-
Enamelled butler's pantry to the dark
Behind us in the south, which coruscates
With watchfire flames of wan stair-landing lights
That hold the island's atoms in their race
Until relieved by dawn. A small, white-faced
Accordionist in black tie and grosgrain
Lapels that send the lamplight glimmering
Tunes up off in one corner, while I, old
Enough to be your father, ask what you —
Erect in untried militance, with blue
Bolts of St. Elmo's Fire at readiness
In the penumbra of your hair, daze on
Your statuary features, Juno eyes,
And vulnerable lips, the weak point through
Which every mortal soul must once transpire,
Or soon, or late — my daughter, junior, my
Impromptu confidante, fresh from the war
Now petering to peace on the burnt shore
Of California, fresh to — in your
Ill-sitting Bonwit suit — this aging coast
Which your vanguard once peopled, plan to do
With your life here, embracing once renounced
Values, a throwback to the time before
Your time, when I and others did a dance
In which form counted all and content not
At all, and played round games. Your answer is,
Amazingly, drowned out in irony —
Too perfectly for life, but irony,
Amazingly, too often salts a life
Devoid of congruence, in flinders, with

Its sole perfection of coincidence —
By a damned chorus of the previous
Management, of these agèd, apple-faced
Young Hotchkiss boys, these vested magazine
Representatives, hail fellows all, in a
Rendition of — their voices quaver! crack!
They're growing younger, men! — of "Going Back
To Nassau Hall," accompanied, of course,
By the small black-and-white accordionist
(Who might just be the Soldat's devil), and,
Of course, of "Our Director," and, of course,
Of "Boola Boola." Silence. I repeat
My query to fair (actually, dark)
Leslie Vandam, embarking in her bark
Canoe for a new shore across the flux
Of overlapping eras: "What do you
Plan for yourself now that you're back here in
New York?" Silence. A tiny minnow-splash
Of slowly parting lips. "I guess I'll do
Exactly what my parents want me to."
Reprise. A movement sinks in distant seas;
A bulldog, raised again at Eli Yale,
Shows us the spectre of his teeth, his tail.

The Mid-Forties:
On Meeting No One in New York

Because I did not opt to ask that blond
Lady the loan of her light, tapered hand
At dinner, at the movies, in her bed,
In marriage, in the grave, I am not met
By her reclusive, comic, beautiful
Face on the dotted line that, dutiful,
I trace, unintersected by the X
Of assignation, unassailed by sex,
Across the city to my sole devoirs,
Uncelebrable in such scant memoirs
As my unerrant, unremarkable
Solo may prompt. The only workable
Scheme, after all, is to refuse the pain
Of pleasure so insufferable; the gain
In pulse rate at such meetings is wiped out
By consequential pangs of hope and doubt,
Guilt and the siren terror of her loss.
Better, assured that our roads cannot cross,
To take my privy way through separate
Crowds of unknowns, the shuttered, disparate
Citizens of the sovereign state of night,
Who pass, like flocks of blackbirds, left and right
Around me and go on to be alone.
In my hotel room the taupe telephone
Is tacit through the night beside the made
Twin bed across from mine. At dawn, a raid
Of color fires the window, and I rise
And walk out through the lobby, where no eyes
Follow my progress to a taxi. None
Sees me down thoroughfares to where the sun
Summons me, inching up the early air,
To end a losing game of solitaire.

Notes Toward a 25th Reunion

"And what do *you* do?" Mrs. Appoplex,
Fat dam of some dim Story Street savant
In baggy Marimekko muumuu and
Barbaric Inca necklet, asks my wife
At some dream sherry party packed with ham-
Strung academics swaying gently in
The wind of Babel. "Why, just cook and fuck,"
My wife does not, so sweetly, tender in
Reply, although I wish like hell she would.
Whose world is real, for Christ's sake, anyway?
Their sculpture gallery of images
That move mechanically in circumscribed
Tangents and — this is a recording — talk
In selfsame selfsongs all the livelong day?
(I must say I have just enough of a
Foot in that world to see its tiny point
Flash in the haystack of irrelevance.)
Or my free-form theatre of absurd,
Unaugurable happenstance, in which —
For gain, my lads, for gain — we businessmen
Risk all upon a nutty and divine
Idea of weal and on our con-man's skill
To sell it to each other. I'll back that
Frail matchstick pyramid of barest will,
On which, to balance, one exposes all
To the black, hithering eye of the abyss,
As realer than the static autoclave
Of academe, full of blunt instruments
Becoming sterile as they sit and steam.
And yet, when I return in steaming June
To my Reunion in the pullulant
Hive of the Yard, I'll look with shuttering
Eyes on my unknown classmates, businessmen
Who have no business with me, and greet
The likes of Mrs. Appoplex and her
Effete levée with a glad, homing cry.
The question is, what kind of fool am I?

Temporary Measures:
A Book of Hours

I. MATINS WITH LAUDS

A Motor City baby derby, and
First down the ways and into this world's weak,
Insolvent waters, cold as the New Year
At 3 A.M. upon its natal day,
Comes Infant Edwards, starproof, mewling, nude
Of words except for an unparsable howl,
To find the place prepared for him and his
Fatal incompetence, the lot of all
Born winners and born losers. Red and green
Clouds halt and march, reflecting city lights
On their soft underbellies stuffed with snow,
And I, returned from tempting Providence —
Dark Brown & Sharpe's, dark double-deckers, dark
State House, all emulous of our new age —
With other freshmen, strike sparks with my steel
Heel taps at 3 A.M. from the Large Quad,
Ascend my entry noisily, disburse
My clothes to the four walls, and fall to bed,
So full of joy as not to fall asleep
At moving, my own man, in a new state
Forever mine, or till the warranty
Expires, whichever may come first. A fist
Of pain, an echo of a fist of sleet
Against the window, pummels me awake
In my uptilted, sweated bed, and I
Inch one hand crabwise to the nurse's call
That breaks the nighttime with a silent scream
Of light above my doorway. Pad, she comes,
A moving flashlight and a shaded face
Some miles from mine. "Pain?" "Um." "O.K., hang on."
The breaking of an ampule, tiny in
That storm of silence; the persistent twinge
Of the steel needle probing for a vein
In the scarred, cratered crook of my forty-
Two-year-old arm, an outgrowth of the one

That Infant Edwards brandished at the world,
So fine and fair. Light dies and crêpe soles slub,
Indefinite, away. The anodyne
Ascends into my higher centers, where
Its tidings cheer my suffering populace
And float me forthwith to the brim of sleep,
Where I put down my pack of grievances.

II. PRIME

A thousand leagues of winter at my back —
Conspiracies of starving men to warm
Cracked hands at trashcan braziers in the dead
Of that unswerving season — I awake
To treble choirs of birds in Florida,
Three times as deafening as anything
The north in spring can offer, and confront
The sun ascended from a green-orange sea
To dazzle me with such rich lenity,
As, fresh-escaped from winter's element-
Ary school, I had not known there was. Such waves
Of song in the high register against
The ground bass of such waves that break and cream
Up to our housestilts argue for divine
Administration, even in the teeth
Of such hard evidence as '34
Can effortlessly marshal. *Tochter aus
Elysium!* massed choruses declare
To me at dawn. Lowell R-34
Jitters and tingles as the radio-Vic,
Its volume knob on 9, jampacks my ears
With affirmation, and I pace and shave,
While spattering Palmolive Shaving Cream
The length of the rag rug. Another March —
I lie awake and wasted as the sun
Comes up to turn the snows to runnels and
Erase the ski trails on the mountains, and
Hear a fresh chorus, ragged, far, and near,
That turns an inanition into a
Hope of a convalescence: the first flock
Of redwings lit, invisibly to me,

In the red-budded branches of a tree
Beside a swamp to descant raucously
On the possibility that life resumes.

III. TIERCE

Morning at Mountjoys'. Waking in the blue,
Disused maid's room, accompanied thereto
Last night by Sally (who, now up betimes,
Has gone down flights of white dust covers to
Gather the May), I still recall her shape
In every fingertip and taste her taste
Upon my tongue. What an authentic ache,
In one eighteen, such being met and left
Behind provides, so that the following day
At the same hour, not having slept, I sit
Alone with Sally's picture — taken at
A booth in Scollay Square, four poses for
A quarter — and devise an undernsong
Upon her eyebrow. Morning at Edwards'. I
Rise up alone to a song-sparrow's song,
Leaving my sleeping wife in grave repose,
One long arm classically curved across
The comforter, and go down to her house
In order, with the imprint of her sweet
Will and deep discipline upon each neat
Arrangement of still life, on each cleared, bare,
And dustless surface. She, although she sleeps,
Is all around me in the frozen dance
Of objects shaped and placed by years of life
Together, and, bespeaking such a love
Of going on as lovers know not of.

IV. SEXT

Upon my windowsill above the Quad
I sit, feet braced against the guttering,
And blot up the noon sun as I indite
My virgin sonnet on that selfsame sun
As seen an evening earlier through rose-

Hued scales of callowness. An overdose
Of Jacobethan diction puffs up my
Stillborn conceits with strange oaths; that ball
Of hollowness clad in glad rags rolls down
The yellow page unto the fourteenth line,
Where, with glad cry — "Here endeth!" — I retract
Myself into my room with hothead haste
To hie me to my classmates to purvey
My clockwork ware to them, my rhyming toy,
And watch them narrowly to see if they
Will think of Chatterton, the marvellous boy.
A matter of a quarter-century
Elapses to denote the passage of
A quarter-century. Discover me
Enthroned in Naugahyde, a No. 2
Eberhard Faber pencil in my hand
Upon a pad upon a clipboard on
My old Peal case upon my lap, and that
Selfsame June sun striding bolt overhead
As I attempt, about the thousandth time,
To set words down on paper in a line
That will lead somewhere other than from left
To right or top to bottom of the page.
Cunning, according to authorities,
Improves with age, but so, alas, does rote:
That well-honed, well-worn bag of burglar's tools
Enables one unguardedly to quote
The words and visions of one's younger self:
Mastery is the last resort of fools.
No, it is needful to apprentice one's
Grey eminence, the counsel of one's age,
To childish, churlish wonder; all blasé
Appraisals, knowing looks, and practiced eyes
Must, like the Phoenix, be quite burnt away
That that sad ash and ember may give rise
At last to a new flight late in the day.

V. NONES

Ah, Mr. Justice in midafternoon —
August, a portly and a portable

Tribunal trundled up to where the fire
Burns brightest, to extinguish it with your
Dry foam, an inert gas, of dusty saws
And modern instances. Is it the same
Young reed who swayed and read before the dames
Of dead Salons of Arts the year the war
Died in a fire storm, unbeknown to them
Who cupped in crippled hands the guttering flames —
The color of a Yellow Book — of art?
Is it the same who once laid down the law
To them — uncomprehending, thinking long
Thoughts of their long-dead dogs and husbands — who
Thrust on them the stale jargon of his view
Of existential action; for his pains,
Reaped a whirlwind of coos and giggles from
His mother-henning auditors; and was
Engulfed, encapsulated in the soft
Breastworks of their indifference, scented by
Synthetic-lavender sachets? Is it
The same who, give or take a trillion cells,
Stands up here now at Sanders, aging, grey,
In the cloud shadow of Commencement Day,
And tries your courtesy with news of him,
At length — please see above, below, passim —
When you and your coordinates might rather
Be out reviewing girls in this loose weather?
Is it the same who one day, should he live
So long, may in the comic motley of
His species — crow-black cassock and a hood
Dyed like a bird of paradise, play out
The courtly rite of honors — bow, dip, scrape
Like Dresden figures in a minuet —
Which, as you know, has less than nothing to
Do with the lonesome life of honor, or
The likelihood of justice under those
Ineffably well-tailored judge's robes?

VI. VESPERS

Homing at evening in the crepuscular
Tristesse of late November is not at all

Like the silk softness of that just-post-war
November night, when Sally in silk and I
Slipped down the Hill in blue and out along
The Esplanade in black to find a bench
Beside the river, where, with world enough
To burn, we burnt each other in the dark.
Novembers now bite deeper with their damp
And send me from the city — an armed camp
Of ignorant infantry whose confused alarms
May sound at any second — to the farms
Where the half-rich and the half-just still sleep
Their half sleep in the drying pools of peace.
Still, home is hope and comfort, the last place
Where order creeps on in its petty pace,
Where topless stacks of letters, papers, books
Demand an answer, where discourse resumes
Its evensong, and, in our inmost rooms,
My wife and I negotiate today
And keep the desert at the door at bay
Until such time as, shrunk-shanked, full of sleep,
We'll break our treaty to defend our keep,
Undo our locks and throw away the key,
And let barbarian night carry the day.

VII.   COMPLINE

Purple and white, three hundred milligrams
Of mere oblivion put paid to day
As mere drink did when I fell late to bed
Twenty-five years ago; and as that mere
Snicker of liquid in the needle did
Last winter in the hospital. But this
Winter, the day's last offices are sung
By courtesy of a white, crystalline
And bitter powder, bitterer than gall,
But not as bitter as the infinite
Spaces of space, the reasonless and cold
Black holes between the stars, which swallow this
Year's end without a sound, which swallow us
In distance now and soon enough in death,
From which no journeyman returns. What now

Remains to do is to apply ourselves
To exercising milligrams of force
To alter the immutable universe;
To work at the pitch of our tiny skills;
To show love to our fellow-passengers;
To put aside the tininess of men;
To give up hope our years will never end;
To sing the temporary measures of
Our night song with such art that our small notes
Will reach across meridians to the ears
Of those who next sing lauds in the small hours.

III

Light and Dreamy

Concerto for the Left Hand Alone

(For Charles Saxon)

Late, late, when BAI played Wittgenstein
Interpreting Ravel, one hand behind
Him in the First World War, I thought of you —
The hand that waited and the hand that drew
My gauche hand drawing on the drawing pad,
A sinister, undextrous fiddler-crab
Claw caught and fixed in the links of your hand,
Left high and dry ashore upon the sand
Of a lost world where all is withershins,
And every left hand sidles for its sins.

Boston–Chicago, May II

The cart thuds up;
The wings embrace
Their element; a pup
Dwindles and barks in a backyard
On a round island; we bank hard
And pack cloud under us. Rock rivers run
North-south, rooted in rose hills
Tainted with maple bud, grow flat,
Meander in brown plains of tilth,
Give rise to that
Young and unsalted sea in blue,
To that pink cloud of filth
We're destined to.

Praeludium, North River

Etch me a drypoint of those old Mack trucks,
Chain-driven, laden with the hidebound trunks
Of England-bound Americans, which pant
On the pavé beside the steam-up ship —
Four-stacker, British registry — which slips
Soon down the river on the Jersey line
And turns its stern on newness, and its head
Toward the old to which the new apply
For precedence and counsel and the wry
Regard of their past masters. All ashore
That's going ashore, and all the rest aboard
The siren-sounding bridge that ends abroad.

Matter of Britain:
Some Fragmentary Souvenirs

S.W. 7

Victoriously, Albert's shade impends
Upon the Iso Grifos rocketing
Their cargo of 2 RADA boys + 2
Girl chattels, barely garnisheed in Quant
Mechanics and Danskins, from mews to mews.
I pause to muse on pullulation in
The nick of evernight, soon to begin.

SALOP

In Clun — faint echoes of "From far, from eve
And morning, from the twelve-winded sky" —
A dotard lifts the hand not on his stick
And halts our Austin to allow an old
Bitch in her terminal pregnancy to cross
The village street. The heaven-bent and bold
Preserve the young idea within the old.

MIDLOTHIAN

Cop cop her loud-shod feet on Saturday night
Spell the one living thing in Princes Street,
All otherwise a quarry of granite
Floored with wet tarmac, walled with blackfaced stone,
Roofed with a lowering cross of smoke and fog.
An empty room unrented for tonight,
Untenanted until tomorrow breaks
And swells with black umbrellas under rain.

NR. OBAN

Plaid Argyll fields here peter down and out
To seas replete with humpback Hebrides,
Black, blue, slate grey, steel grey, French grey, off-white,
As they recede toward the falling night
To windward. Here, on burning green, a black
Stone kirk attracts a shorthand funeral:
One Humber hearse, one Riley Imp is all
The worm that winds its way to burial.

A Private Line

Hearing you two talk on the telephone
Long distance — the two hundred give-or-take
Miles separating Weston from Saltaire,
And the inordinance of miles that separate
Person from person — I rejoiced that two
Gifts dressed in persons like the ones that you
Possess need not be solitary, but
May talk and touch each other, eye to eye,
And stand upon one footing: not a lie
Marked love, but love of an uncommon kind,
A sympathetic symptom of the heart
Moving in unison with alien art.
"Hi, Tony Baloney!" A fine how-d'ye-do,
Filling the trilling wire from you to you.

To Your Uterus;
an Uncompleted Call

«Allo, allo, down there. Is this Odéon
96-69? Ever since the hasty erection
Of the Central Exchange, I can't get through to you
Without static or overheard conversations
Of furious businessmen or busy signals.
The line's engaged a lot. It must be you —
Your head, that is — in motherly colloquy
With your otherwise unemployed womb, both gossiping
Of potentialities. But that's an inside call.
No wonder I can't get through to you at all.
And here I thought that we just had a bum connection.»

Packing Material: Excelsior

Saul Steinberg,
Our Pelikanic Hillary,
Surmounts a fine berg
Of flesh and ice, the human spirit.
Look up from our pillory
At the summit
And see that, on it,
His nibs,
With light squibs,
Have set his flag, an unintelligible escutcheon
(Wyverns and such on
A field of curlicudinous cucurbits
In elongated orbits),
And, near it,
A human figure,
Scarcely bigger
Than a midge;

A rubber-stamped
Assign of us
Encamped
High on the ridge.

October 28, 1970

Dear John

L. E. Sissaman wakes at dawn,
Showers, shaves, calls William Shawn
(Busy), boards his motorbike,
Stops at a truck stop truckies like,
Meets and chats up Steve McQueen
Anent the Baja sickle scene,
Remounts and powders to the shop,
Ingests the work on his desk top,
Rewrites two campaigns, reads his mail,
Tweaks a typist by the tail
And by the bodice, phones the press,
Tells them he is L.E.S.,
Gets a rude rejoinder, sacks
A lacquey, reads the Telefax
Edition of *New Statesman,* sees
The Old Man, sunk in solving seas,
Receive his final judgment, cranks
A note into his Hermes, franks
The envelope (a call to Blount
Squares everything), replaces "cunt"
With "pudend" in a poem in proof,
Enters a time-warp (or time-woof)
To dine in London with S.J.P.,
Returns to redact la nuit.

Best,

Ed

269

Cockaigne: A Dream

CHORUS OF ALL: Then our Age was in it's Prime,
Free from Rage, and free from Crime,
A very Merry, Dancing, Drinking,
Laughing, Quaffing, and unthinking Time.
(*Dance of Diana's Attendants. Enter Mars.*)
— *"The Secular Masque,"* by *John Dryden*

Coming around the corner of the dream
City I've lived in nights since I was ten —
Amalgamated of a lost New York,
A dead Detroit, a trussed and mummified
Skylineless Boston with a hint thrown in
Of Philadelphia and London in
An early age, all folded into a
Receipt (or a lost pawn slip) for a place
That tasted of a human sweetness, laced
With grandeur and improbability —
I passed the old cast-iron hotel where I
Had sat and talked and sipped a cheap cognac
In many a dream, and came out on the fore-
Side of a wide white river promenade
Crossed by a dun-green "L" stark overhead
And paralleled, across the river, by
Another larger elevated steel
Conception of sequoia girders — a
Throg's Neck usurping all the western air
And staining it its brighter green. The east
Bank, though, was still its unprogressed,
Arrested older self. To learn the time,
I detoured down an alleyway between
Two ranks of small, chapfallen shops, and off
A rusty paper rack chained to the steps
Of a moribund grocerette I bought — five cents —
A copy of the Boston *Morning Globe*
For April 7th, 1953.
Northbound again upon the promenade,
I caught an air of spring, a clef or key
Of untuned song, a snatch of melody
In untrained voices carrying no tune
But the light burden of the first warm day
Set loose, light-headed, in the open, to
Salute the single minute of the year

When all's forgiven life, the garroter
Who still stands sentry on the darkening stair
In every stifling rooming house. Alone,
But only literally, I proceed
Past faces that have all the love they need
For once, and can, for once, give some away,
As their smiles give away, their eyes betray,
Level, for once, with mine, and not cast down.
A great glass café, half a riverboat,
Half Crystal Palace, beckons; I step in
To ranks of white enamel tables, wire,
Wood-seated ice-cream-parlor chairs,
And, in the place of honor by the door,
A towering cardboard mockup, like a cake
Of a French battleship, the *Richelieu,*
Around which sailors cluster, jabbering
In French, which figures, since the French fleet's in.
Uproom, in the glass-ceilinged, vasty hall,
Quite like a Continental station, all
The places have been set at an oblong
Long banquet table. As I approach it, all
My dearest friends, looking, in 1953,
Precisely as, in fact, they look today,
Rise from some ambush and, laughing, welcome me
To the fraternal order of the spring.
A pause; an unheard drum roll; from the other side
Of the table steps forth, smiling, Anne, my wife,
And I awaken at twelve-fifty-five
A.M., according to the bedside clock,
On February 14th of this year,
Elated, desolate it could not spell
Me any longer, being but a dream,
Its only evidence being my tears
Of joy or of the other, I can't tell.

Three American Dreams:
A Suite in Phillips House

I. OLD COPY CHIEFS

When Phillips lay in Phillips House, his brain
Drowned in a jigger of his incontinent
Blood, and death's door ajar in front of him,
He dreamt indomitable dreams of death,
Of failure in men's eyes and in his own,
Shut, swollen, on the pillow where pale tubes
Poured air and glucose ever into him.
The first dream saw him out of Phillips House
And back at work in the bone light of his
Old agency, where everything had changed:
Gone his employees, booted, bearded, jeaned
Young copywriters; in their offices,
New reft of Peter Maxes, sat and tapped
On pipes and typewriters a podgy race
Of pawky, dottled former copy chiefs
In faded red suspenders and age-green,
Age-frayed grey-flannel bags, all glad to make
Eight thousand now and be again employed
After so many a winter in a room
Of that sort where one's world's goods creak and shrink
To piles of mildew and one's hair goes grey.
In his own office, Phillips found a man
Like these, but more so, who directed him
To talk to the director, in whose suite
He got his walking papers for the street
Of dreams, where every manliness has its
Distress price, honor is hurt merchandise,
And talents are knocked down and given away.

In life, not far behind his dreams, he was
Discharged one day as cured, the misled blood
Sponged from his brain, and found himself again
Behind his brown desk at the agency,

Still feeble, muscles toneless, memory
Flown over the cuckoo's nest. One afternoon,
Having been summoned to the director's room
Summarily, he was told his work was not
Up to his former standard, and was fired.

II. KID WOMBAT

There is a low-down bar in Phillips House —
Brown-varnished plywood, plastic brewers' signs,
A feral stench of filthy urinals,
Smoke stratified before the blinking blue
Eye of the television jammed by noise
From the contending jukebox — where, between
Sleeping and sleeping, Phillips would repair
To the old world for a greasy glass of beer.
One night in there — or was it day? It's al-
Ways night in there — he was accosted by
A senile, drooling bruiser whose sateen
Battledress jacket read "Kid Wombat" in
Green letters on the back. This dying man —
Râles punctuating his Australian
Subaccent with a rattling, phthisic wheeze —
Did not like Phillips' looks and told him so
And challenged him to a fistfight and lunged
To overtop him and then knocked him down
With a clanging great right cross, and the bar laughed
As one demented throat to see such sport:
The clean young athlete, hated college man,
Supine upon the floor; the leering, brown,
Web-faced old stager gloating over him.

Later, on business in Albany,
Phillips, still fragile as a pullet's egg,
Stopped by a workmen's bar for a quick drink,
And was accosted by a drunk old man
Who challenged him to fight and was talked out
Of it, but only barely, by his friends,
Who sent Phillips packing out into the night
On a hostile street he'd never dreamt of, where

The mystery of life — aloneness — was
Disclosed in full to him and his footfalls.

III. DEATH BY BLACKNESS

In Phillips House old dreams recur. A dream
That visited him first — like an old aunt
In sinister bombazine — at seventeen
Came back to call again. Imagine that
Ink night in Tennessee, when Bessie Smith —
Her forearm crushed on the coaming of her car
When it was sideswiped, then torn off and flung
Into the road behind her — bled to death,
Her voice going out like a guttering candle stump
That breathes its last surrounded by the dark,
Which can afford to wait; imagine that
Old Arthur Rothstein photo of a Ford
Crushed in on some grey, straight Midwestern road,
Its injured driver being comforted
By citizens in a fedora and
A derby hat against the coming night;
Imagine that bright day that Phillips dreamt —
At first at seventeen and once again
In Phillips House — when a vast impact smashed
His father's car, and Phillips, thrown into
A roadside ditch among the thistles, tried
To raise his head, but was prevented by
An access of matt black that overspread
The earth from the horizon, pushing down,
With atmospheres of pressure, his light head
And all the reeds around, a blackness that
Shut, in an undertaker's gesture, his
Blue eyes with black lids, leaving him for dead.

That dream has not come true yet. Knowing what
Inexhaustible patience genuine darkness is
Capable of, I'd say, though, that it will.

IV

Hello, Darkness

Negatives

Hello, black skull. How privily you shine
In all my negatives, white pupils mine
Stock-staring forward under the white shock
Of straw, the surrogate for a forelock
To tug and be made free of Schattenland,
Where dusty Freiherren and Freifrauen stand
About apart in independent pools
Of absolute aphosis by the rules
That govern all reversals. Au contraire,
My awesome, glossy X-rays lay me bare
In whited spades: my skull glows like a moon
Hewn, like a button, out of vivid bone;
The tubular members of my rib cage gleam
Like tortile billets of aluminum;
My hand shines, frozen, like a white batwing
Caught in a strobe. The ordinary thing —
The photo-studio-cabinet-portrait shot,
The positive, quite empty of the not-
So-prepossessing characteristics of
Its subject, featly lighted from above
To maximize the massif of the brow
And minimize the blunt thrust of the prow
Above the smiling teeth clamped on a pipe
In smoking, stiff, still smugness, overripe
To fall — is the extraordinary thing.
When I am dead, my coroners will bring
Not my true bills, those rigorous negatives,

Nor those transparently pure fluorographs,
But this dishonest botch in evidence.
Ecco! they'll say, keeping the wolf far hence.

December 27, 1966

Night sweat: my temperature spikes to 102
At 5 A.M. — a classic symptom — and,
Awake and shaken by an ague, I
Peep out a western window at the worn
Half-dollar of the moon, couched in the rose
And purple medium of air above
The little, distant mountains, a black line
Of gentle ox humps, flanked by greeny lights
Where a still empty highway goes. In Christmas week,
The stars flash ornamentally with the
Pure come-on of a possibility
Of peace beyond all reason, of the spheres
Engaged in an adagio saraband
Of perfect mathematic to set an
Example for the earthly, who abide
In vales of breakdown out of warranty,
The unrepairable complaint that rattles us
To death. Tonight, though, it is almost worth the price —
High stakes, and the veiled dealer vends bad cards —
To see the moon so silver going west,
So ladily serene because so dead,
So closely tailed by her consort of stars,
So far above the feverish, shivering
Nightwatchman pressed against the falling glass.

Homage to Clotho:
A Hospital Suite

1

Nowhere is all around us, pressureless,
A vacuum waiting for a rupture in
The tegument, a puncture in the skin,
To pass inside without a password and
Implode us into Erewhon. This room
Is dangerously unguarded: in one wall
An empty elevator clangs its doors,
Imperiously, for fodder; in the hall,
Bare stretchers gape for commerce; in the air
Outside, a trembling, empty brightness falls
In hunger on those whom it would devour
Like any sparrow hawk as darkness falls
And rises silently up the steel stairs
To the eleventh and last floor, where I
Reside on sufferance of authorities
Until my visas wither, and I die.

2

Where is my friend, Rodonda Morton Schiff,
Whose hulk breasts, cygnet-like, the Totensee,
Shrilling her bosun's whistles, piping Death —
The Almirante of the Doldrums in
His black cocked hat and braided cape — aboard
Her scuttling vessel with such poems as just
Escape confounding his gaunt rape with lust?
She should be singing my song at this hour.

3

It is a simple matter to be brave
In facing a black screen with a white FIN —
The final title — fading out as all
Credits have faded in the final crawl,

To which the audience has turned its back
And mumbled, shuffled, struggled into coats
On its way out to face a different night;
It is far harder, in the light of day,
Surrounded by striped student nurses, to
Endure a slight procedure in which you
Are the anatomy lesson in pink paint
Splashed by some master on the tinctured air,
Complete, in gross detail, to the grimace
Denoted by a squiggle on your face
As the bone-marrow needle sinks its fang
Through atomies of drugged and dullard skin
And subcutaneum to pierce the thin,
Tough eggshell of the pelvic arch, wherein —
After steam-hammer pressure — it will suck
Up sips of specimen tissue with a pain
Akin to an extraction under gas,
All gravity against all hollowness.
Affronted and affrighted, I can't pass
This episode in silent dignity
Or bloodless banter; I must sweat and grunt
And moan in corporal fear of corporal pain
Too venial to be mortal, making a fool
Of my lay figure in its textbook pose
(Fig. 1) before these starched and giggling girls
Too young to be let out of simpering school
To meet live terror face to face and lose.

4

Why must the young male nurse who preps the plain
Of my knife-thrower's-target abdomen
With his conversant razor, talking snicks
Of scything into my sedated ears,
Talk also in his flat and friendly voice,
So far from showdowns, on a blasé note
Of reassurance, learnt by classroom rote?
It is that he must make his living, too.

5

If Hell abides on earth this must be it:
This too-bright-lit-at-all-hours-of-the-day-
And-night recovery room, where nurses flit
In stroboscopic steps between the beds
All cheek by jowl that hold recoverers
Suspended in the grog of half-damped pain
And tubularities of light-blue light.
For condiment in this mulled mix, there are
Assorted groans and screams; and, lest repose
Outstrip the sufferer, there is his own
Throat-filling Gobi, mucous membrane gone
Dry as Arabia, as barren of
Hydropsy as a sunburnt cage of bone
Perched on parched rocks where game Parcheesian
(A devil figure, this) went, wended his
Bent way to harvest, for a shekel, rugs,
And pack them back by camel over sands
Of nightmare to transship to richer lands
Where millions of small rills plash into streams
That give rise to great rivers — such wet dreams
Afflict the desiccate on their interminable way
Up through the layers of half-light to day.

6

The riddle of the Sphinx. Man walks on three
Legs at the last. I walk on three, one of
Which is a wheeled I.V. pole, when I rise
From bed the first time to make my aged way
Into the toilet, where, while my legs sway
And the pole sways, swinging its censer high,
I wait to urinate, and cannot make
My mortal coils distill a drop, as time
Stumps past and leaves me swaying there. Defeat:
I roll and hobble back to bed, to the
Refrain of cheeping wheels. Soon the young man
With his snake-handler's fist of catheters
Will come to see me and supply the lack
Of my drugged muscles with the gravity

Of his solution, and I'll void into
A beige bag clipped to the bedside, one of
The bottles, bags, and tubes I'm tethered to
As a condition of continuance.
The body swells until it duns the mind
With importunities in this refined,
White-sheeted torture, practiced by a kind,
Withdrawn white face trained in the arts of love.

7

Home, and the lees of autumn scuttle up
To my halt feet: fat, sportive maple leaves
Struck into ochre by the frost and stripped
From their umbilic cords to skate across
The blacktop drive and fetch up on my shoes
As if including me in their great fall,
Windy with rumors of the coming ice.
Though fallen, frostbit, yellowed also, I
Cannot participate in their late game
But must leave them to hide and seek a place
To decompose in, while I clamber up
Long enneads of stairs to the room where
I'll recompose myself to durance in
A world of voices and surprises, for
As long as Clotho draws my filament —
To my now flagging wonder and applause —
From indefatigable spinnerets,
Until her sister widows, having set
The norms for length and texture of each strand
And sharpened their gross shears, come cut it off
And send me to befriend the winter leaves.

Cancer: A Dream

1. INT.

After the morning shooting, I repair
To my makeshamble dressing room between
The stage and the backstage and the machine
For life support just outside, called a street
And also a location. Inside, air
Is fumed and darkened from a sightless age
Of cave-fish audiences goggling at
Alarms from the direction of the stage,
Now tarnished and festooned with cables. Rage,
Now torn to dated tatters, is replaced
By decorous muttering of a host of crews.
My blacked-out dressing room: a Bernhardt bed,
Swaddled in grubby cloth of gold, holds a
Late *levée* for a rabble of old props —
Drapes, swags, flats, hassocks, bunting, a malign
And lame old vanity with one short leg,
An easel with a bogus portrait of
Some doe-faced buck or beau, a cellarette
Dwarfed by a tottering stack of film cans —
Reclaimed to servitude as furniture.
I feel ungodly weak and sick for noon;
I undress shakily and lie me down
In dust on the vast desert of the bed.

2. INT.

Sound is a kind of pain to which all pain
Responds, as when the prompt boy knocks and calls,
And my insides reply in pain, and I
Sit up in my pyjamas and then stand
And make my way toward the toilet, and,
Returning through a ruinous anteroom
With sand upon the floor and masons' tools,
A length of cast-iron pipe, a dwarf sawhorse,
Discover on the floor, all befouled,
My blue-and-white pyjamas, the immemorial

Stench the pilots smelt in closed cockpits
Over the killing ground above Berlin.
I wash and dress. I walk like a whole man —
The captain on the bridge — to the next scene.

3. EXT.

A visiting fireman. The woman is introduced
By the second-unit man. I miss her name.
She looks familiar. Smokes her cigarette
In a long holder. Waves her hands a lot.
Talks in an accent. Russian. Sixty. Tall.
Not fat but solid. Some kind of beauty once.
Long catlike jawline under jowls. Stiff white
Straight hair tinted a shocking green. Green eyes,
And those not older than before. Nice legs.
Her character comes back. The wife of an
American avant-garde little-magazine
Editor, once a big bug, now passé.
Herself not quite passé — the author of
One book of verse that, less than moribund,
Keeps a fierce toehold on its shelf. Her name
Is Olga Verushkova, and she's here
(Returning to the moment) to research
A piece on movies. Walls of urban air
Weave a small room, made out of light and noise,
Around us and our small talk, which grows dark
And meaning. And, if I were still a man
Of any age, I'd know precisely what
To do when she quite lightly kisses me
Upon the lips and I respond by rote,
And she responds, and I, as if I had
A backbone for my keelson, and were not
Just a façade, a shield upon a stick,
Feel her electric zone impinge on mine
And hear her say, "I am obsessed with you,"
To her amazement, as I break the field
Of force forever, and turn soft away,
One stiffening hand left on her shoulder, and,
Shaking my head to throw the tears away,
Excuse the lateness of the shining hour.

4. EXT.

Dissolve. A rank of crew approaches me.
One tall girl, quite superb in her neat skirt
And modest sweater, looks up from her clip-
Board with grey eyes that will not ever age
And smiles professionally straight at me.
"You're wanted on Stage R. We're running late."
I turn to face the music. I awake.

5. INT.

And go now to the center of the stage
To execute a solo *pas de deux* —
The crab dance — on the black-and-white parquet
Under all eyes and lenses. Partner mine,
With your pink carapace coterminous
With mine, your hard two-fingered hands contained
In mine, your long legs telescoped inside
My legs, your entire *Geist* the work of my
Own brain, why do you lead me such a dance,
So painfully and clumsily drawn out
Of step with the macabre music of
The tiny chamber orchestra that winds,
Diminuendo, down to the last scratch
Of gut, like an old gramophone, leaving
The *premier* — and the only — *danseur* there,
Alone, supine upon the checkered floor,
Where lights — undamped, undimmed — burn on and on,
And eyes — undamped, undimmed — and lenses turn
To other scenes, fresh fields and pastures new,
As I sink into union with you?

Tras Os Montes

I. MOTHER (1892–1973)

My mother, with a skin of crêpe de Chine,
Predominantly yellow-colored, sheer
Enough to let the venous blue show through
The secondarily bluish carapace,
Coughs, rasps, and rattles in her terminal
Dream, interrupted by lucidities,
When, suctioned out and listening with hard
Ears almost waned to stone, she hears me say,
"Mother, we're here. The two of us are here.
Anne's here with me," and she says, "Anne is so —
So pretty," as if abdicating all
Her principalities of prettiness —
So noted in her teens, when she smote all
Who saw her shake a leg upon the stage
Of vaudeville — and sinking into deeps
Where ancience lurks, and barebone toothlessness,
And bareback exits from the centre ring
Of cynosure. Of little, less is left
When we leave: a stick figure of a once
Quite formidable personage. It is,
Therefore, no shock, when next day the call comes
From my worn father, followed by the spade
Engaged upon hard January earth
In Bellevue Cemetery, where he sways
And cries for fifty years of joint returns
Unjointed, and plucks one carnation from
The grave bouquet of springing flowers upon
The medium-priced coffin of veneer,
To press and keep as a venereal
Greenness brought forward from the greying past.

II. FATHER (1895–1974)

Whether the rivals for a wife and mother can
Compose their differences and timely warp
Into concomitant currents, taken by

The selfsame tide when taken at the flood —
Great waters poured black downhill at the height
Of melting in the middle of the night —
Is to be seen. We did not find it so.
My father, whom I loved as if he'd done
All his devoirs (though he had not), and shone
Upon my forehead like a morning sun,
Came home out of his hospital to stay
In our rich, alien house, where trappings tried
His niggard monkishness. Four days he stayed
In his ashen cocoon; the fifth he died
Under my ministrations, his pug jaw
Thrust out toward the port of hopelessness,
Where he (I hope) received the sirens of
All possible welcoming tugs, even as I
Felt under his grey, waxen nose for breath
And called the doctor to record a death
That made shift rather easier for me,
Staring at nothing standing out to sea.

III.   TRAS OS MONTES (197–)

1. In Company

Inspecting their kit and equipment at first light,
I am glad the dawn is behind me, so my friends
Cannot reflect upon my tears. The province I
Move on across the mountains is still night-
Bound, deep beneath the reaches of the sun
Across the passes; so it will remain
All of this long and dusty day, while we —
Will, Joe, Bob, Jonathan, Garth, Peter, Paul,
Ed, John, Phil, Harry, and a droptic me —
March up the sunstruck slopes, dots on the rock
That jags two thousand metres high ahead
Of us above the passes where the dead
Take formal leave of life: a kiss on both
Cheeks of the dear departing, medals stripped,
With all due ceremony, from his breast,
Both epaulets cut loose from their braid stays,
His sword, unbroken, pommelled in the hand

Of his reliever; lastly, a salute
Fired by the arms of officers, the guns
Of other ranks, and a flat bugle call
Played on a battered Spanish instrument
With ragged tassels as the body falls
Over the parapet — gaining weightlessness
As its flesh deliquesces, as its bones
Shiver to ashes — into an air that crawls
With all the arts of darkness far below.

2. *A Deux*

A new scenario: on upswept slopes
Of ripe green wheat — rare in this country — we
Take, linked, a last long walk. In late July,
The landscape waits, breath bated, on the whim
Of cumulonimbi in the west, which roll
In with deceptive stealth, revealing a
Black heart cut with a cicatrice of fire,
Zigzagging to its ground: a naked peak
Kilometres away, a *serra* out
Of mind. I fix your face with a wax smile.
Our hands articulate our oneness, soon
To dissipate, in a stiff splay of joints.
Is all the language at my tongue's command
Too little to announce my stammered thanks
For your unquestioning hand at my side,
Too much to say I know the lowly deuce
Is a poor card to play beside the ace,
Black with his curlicues and his strong pulse
Of *sauve qui peut* ambition? Calling a spade
A spade, I'm pierced with the extreme regret
Of one who dies intestate; as I'm snatched
Into the stormcloud from the springing field,
From green to black, I spy on you, below,
A lone maid in green wheat, and rain farewells
And late apologies on your grey head,
And thunder sorrows and regrets. The storm
Goes east, and the sun picks out my remains
Against the cloud: a tentative rainbow,
An inverse, weak, and spectral kind of smile.

3. Alone

The long march up the fulvous ridgebacks to
The marches, the frontiers of difference —
Where flesh marches with bone, day marches with
His wife the night, and country marches with
Another country — is accomplished best,
By paradox, alone. A world of twos,
Of yangs and yins, of lives and objects, of
Sound grasses and deaf stones, is best essayed
By sole infiltrators who have cast off
Their ties to living moorings, and stand out
Into the roads of noon approaching night
Casting a single shadow, earnest of
Their honorable intention to lay down
Their lives for their old country, humankind,
In the same selfish spirit that inspired
Their lifelong journey, largely and at last
Alone, across the passes that divide
A life from every other, the sheer crags
Of overweening will, the deepening scarps
Like brain fissures that cunningly cut off
Each outcrop from the main and make it one
While its luck lasts, while its bravura holds
Against all odds, until the final climb
Across the mountains to the farther shore
Of sundown on the watersheds, where self,
Propelled by its last rays, sways in the sway
Of the last grasses and falls headlong in
The darkness of the dust it is part of
Upon the passes where we are no more:
Where the recirculating shaft goes home
Into the breast that armed it for the air,
And, as we must expect, the art that there
Turned our lone hand into imperial Rome
Reverts to earth and its inveterate love
For the inanimate and its return.

FINIS

Index of Titles

Amazing Grace, 1974   224
American in Evans Country, An   160
American Light: A Hopper Retrospective   220
Among Schoolchildren   156
Anniversary, An: A Lucubration   227
Arundel Footnote, An   198
At the Bar, 1948   241
August: A Jingle Man   215
Bathing Song   106
Bethlehem State   61
Better Half, The   230
Big Rock-Candy Mountain, The   151
Birdman of Cambridge, Mass., The   18
Boston–Chicago, May 11   265
Cancer: A Dream   281
Canzone: Aubade   87
Chamber Music, Bar Harbor, Off-Season   54
Cinematographers, The, West Cedar Street   111
Clearing in the Woods, The   219
Clever Women   112
Cockaigne: A Dream   270
Cock Robbins Opens in New York   159
College Room, A: Lowell R-34, 1945   16
Comedy in Ruins, A   232
Common Prophecy, A   61
Concerto for the Left Hand Alone   264
Convenient to Victoria   197
Day in the City, A   33
Dear George Orwell, 1950–1965   52
Dear John   269
Death City, 1949   31
Deathplace, A   93
December 27, 1966   276
Dump, The: A Dream Come True   167
Dying: An Introduction   83
Dying: A Resurrection, 1969   179
East Congress and McDougall Streets, Detroit, May 25   13
Edward Teshmaker Busk Obiit Aet. 28, 5 Nov. 1914   113
Elegy: Evelyn Waugh   107
Empson Lieder   206
Escapists, The, August, 1949   242
E-Type on the Interstate, An   156

Excuse for an Italian Sonnet   201
Fall Planting   126
First N.Y. Showing   161
Getting On: Grave Expectations   213
Going Back: A Word with Leslie Vandam in New York 253
Going Home, 1945   3
Harvest, The, State Street   94
Harvest Home   141
Henley, July 4: 1914–1964   15
High Summer   136
Homage to Clotho: A Hospital Suite   277
In and Out: A Home Away from Home, 1947   26
In and Out: Severance of Connections, 1946   24
In Baltimore — Why Baltimore? — Did Kahn   203
In Bardbury   196
Inflation   204
In the New Year   147
J.J.'s Levee, 1946   202
Just a Whack at Empson   51
Late Good Night, A   251
Letter from Coast to Coast   170
Lettermen   118
Life in Alabaster Street, A   199
Loss of Largesse, A; Its Recapture (And Point After)   200
Love Day, 1945   234
Love-Making; April; Middle Age   82
Lüchow's and After   101
Man and Wife   67
Manchester: Night   161
Man in the Street   225
Marschallin, The, Joy Street, July 3, 1949   55
Matter of Britain: Some Fragmentary Souvenirs   266
Mid-Forties, The: On Meeting No One in New York   255
Midsummer Night, Charles Street   28
Model Rooms   223
Mouth-Organ Tunes: The American Lost and Found   165
Museum of Comparative Zoology, The   20
Nanny Boat, The, 1957   77
Negatives   275
New England: Dead of Winter   23
New Year's, 1948   174
New York: A Summer Funeral   244

New York Woman, The   163
Nocturne, Central Park South   120
Notes Toward a 25th Reunion   256
On Picking and Smelling a Wild Violet While Wearing
   Driving Gloves   216
On the Island   37
Our Literary Heritage   46
Packing Material: Excelsior   268
Parents in Winter   11
Patrick Kavanagh: An Annotated Exequy   99
Peace Comes to Still River, Mass.   53
Peg Finnan's Wake in Inman Square   32
Pepy's Bar, West Forty-eighth Street, 8 A.M.   116
Persistence of Innocence, The   231
Praeludium, North River   265
Private Line, A   267
Provincetown, 1953   70
Pursuit of Honor, 1946   180
Safety at Forty: or, An Abecedarian Takes a Walk   114
Savage, The, Gore Hall G-31   18
Scattered Returns: Three Derivative Poems   95
Small Space   103
Solo, Head Tide   115
Sonatina: Hospital   98
Sondra Dead or Alive   65
Spring Song   214
Stillman Infirmary   22
String Song   44
Sweeney to Mrs. Porter in the Spring   35
Tears at Korvette's   169
Temporary Measures: A Book of Hours   257
Three American Dreams: A Suite in Phillips House   272
Time in Venezuela, The   170
To Your Uterus; an Uncompleted Call   268
Tras Os Montes   284
Tree Warden, The   42
20th Armored, The: A Recurrent Dream   110
Two Encounters   29
Two Happenings in Boston   67
Under the Rose: A Granfalloon for Kurt Vonnegut, Jr.   217
Unknown Western-Union Boy, An   101
Up All Night, Adams House C-55   20

Upon Finding *Dying: An Introduction,* by L. E. Sissman,
  Remaindered at 1*s.*   109
Veterans, The: A Dream   104
Village, The: The Seasons   120
Visiting Chaos   108
War Requiem, A   125
West Forties, The: Morning, Noon, and Night   73
Wintertime and Spring   131
With Dr. Donothing at Farney End   116
Work: A Sermon   226